# CAMBRIDGE PAPERS IN SOCIAL ANTHROPOLOGY

General Editor: Jack Goody

No. 11  Inequality in New Guinea Highlands Societies

Edited by Andrew Strathern

T0370906

# CAMBRIDGE PAPERS IN SOCIAL ANTHROPOLOGY

# *Inequality in New Guinea Highlands Societies*

Edited by Andrew Strathern

CAMBRIDGE UNIVERSITY PRESS
CAMBRIDGE
LONDON    NEW YORK    NEW ROCHELLE
MELBOURNE    SYDNEY

CAMBRIDGE UNIVERSITY PRESS
Cambridge, New York, Melbourne, Madrid, Cape Town, Singapore, São Paulo, Delhi

Cambridge University Press
The Edinburgh Building, Cambridge CB2 8RU, UK

Published in the United States of America by Cambridge University Press, New York

www.cambridge.org
Information on this title: www.cambridge.org/9780521107846

First published 1982
This digitally printed version 2009

A catalogue record for this publication is available from the British Library

Library of Congress Catalogue Card Number: 82–4203

ISBN 978-0-521-24489-3 hardback
ISBN 978-0-521-10784-6 paperback

# CONTENTS

# NOTES ON THE CONTRIBUTORS

MAURICE GODELIER was born in 1934. He worked with Fernand Braudel at the Ecole Pratique des Hautes Etudes (VIe section), and with Claude Lévi-Strauss at the Collège de France, before becoming Director of Studies in economic anthropology at the Ecole des Hautes Etudes en Sciences Sociales in 1975. Between 1967 and 1980 he carried out extensive fieldwork among the Baruya of New Guinea. He is Doctor Honoris Causa of the University of Louvain, Belgium, and is also Vice President of the Scientific Society for the Study of Oceanic Cultures. He has published a number of books and articles on economic anthropology and on his field research in New Guinea.

JACK GOLSON has been Professor of Prehistory at the Australian National University since 1969. He read history and archaeology at Peterhouse, Cambridge, and in 1954 was appointed the first lecturer in Prehistory in the newly established Department of Anthropology at the University of Auckland. While there he worked archaeologically in New Zealand, Tonga, Samoa and New Caledonia, and helped to found the New Zealand Archaeological Association. Since his move to Australia in 1961 he has been concerned with research on New Guinea and the Melanesian Islands. He is currently President of the Indo-Pacific Prehistory Association.

NICHOLAS MODJESKA was born in Southern California in 1942. He studied anthropology at Reed College in Portland, Oregon (where he wrote a B.A. thesis on the anthropology of E.R. Leach), and also at Oxford and at the Australian National University. He began field studies among the Duna people of the Southern Highlands in 1969 while a tutor at the University of Papua New Guinea. He now teaches anthropology at Macquarie University, and is currently working on a book about Duna mythology and dreams.

ANDREW STRATHERN was born in 1939. He was educated at Trinity
College, Cambridge, and received a B.A. in 1962 and a Ph.D. in 1966. He
has held research fellowships at Cambridge and Canberra between 1965
and 1972. He was Professor of Anthropology at the University of Papua
New Guinea between 1973 and 1976. Since 1976, he has been Professor
of Anthropology at University College London. He is also currently
Director of the Institute of Papua New Guinea Studies, Port Moresby. He
has written several books and articles on his field research in the New
Guinea Highlands.

# Preface to the Paperback Edition

## Inequality Reconsidered: Models and Histories of Change

Andrew Strathern and Pamela J. Stewart[1]

The essays included in this volume were brought together as a way of exploring how analytical views of Papua New Guinea Highlands social processes were changing, and how the Highlands societies themselves were changing in response to the introduction of cash cropping, state money, and new forms of political leadership. The essays stood out in the literature at the time for their innovative probing of significant patterns of production and exchange and how these correlated with diachronic shifts as well as synchronic patterns, keeping in mind material circumstances and relations of production as an analytical focus; and today they serve as a foundational set of readings in this arena of scholarship.

Anthropological discussions on the Highlands region have moved on since the early 1980s into a wider sphere of interpretive and comparative concerns. This does not mean that the concerns of the 1980s are outmoded. On the contrary, the earlier discussions remain important benchmarks for the study of change in general, especially with regard to the issue of the development of social classes in response to capitalist enterprise. However, further enduring and shifting patterns of response, adaptation and creativity have claimed attention. We give here a small selection of references from our own work since the 1980s and its relationship to earlier writings, including those in this volume. These references also reflect wider trends in the overall literature, and stand here as a mark of these trends.

First, the theme of historical change has itself been updated in our book *Arrow Talk* (Strathern and Stewart 2000a). Longer term processes of prehistory, discussed in Golson's chapter in the volume, have also been explored further (Strathern and Stewart n.d), as well as the comparative study of horticulture (Sillitoe, Stewart, and Strathern 2002). Cultural heritage issues relating to the famous Kuk site were explored in a unique edited volume (Strathern and Stewart eds. 1998), and in a collection of oral histories (Strathern and Stewart 2000b).

Second, the long-term work that we have conducted on the Hagen area has been significantly added to by our in-depth work on the Duna area, which was the focus of Modjeska's paper in the volume. Duna social structure and oral history were the focus of one book (Strathern and Stewart 2004a) and Duna religion and ritual change in response to mining activities were the theme of another book (Stewart and Strathern 2002a). Duna speeches are also studied in Stewart and Strathern 2000a.

The above works also took in a further significant arena of contemporary discussion in anthropology, i.e., religion and religious transformations, especially in relation to Christianity. Reconsiderations of the histories of earlier practices have been further addressed (e.g., Strathern and Stewart 1999a; Stewart and Strathern eds. 2008). Significant approaches to the study of Christian conversion and practice are incorporated in Stewart and Strathern eds. 2000b.

The essays in the *Inequality* volume extensively discussed matters such as gender relations, partly from the perspective of "male domination". This approach has been modified considerably in later work (e.g., Stewart and Strathern 1999, 2002b; Strathern and Stewart 2004b). We introduced the concept of the "collaborative model" of gender relations in these works. Other wide-ranging themes have been broached on a comparative front (Strathern and Stewart 2000c); on ideas of the body and embodiment (Stewart and Strathern 2001); on processes of historical change in ideas of personhood as seen in life histories (Stewart and Strathern eds. 2000c; Strathern and Stewart 1999b); on violence and peace-making (Stewart and Strathern 2002c); and on genres of aesthetic expression (Stewart and Strathern eds. 2005).

Taken all in all, these contributions have greatly expanded the earlier contexts in which social inequalities were examined, going beyond materialist models into the broader spheres of cultural and historical analysis, in which indigenous meanings and observers' analyses are blended together in an enriched picture of the complexities of Highlands New Guinea societies in their historical contexts, for which this *Inequality* volume serves as an important set of analyses.

The project and rationale for the reprinting of these essays in this new edition are in line with the recent reprint of another early classic study, first published in 1971, *The Rope of Moka: Big-Men and Ceremonial Exchange in Mount Hagen, New Guinea*, for which we also wrote an updated preface (Strathern 2007, with new preface by Strathern and Stewart, "Waves of Change"). That volume's detailed synchronic analyses of local competitive leadership and struggles for prestige and pre-eminence led naturally to the more comparative and diachronic studies exemplified in this *Inequality* volume, which also engaged with materialist models that came into vogue during the 1970s (e.g., in Godelier's work). Later studies have broadened the basis in terms of which axes of equality or inequality can be considered, and have also broadened the scope of topics under the rubric of historical change. The closely considered dimensions of analysis exemplified in *Inequality* remain, however, highly relevant for understanding the contemporary trajectories of the Highlands societies, as for many other societies around the world enmeshed in what is now often discussed in terms of global economic and social forces.

AJS and PJS
September 2008
Cromie Burn Research Unit
University of Pittsburgh

NOTE

(1) A. Strathern and P.J. Stewart are a husband and wife research team who have spent many years as long-term researchers working on Papua New Guinea topics. They have published extensively and widely. For a list of relevant examples of their work visit their website (www.pitt.edu/~strather/sandspublicat.htm). They also have over many years served, and continue to serve, as Co-Editors on a number of scholarly book series, assisting researchers in Pacific Studies to publish their findings.

REFERENCES

Sillitoe, Paul, Pamela J. Stewart, and Andrew Strathern (2002) <u>Horticulture in Papua New Guinea: Case Studies from the Southern and Western Highlands</u>. Ethnology Monograph Series. No. 18 University of Pittsburgh, Pittsburgh.

Stewart, Pamela J. and A.J. Strathern (1999). Female Spirit Cults as a Window on Gender Relations in the Highlands of Papua New Guinea. <u>The Journal of the Royal Anthropological Institute</u> 5(3): 345-360.

Stewart, Pamela J. and Andrew Strathern (2000a) <u>Speaking for Life and Death: Warfare and Compensation among the Duna of Papua New Guinea</u>. Senri Ethnological Reports 13: National Museum of Ethnology, Osaka, Japan.

Stewart, Pamela J. and A. Strathern (eds.) (2000b) <u>Millennial Countdown in New Guinea</u>. Special Issue of <u>Ethnohistory</u> Vol. 47(1), 2000. Durham, N.C.: Duke University Press.

Stewart, Pamela J. and Andrew J. Strathern, eds. (2000c) <u>Identity Work: Constructing Pacific Lives</u>. ASAO (Association for Social Anthropology in Oceania) Monograph Series No. 18. Pittsburgh: University of Pittsburgh Press.

Stewart, Pamela J. and A. Strathern (2001) <u>Humors and Substances: Ideas of the Body in New Guinea</u>. Westport, Conn. and London: Bergin and Garvey, Greenwood Publishing Group.

Stewart, Pamela J. and Andrew Strathern (2002a) Remaking the World: Myth, Mining and Ritual Change among the Duna of Papua New Guinea. For, Smithsonian Series in Ethnographic Inquiry, Washington, D.C.: Smithsonian Institution Press.

Stewart, Pamela J. and A. Strathern (2002b) Gender, Song, and Sensibility: Folktales and Folksongs in the Highlands of New Guinea. Westport, CT and London: Praeger Publishers (Greenwood Publishing).

Stewart, Pamela J. and Andrew Strathern (2002c) Violence: Theory and Ethnography. London and New York: Continuum Publishing.

Stewart, Pamela J. and Andrew Strathern (eds.) (2005) Expressive Genres and Historical Change: Indonesia, Papua New Guinea and Taiwan. For, Anthropology and Cultural History in Asia and the Indo-Pacific Series, London, U.K. and Burlington, VT: Ashgate Publishing.

Stewart, Pamela J. and Andrew Strathern (eds.) (2008) Exchange and Sacrifice. For, Ritual Studies Monograph Series, Durham, N.C.: Carolina Academic Press.

Strathern, Andrew (2007) The Rope of Moka: Big-Men and Ceremonial Exchange in Mount Hagen, New Guinea. Cambridge: Cambridge University Press.

Strathern, A. and Pamela J. Stewart (eds.) (1998) Kuk Heritage: Issues and Debates in Papua New Guinea. The National Museum of PNG and the JCU-Centre for Pacific Studies and the Okari Research Group, Department of Anthropology, University of Pittsburgh.

Strathern, A. and Pamela J. Stewart (1999a) The Spirit is Coming! A Photographic-Textual Exposition of the Female Spirit Cult Performance in Mt. Hagen. Ritual Studies Monograph Series, Monograph No. 1. Pittsburgh.

Strathern A. and Pamela J. Stewart (1999b) Collaborations and Conflicts. A Leader Through Time. Fort Worth Texas: Harcourt Brace College Publishers.

Strathern, A. and Pamela J. Stewart (2000a) Arrow Talk: Transaction, Transition, and Contradiction in New Guinea Highlands History. Kent, Ohio and London: Kent State University Press.

Strathern, A. and Pamela J. Stewart (2000b) Stories, Strength & Self-Narration. Western Highlands, Papua New Guinea. Adelaide, Australia: Crawford House Publishing.

Strathern, A. and Pamela J. Stewart (2000c) The Python's Back: Pathways of Comparison between Indonesia and Melanesia. Westport, Conn. and London: Bergin and Garvey, Greenwood Publishing Group.

Strathern, Andrew and Pamela J. Stewart (2004a) Empowering the Past, Confronting the Future: The Duna People of Papua New Guinea. For,

*Preface to the paperback edition*

Contemporary Anthropology of Religion Series, New York: Palgrave Macmillan.

Strathern, Andrew and Pamela J. Stewart (2004b). Cults, Closures, Collaborations. In, <u>Women as Unseen Characters. Male Ritual in Papua New Guinea</u>, for Social Anthropology in Oceania Monograph Series, edited by Pascale Bonnemere, pp. 120-138. Philadelphia, PA: University of Pennsylvania Press.

Strathern, Andrew and Pamela J. Stewart (n.d.) Hagen Settlement Histories: Dispersals and Consolidations. In, J. Golson, T. Denham, P. Swadling, and J. Muke (eds.), *Nine Thousand Years of Gardening: Kuk and the archaeology of agriculture in Papua New Guinea*

# *Introduction*

~~~~~~~~~~~~~~~~~~~~~~~~~~~~~~~~~~~~~~~~~~~~~~~~~~~~~~~~~~~~~~~~~~~~~~

The five essays in this volume explore in different ways the themes of
social inequality and historical change in New Guinea Highlands societies.
They are concerned largely with the 'pre-capitalist' context, but this is not
done for antiquarian purposes: rather, the focus is necessary in order to
develop schemes of analysis which will enable us to move continuously
through discussion of these societies over extended periods of time, from
the pre-colonial through to post-independence phases. Another purpose
also runs through the papers: an attempt to engage critically with the
models for Highlands societies which were produced during the upsurge of
anthropological writings in the 1960s and 1970s. The Highlands have
proved a testing-ground, if not a graveyard, for many an approach: descent
and exchange theory, ecological functionalism, and neo-marxist analysis,
for example. In order to make further progress, we need to do two things:
first, to produce sharp and defensible synchronic accounts of the kind
which Maurice Godelier gives us in this volume; and second, to set such
accounts into a comparative context which will facilitate argument about
processes of long-term change in the wider region to which local societies
belong. Godelier provides some hints as to how this second stage should be
tackled, for example by considering marriage practices and the exchanges
of wealth against persons. Modjeska, while not concentrating explicitly on
marriage rules as a variable, takes the discussion a good deal further with
his concept of an evolving lineage mode of production and its implications
for gender inequality and big-manship. In Modjeska's terms, big-manship
belongs to high-intensity horticultural production systems, and is correlated with the principles of increment and enchainment of exchanges
which I pointed to in my original analyses of Hagen society (e.g. A.J.
Strathern 1971). The Baruya, studied by Godelier, should fit into
Modjeska's scheme as a people with a moderate-to-low-intensity production system, but in addition they have developed an ethic of the 'great-
man' as a warrior or shaman, and this stands in positive counterpoint,

Godelier argues, to the big-man model which has tended to predominate in the ethnography. It will be interesting to see whether the 'great-man' model proves to be generalisable in the same way as the big-man model.

The paper by Golson gives archaeological depth and control to some of the more speculative suggestions in Modjeska's work; in turn, it has been influenced by Modjeska's critical ideas and by my own ethnography from the Hagen area. Golson's work has shown that intensive horticulture goes back much further in the Highlands than was earlier supposed, and it raises the question of the interplay between technology and social organisation over time. Did swamp control imply authoritative leadership and social hierarchy in the past? A definite answer is not available, but we can argue that the introduction of sweet potato in place of taro may have liberated the local system from certain constraints entailed in the production of taro and have enabled more men to compete for status, just as the colonial introduction of large numbers of shells brought on the demise of big-men's monopolistic control of shell-*moka* and re-opened the competition to those who gained best access to the European intruders. We can therefore view the historical processes as in some ways repetitive although in other ways they are cumulative and directional.

These papers are intended as exploratory contributions rather than definitive statements: the aim is to bring Highlands data to bear on issues of gender, production, and change in social systems which are exercising scholars in many other parts of the world, including Africa, but without succumbing to a second wholesale importation of 'African models'. Two of the papers were given in a preliminary form as seminars in the Department of Social Anthropology at Cambridge in 1978 (Golson, Godelier); my papers are closely related in theme to a seminar given there in the same year also (published separately as A.J. Strathern 1979b); and Modjeska's paper completes the set because his work is crucial to ideas expressed throughout the volume.

Cambridge,                                                        ANDREW STRATHERN
*June 1981*

# 1 Social hierarchies among the Baruya of New Guinea

*Maurice Godelier*

～～～～～～～～～～～～～～～～～～～～～～～～～～～～

## INTRODUCTION

In this paper I propose to reconstitute the manner in which the Baruya, a people of the Eastern Highlands, governed themselves before 1960, the date at which they submitted to Australian colonial power. I shall then briefly show the transformations which arose from the founding of a form of direct colonial administration, which came to an end with Papua New Guinea's accession to independence in September 1975. Hardly a quarter of a century had elapsed since 1951, when James Sinclair, then a patrol officer at Mumeng, made up his mind to mount an expedition to discover the Batya. This was the name given, in the Mumeng region, to the unknown tribe which manufactured a famous salt, and which was, in fact, the Baruya (Sinclair 1966).

As I hope to demonstrate, my analysis reveals the existence of a global social logic among the Baruya, which places 'great-men' in the first rank of society. These men perform, to an exceptional degree, specific roles, among which warriorhood and shamanism are the most important. I shall show that this society of great-men contrasts fundamentally with those which have big-men as the principal personae in their midst. I shall finally suggest that societies with big-men, which, since Marshall Sahlins' work, now tend rather too easily to be considered typical of Melanesian societies, constitute one variation among others, and that the reasons why these appear and develop should be sought. In order to make the contrast more discernible, I shall provide a brief summary of the elements which, according to M. Sahlins, go to make up the power of a big-man, and which draw the portrait of a personage whom I have not encountered among the Baruya (Sahlins 1962–3).

A big-man, according to Sahlins, is a man who possesses personal power acquired by his own merits, which is not inherited and cannot be passed on. These merits arise from the exercise of several talents: magical powers,

3

Maurice Godelier

oratorical gifts, courage in war, competence and effort in agricultural work, which have proved his superiority in these various contexts. Yet, according to Sahlins, these talents are *not* sufficient to make a man a big-man. It is still necessary that he should add to them a capacity which seems to play a decisive role in the formation of his prestige and power: the capacity of knowing how to accumulate wealth and distribute it with calculated generosity. Little by little, these talents, this wealth and this generosity make this man worthy of the respect of a large number of individuals who belong to his own and neighbouring tribes. And soon, for some of them, the respect and admiration are transformed into loyalty and active support. These people are in general close and distant relatives, affines, and neighbours who consent to help this man in his enterprises and thus form a 'faction', upon which he depends to make the fame of his name spread far beyond the frontiers of his tribe.

For Sahlins, this type of power and personage does not appear by chance. It is born at the heart of certain *acephalous* tribal societies without central power, composed of a certain number of local groups which are equally matched in the political sphere. They govern their own material resources and are organised according to relationships of segmentary kinship which, by contrast with African segmentary societies, do not entail the automatic attribution of functions and positions of power to individuals occupying, through birth, geneological nodes of segmentation in these relations of kinship. At the heart of these societies, the big-man and his power constitute an institutional response to the need to be equipped with supralocal political powers in certain circumstances: war, organisation of religious ceremonies and exchange with distant tribes. Through his ambition and his initiative, the big-man seems to act as the instrument for satisfying these general social interests. He becomes the support and personification of the supralocal political relations which the society, because of its own structure, cannot organise *directly* in the form of a *permanent* institution. Following his analysis, Sahlins emphasises how contradictory is the basis of this power. Although it commences within reciprocity, the big-man's power rapidly involves an opposing practice. Little by little, the big-man will come to receive without ever repaying; in brief, he will end by making levies on the work and wealth of those who constitute the social basis of his power: his supporters, his faction. Reciprocity partly gives way to exaction. Finally, undermined and cracked, his social and material base collapses beneath him and his faction disperses, to rally around one or other of his rivals, who is thus raised by his fall.

I will not dwell on the point that Sahlins contrasts the dynamics of big-

4

men societies with the chiefly societies of Polynesia, in which a hereditary aristocracy exercises power in a permanent manner, to the extent that it has the monopoly over the conduct of ritual, war and trading activities.

After this brief synopsis of Sahlins' stimulating article, which has allowed me to outline the principal traits of the personage of a big-man, I shall now turn to the analysis of Baruya society.

## BARUYA SOCIETY

In September 1979, the Baruya formed a group of 2,159 individuals, divided among 17 villages and hamlets, located at altitudes of between 1,600 and 2,300 metres in Marawaka and Wonenara, two high valleys of the Kratke Range, a chain of mountains with peaks of up to 3,720 metres. In June 1960, this region was the last part of the province of the Eastern Highlands to pass under the control of the Australian Administration. In 1965, the region was declared pacified and opened to free movement for Whites.

By language, material culture and social organisation, the Baruya belong to an original group of local tribes and groups which have long been designated Kukakuka, a derogatory term which is not used by the Baruya themselves. *Kuka*, in their language, signifies 'to steal' or 'a thief'. Today, linguists, anthropologists and missionaries are endeavouring to get this insulting term banned from official texts and usage, and propose to replace it with the word *anga*, which, in all languages of this vast ethnic group, means 'house'. But it is fundamentally up to these groups themselves to decide what one should call them. Linguistically, they speak a group of related languages which one cannot link with the Melanesian languages of coastal groups in Papua New Guinea. Wurm (1975) has tried to link them to the phylum of non-Austronesian languages of the interior of New Guinea, but this is not yet completely proven. According to the work of the linguist Richard Lloyd, the Anga populations speak 11 languages, which might have become differentiated from a common root at the end of a process taking more than a thousand years to accomplish. The origin of these groups points in the direction of the south of Menyamya, which was probably the location of a great secular expansion of the Anga (Lloyd 1973).

The Baruya themselves arose from the misadventures of a fratricidal struggle, which took place within a tribe living near to Menyamya. This was over two centuries ago, according to my estimate. This tribe, the Yoyue, exploded into different fragments which became refugees with

Maurice Godelier

neighbouring groups. The Baruya were descended from a group of fugitives who were received by certain lineages of the Andje, a tribe living in the valley of Marawaka. Later, the Baruya, with the complicity of these Andje lineages, seized the territory of their hosts and drove them back towards the south.

Briefly, the social organisation of the Baruya is that of an acephalous tribe, composed of fifteen patrilineal 'clans' of which eight are descended from refugees coming from Menyamya, and seven from absorbed local groups. The clans are divided into lineages, which are themselves segmented. Residence, it seems, was patrilineal at first, and each of the lineages was grouped around a distinct location. But internal divisions, feuds, the possibility and, in certain cases, the urgent necessity of having to take refuge among affines or maternal kin, have entailed that several segments of lineages, belonging in fact to different clans, coexist in each village.

Agriculture is the principal economic activity, accompanied by pig-raising and a considerable production of vegetable salt. The main agricultural production is that of the sweet potato, cultivated in a relatively intensive fashion in the deforested area surrounding the villages, or in secondary growth. Taro comes a rather long way after sweet potato in the diet, but it is of first importance in ritual. It is cultivated sometimes in primary forest on newly tilled, cleared soil, sometimes in irrigated gardens. Hunting and gathering play a minimal role in subsistence, but have great social and ritual importance.

Land ownership is collective, in the sense that the descendants of a common ancestor are co-owners of the lands which he first cultivated. Everywhere, stems of cordyline trees planted by the first settlers mark the limits of property. But the use of land is very flexible and everyone easily obtains from his maternal relatives or his wife's brothers permission to use a piece of their land to make a garden, in exchange for returning the same service upon request. Women retain the right to use ancestral land all their lives, but they can neither inherit it nor pass it on to their children (Godelier 1969).

After this short account of Baruya society, let us go on to study the forms of authority and power which exist between the individuals and groups of which it is composed.

THE HIERARCHY OF THE SEXES: MALE DOMINATION

When I visited the Baruya for the first time in 1967, sleeping in the men's houses, one of which stands outside each village, what struck me immedi-

6

ately were signs of the existence of a double hierarchy: between men and women on the one hand, and among men on the other hand – between those who were described to me as the 'great warriors' and the others. Since then, several years spent among the Baruya have confirmed these first impressions. They have also allowed me to discover other forms of hierarchy, less visible and more complex, which I shall now proceed to sketch.

**The signs and forms of male domination**

There are many outward signs of the domination of men over women. At the level of body decoration, it is a fact that men are the beautiful sex among the Baruya. Their forehead is bound by a red band the colour of the sun, of which all the Baruya say they are sons. The head is decorated with different bird feathers, according to the man's stage of initiation and functions. The feather of an eagle, for example, is the mark of a shaman. By contrast, the women's appearance is much less colourful, and they are forbidden to wear or touch the feathers which adorn the heads of men (Godelier 1976).

Formerly, the Baruya space was traversed by double tracks, the track of the women meandering below the track of the men. When passed by a man, the women stopped, and hid their faces under a flap of their bark capes. As for the young initiated boys, they used to hide themselves in the bush when a group of women suddenly appeared round a corner of their route. The village space is divided into three sub-spaces. Dominating the village are one or more men's houses, where the young initiates live, and this constitutes a space which is strictly forbidden to women. Opposite this, at the lower end of the village, in an area of brushwood and jungle, the women go to bring their children into the world in shelters of branches and foliage, which they burn after use. This space is strictly forbidden to men, and when one suggests the idea of penetrating it they react with cries and strident laughter, in short, a form of behaviour which would qualify as hysterical in Europe. Between these two spaces, the village itself is a space occupied by both sexes. Here are the houses, inhabited by families composed of the husband, the wife or wives, the unmarried daughters and uninitiated sons. But as soon as one enters one of these houses, one can see once more the evidence of segregation between the sexes, since the interior space is divided by an imaginary line, passing through the middle of the hearth, which is constructed in the centre of the house. In the semi-circle near the door, the wife and her children live and sleep. At the other side of the hearth is the space for her husband and the men who come to pay him a visit. A woman must avoid going into the male part of the house, and must not in any case step over the hearth, because her genitals would then open over the fire and would pollute the food which goes into the man's mouth. But one must go beyond these exterior signs of male domination, such as bodily postures and gestures and the movements permitted or forbidden to each sex.

The picture of male domination becomes more explicit when one begins to analyse the place occupied by women and men in the various activities which produce their material and social existence. Briefly, women are excluded from land ownership, but not from usufruct rights. They are excluded from ownership and use of the most efficacious tools for clearing the forest: stone adzes and, these days, steel axes (Godelier 1973a). Women are excluded, in a general way, from ownership and use of weapons: for example, bows, clubs and shields. The monopoly over the main means of production and over the means of destruction and armed violence is thus found in the hands of men.

In addition, women are excluded from manufacturing the principal Baruya means of exchange, which is salt, and have no responsibility in the organisation of trading expeditions, in which men go to exchange this salt with neighbouring tribes. They depend upon men to obtain bars of salt (and, today, money) which they nevertheless dispose of as they wish, for example, for purchasing clothes or ornaments. In passing, I must point out that the production of salt is not a secondary aspect of the Baruya economy. It permitted them to procure stone axes, black palm wood for making their bows, feathers and pigs' teeth for decorating initiates, magical nuts for success in hunting, etc. Briefly, the production of this means of exchange is indispensable for the reproduction of the conditions of their material and social existence. The Baruya tribal economy can thus exist and reproduce itself only within the framework of a regional economy of diversified production and exchange.

Finally, women are excluded from the ownership and use of the sacred objects which, according to the Baruya, allow the production of social order (Godelier 1973b). They are entirely forbidden to see, touch or use the musical instruments, bullroarers and bamboo flutes, which are the voices of spirits that speak to men in the forest when they are initiating the boys whom they have just separated from their mothers.

In addition to this subordination of women in the various processes of production and exchange of the material means of social existence, the women likewise occupy a place subordinate to men in the process of reproduction of life, which is to say, within the functioning of kinship relations and rules of marriage. Descent among the Baruya is patrilineal and their kinship terminology is of the Iroquois variety (Lloyd 1974). They distinguish between parallel and cross cousins and, in ego's generation, senior:junior relationships are marked. The kinship terms extend into the generation of ego's great-grandparents and descend to his great-grandchildren. The term for the great-grandfather is the same as that used for older brother.

In this system, the locus of male domination is situated first in marriage rules. Marriage rests fundamentally on the principle of direct exchange of women between two lineages or segments of lineages. This type of marriage is considered the norm, and has a name: *ginamare*. Marriages with a close patrilateral parallel or close matrilateral cross cousin are forbidden. Marriage with a distant patrilateral parallel cousin is possible. The lineage and the clan are thus not exogamous units. The preferred form of residence is virilocal, but it is possible and common for the new couple to set up home with the woman's parents if the young husband wishes to get away from his brothers. This is a practice intended to restrain oppositions between brothers or parallel cousins, who are co-resident in the same village and invite one or other of their brothers-in-law to come and live among them. It leads rapidly to a complex entanglement of lineages within a village.

Alongside this first type of marriage exists a second, which is derived directly from it. It is called *kourémeundjinaveu*, literally 'to follow (*mandjinaveu*) the banana tree (*kouré*)', referring to the shoot which thrusts from the foot of a banana tree and replaces it when it dies. This image, in fact, depicts marriage with the father's sister's daughter, the patrilateral cross cousin. This marriage takes place when a man has given his sister without receiving a wife in exchange. He has then the right to claim one of his sister's daughters for marriage with one of his sons. This type of marriage thus points to the same principle as the preceding type, but the exchange, instead of being immediate, takes place within the short cycle of one generation.

Several other forms of marriage exist, upon which I shall not elaborate. The important thing to note is that they also issue, sooner or later, in the formula of exchange of women. For example, a man, by agreement with a young girl, decides to elope and marry her; later, after having been beaten by the wife's parents, he most frequently arranges to give them back one of the daughters born from this forced marriage. But the most important fact to underline is that the Baruya practise a type of marriage by payment

9

of bridewealth with distant tribes, with whom they have established or want to establish trading relations. They propose the exchange of salt bars and fathoms of cowries for a woman, or they hand over one of their women for a certain quantity of wealth. This marriage is called *apmwé tsala iraveumatna* (*apmwé*: 'woman'; *tsala*: 'salt'; *irata*: 'resemble'; *matna*: 'to take'). This type of marriage is never practised internally among the Baruya themselves.

Thus the relationships of Baruya kinship rest fundamentally on the principle that only a woman is worth a woman. When wealth intervenes to knit the matrimonial alliance, it is not in the interior of the group, nor likewise at the boundary with nearby tribes, but at the frontier of the economic region to which these tribes belong. We already catch a glimpse of one of the bases of the contrast between Baruya-type societies and big-men societies because, among the latter, the production of pigs, or of other forms of material wealth, is vital to the reproduction of life and the establishment of affinal alliance. Thus the social logic becomes meaningful which consists in accumulating goods in order to accumulate women or, conversely, in accumulating women in order to accumulate goods. The Baruya understand the principle of exchange of wealth for a woman but this principle plays only a subordinate role in the functioning of kinship relations. The difference between Baruya-type society and big-men societies is thus not really a difference consisting of the presence or absence of the principle of equivalence: women equal wealth. It is a difference in the relative importance of this principle in the reproduction of life.

Let me specify one essential fact. One might have the impression, on reading this brief description of Baruya social structure, that women have nothing to say in the making of matrimonial alliances, that they are passive instruments in them, that they submit docilely to the will of men in their lineage; but in fact it is nothing like this. Certainly a Baruya woman cannot refuse to marry and decide to remain single, but she can refuse to marry someone who has been chosen as her spouse. If this is the case, she reveals her decision after the initiation which she undergoes following her first menses. She then refuses the presents which are sent to her by the family of her fiancé, signifying by this that she refuses the alliance. It is a grave decision, difficult to take, above all because upon her marriage depends that of one of her brothers, who waits for her exchange to find a wife. But it does happen. It is likewise common, when a girl is born to a family and her parents are approached by another family, which already contemplates requesting her as future wife for one of their sons, that the mother refuses. Furthermore, nothing can begin, no engagement can be made, without the agreement of the girl's mother, who can dismiss a projected alliance without her husband being able to oppose her. This means two things; that the mothers have a solidarity with their daughters and intervene in their matrimonial fate; and then, because the mother consults the members of her lineage, that maternal relatives play their role in the conclusion of alliances between patrilineal lineages. Nevertheless, and this testifies again very clearly to the subordination of women to men, once the woman is married she cannot leave her husband, while he has the complete right to repudiate her or to give her to one of his brothers. On the death of a husband, the widow is inherited by one of his brothers or patrilateral parallel cousins.

Baruya women are thus subordinate to men materially, politically and symbolically. This subordination does not mean, in any way, that women do not possess specific rights. They have their own rights which the men have to recognise and to acknowledge. This does not imply at all that women consent without resistance to the social order which dominates them and often oppresses them. I shall return before long to their forms of resistance and to the forms of repression which their resistances trigger off on the men's part. But, before this, I must emphasise the point that men and women do not exercise full rights until they are married, and they cannot marry unless they are initiated. Initiations are thus the means of social production of men and women as subjects of rights and duties known to all, but which are not the same for all. It is this inequality which simultaneously produces and legitimates the apparatus of socialisation of individuals – male and female initiations.

### The institution and legitimation of male domination: initiations and the separation of the sexes

In the course of their lives, Baruya men and women pass through various stages, each of which has a distinct name. But the fundamental moments in the life cycle are the moments of initiation. I cannot go into details about the many rituals which make up male and female initiations, and will have to be content to present a schematic résumé.

Until he is 9 or 10 years old a boy lives with his parents. Then he is brutally severed from the female world to undergo the tests of the first stage of initiation, in the course of which his nose is pierced. Until then, he has been dressed in a manner fairly similar to a young girl. From now on he wears male insignia, but meanwhile he retains a certain part of the costume which recalls his former appearance in the female world. At about 13 years of age he becomes a *kawetnie* and is this time dressed completely like a man. At about 15 years of age he attains adolescence and becomes a *tchouwanie*. He is initiated into the secret principles of male domination and after this stage he can participate in combat by the side of adult warriors. At about 18 years of age, if he is engaged, and if his fiancée has had her first menses and is thus initiated, he becomes a *kalava* and stays in the men's house two or three more years until his marriage. Then he definitely quits the exclusively masculine world of the men's house and enters once more the bisexual world of the village, where he usually lives beside his older brothers or his father. On the birth of each one of his children he undergoes a ceremony, but his status as an adult man is not truly acquired until after he has become the father of four children. In old age, he will become an *apmwenangelo*: a 'great-man'. The two most important moments in the cycle of male initiation are the passages to the first and third stages. The first achieves the severing of the boy from the female world. The other gives the young initiate access to the world of warriors and future married men. One of the most secret and sacred rites of the initiation into the third stage, the *tchouwanie*, is when a huge horn-bill's beak is put on top of his head, overhanging a framework of rattan ending in two pointed pig's tusks, which are forced down on to the initiate's forehead. This painful headdress signifies male domination, because the secret meaning of the hornbill's beak and pig's tusks is that the first represents a man's penis and the second a woman's vagina.

The mother is thus the first woman that a man leaves. But she is also the last whom he recovers, in the sense that a Baruya man has to wait several years and have children before offering game to his mother and lifting the taboo, which had until then prohibited him from eating in her presence and addressing her directly.

If it takes ten years and four stages of initiation to produce a Baruya man, it seems to take only a few weeks to produce a woman. It is in fact when a young girl has had her first menses that she undergoes the tests of her initiation. She is isolated in a menstrual house, where she stays fasting for several days, until the moment when she is led out to the bush to participate in the various rituals of her initiation. These rites are, for the most part, at night; but some take place at dawn and at dusk.

With the permission of the women, I was able to participate, as an exception, in several female initiation ceremonies. Without going into detail, I can say that these ceremonies take place around a gigantic fire, lit by the young girl's sponsor and newly married women. At night, the initiate is led close to the intense heat and they make her sit down very near the flames, on the lap of her sponsor, who attends her all through the night. The heat is appalling and is intended to cleanse the young girl of her impurities and give her a new skin: more beautiful, glossy. This is achieved during hours of long speeches delivered by old women who address themselves to the initiate, menacing her with long digging sticks. From time to time these harangues are interrupted by dances and little scenes played by groups of recently initiated girls or young married women. The general meaning of these speeches and dances is an appeal for the submission of women to men: do not resist your husband when he wishes to make love; do not cry out, or it will be heard, and he will hang his head in shame; do not laugh if your husband's loincloth is badly placed and allows his genitals to be seen — he will be ashamed; do not kill your child when you have brought it into the world — men are more attached when they have children . . . In the middle of these sermons a young girl appears disguised as a man, a warrior. She is the sister of the initiate's fiancé, or a young woman chosen by the father of the initiate, and she comes to represent the groom. The old women then shout, to catch the young initiate's attention: 'Well, see who comes, see [and here follows the name of the young man she will marry].'

At a certain moment — one of the most important of the ceremony — they give the young girl a piece of sugar cane, with the peel removed, to suck. For the Baruya, sugar cane is a plant exclusively cultivated by men, in special gardens, and it represents the penis. The juice of sugar cane is thus like the sperm which men disseminate not only in women's wombs to make children, but also in their mouths, since they give their semen to women to drink when they need to recover strength after having given birth.

There is a major difference between male and female initiations. Young boys, once separated from their mothers, find themselves for at least ten years in a truly different world, exclusively masculine, where they will be reborn. Young women spend only a few days in an exclusively female world, to find themselves afterwards back with their mothers, living the same family life as before. Then they wait to leave one family for another: that of their father for that of their husband. Nevertheless it would be wrong to consider female initiation as a way in which women either imitate or oppose men. Indeed, if one examines the content of the messages of which female rites are the vehicle, one sees that these are the complement or extension of male initiation rites within the world of women. It is the portion reserved for women so that they affirm the same order, the same law, the law of male domination. It is the performance, by the women themselves, of their consent to the order that dominates them.

All these ritual practices are, of course, expressed, interpreted and marked off by a system of representations which legitimates them in Baruya thought. To give an idea of the nature of these representations, I will refer to two of the theoretical schemes which occur. In one, there are myths, which explain how women invented the bow, the sacred flutes, etc., which they do not now have the right to handle and which have become a male monopoly. These myths also explain, for example, that women held the bow wrongly and killed too much game in a disordered manner. The men themselves discovered the *right* usage of the bow and since then they have had the monopoly of it. These myths thus clearly affirm that women possess a creativity which is profound, but a source of disorder, and that order is the order of masculine domination. In other myths, it is said that taro and other cultivated plants came out of the body of a woman who had been murdered and secretly buried by a man. Here again the message is the same: the cosmic order cannot be founded without doing violence to women and appropriating their creativity.

If one considers, in another connection, Baruya representations of the process of conception of a child, one rediscovers the same inequality in the contribution of each of the sexes to this process. Indeed, for the Baruya, the child is made in the female's womb by the double intervention of the man and the sun. The man makes the embryo with his sperm and 'feeds' it afterwards by repeated intercourse. But the man makes only the body of the child: it is the sun who makes the eyes, the nose, the mouth, the hands and the feet. Each child therefore has two fathers: his natural father and the supernatural father of all human beings, the sun. The woman herself becomes fecund only after the moon has 'pierced' her and caused her first menstrual blood to flow. Yet the child who emerges from the woman's womb must, if he is a boy, be reborn by the work of men and in an exclusively masculine world. This is the meaning of initiations, of the separation of sexes and the extended existence of boys in the men's house.

Thus the Baruya combine two principles of exchange in order to make a man: the direct exchange of women between men belonging to distinct lineages, and the generalised exchange of sperm between young men of distinct cohorts who have not yet left the exclusively masculine universe of the men's house. Whereas in the exchange of women the givers are also the takers, in the exchange of sperm the seniors give to their juniors a vital substance which they themselves received from their elders. I shall not go further in this analysis of fundamental representations of Baruya thought, but I must indicate that this thought is much more ambiguous and complex than I have suggested. Even as men exchange their vital substance between themselves, the women exchange their milk between themselves — but this is not supposed to be known to men. There are thus elements of a certain autonomy of the female world, an autonomy which the Baruya male world strives unceasingly to deny. It is thus not by chance that several versions of the identity of the sun and moon exist. In the current version, the moon is the wife of the sun, and it is she who penetrates the young girl at the time of puberty. In another, known only to some shamans, the moon is the younger brother of the sun. At the level of supernatural powers the universe again becomes more strongly male, or at least the male aspect of the universe once more appears larger, ideationally amplifying and ideologically magnifying the powers lent to men in society.

Finally, at the end of this analysis of the place of men and women in pre-colonial Baruya society, I can confirm that the role of male and female initiations is to produce, and at the same time legitimate, the general domination of men, of *all* men, whatever may be their personal aptitudes, over women, *all* women, whoever they are. It is this general rendering of the subordination of women which perfectly illuminates the fact that, among the Baruya, as soon as a young man is initiated and enters the men's house, his older sisters stop calling him little brother, our junior, as they have until now, but call him henceforth *dakwe*, older brother. Male initiation thus transforms all women into juniors of their juniors, and displaces the real, genealogical, order of women within kinship relations.

This superiority in general and in principle of men over women is not the only form of social hierarchy among the Baruya. Others exist alongside this, but all of them have this first inequality as their basis, a basis they are unable to overstep.

## THE PRODUCTION OF GREAT-MEN AND GREAT-WOMEN

I am now approaching the analysis of two groups of hierarchical relations which are additional to those of male domination and at the same time proceed from them. These two forms of hierarchy are organised around different social functions, which finally distinguish the individuals among themselves, according to their capacity or incapacity to assume them.

The first hierarchy is that which sets apart, among men, those responsible for rituals of male initiation. These individuals possess this function because they have inherited it from their ancestors who have transmitted to them the sacred objects and indispensable magico-religious formulae for the accomplishment of initiation rites. It is said that their ancestors themselves received them from the sun and the moon; but not all lineages possess sacred objects. Behind the distinction between the masters of rituals and others is the outline of a hierarchy between those lineages which assume responsibility for initiation rites and the other lineages which do not perform them and do not have the right to perform them. Beyond this hereditary lineage hierarchy, another domain opens up, in which it is possible to express the unequal capacities of individuals of each generation to assume three roles required for the reproduction of society: warriorhood, shamanism and cassowary hunting. It is here that great-men are selected who distinguish themselves in the course of their lives from the mass of their contemporaries, men of more ordinary capacities and qualities, whom the Baruya themselves call by the rather unflattering term *wopaie*, sweet potatoes.

One of these three functions, shamanism, occupies a distinct place, in that it is equally accessible to women and constitutes the only domain of social practice in which the powers of the two sexes can to a certain degree confront each other. It is in this domain that some women emerge who are greater than others: shamans who, while becoming great-women, none the less cannot also maintain that they are as great as the great male shamans.

One can already guess in the course of this résumé that, within Baruya society, individual differences between men are at the same time sought and produced, while the same society seems to be content with a female world far more homogeneous and dull.

## Hereditary status and interlineage hierarchy: the *kwaimatnie* men

Every three years, a new age-group enters the great ceremonial house (*tsimia*) which is specially constructed for the performance of male initiations. This house assumes a very precise meaning for the Baruya. They visualise it as the 'body' of the tribe, in which the 'bones' are the posts, each of which has been planted by an adult man and each of which represents an initiate. The thatch of the roof is considered to be the 'skin' of this body, which is the symbolic body of the political and religious unity of all Baruya, whatever may be their membership of such kinship groups or villages as make up the tribe. And yet this ceremony, celebrated for all, is not celebrated by all, because only men of the lineages that possess a sacred object, a *kwaimatnie*, have the right to perform and assume this duty on behalf of the general interest.

A *kwaimatnie* is an object carefully concealed from public gaze by a piece of bark cape. The word means 'to increase and multiply men', 'to raise their skin'. In general, the *kwaimatnie* exist in pairs and the more powerful of the two is considered to be female. This is unknown to women, so that, once again, one can see that male power is constituted by the appropriation, the capture of a female power.

When one analyses the list of lineages that possess *kwaimatnie*, one is immediately struck by the fact that they belong, with one particular exception, exclusively to the Baruya clans which fled Menyamya two centuries ago and became refugees in Marawaka, amongst populations whose territory they have finally conquered. The exception confirms this rule, because it concerns precisely that clan of the autochthonous Andje which helped the Baruya refugees to seize the land of their hosts. It is in repayment of their treason and inestimable help that the principal clan of refugees, the Baruya clan — which has given its name to the new tribe — has granted one of its *kwaimatnie* to them. It is thus a fundamental political distinction between conquerors and conquered which explains the distinction between the lineages with *kwaimatnie* and those which are bereft of them.

According to the Baruya, all the sacred objects appeared when they were still in their ancestral territory, before the disruption of their tribe and the flight to Marawaka. They attribute their military and magical superiority over the autochthons to the possession of these sacred objects. I will not enter into the problems which are posed by this Baruya claim to possess incomparable powers and sacred objects and to deny possession of true *kwaimatnie* to the autochthons. In fact, my researches allowed me to discover that the autochthons now absorbed by the Baruya formerly possessed sacred objects of the same type which they have been forced to hide, to bury in the ground after the Baruya conquest.

What are the functions of *kwaimatnie* men? They are mediators between the sun and men. In the course of ceremonies, they beat the chests of initiates with the sacred object, while pronouncing the secret name of the sun in an inaudible fashion. This then emits its force, which flows into the body of each one. But, when they are officiating, the masters of ritual also have the power of divining the future of each initiate, of predicting his life for him to a certain degree. This gift of prescience is possessed by them only at the ritual moment, and this distinguishes them from shamans. As mediators and seers, the possessors of *kwaimatnie* are also those who set rituals in motion and watch scrupulously over their celebration. They are surrounded by respect and recognition for the ser-

Maurice Godelier

vices which they render to the tribe; but this respect comes more from their function than from their person.

Besides respect and recognition, the psychological aspects of his authority, the possessor of *kwaimatnie* benefits from several less psychological advantages. People see to it that he finds a spouse easily in order for him to have sons to whom he can transmit his ritual knowledge. Above all, in a society which puts the warriors and the values of warfare in the first rank, the *kwaimatnie* man is not authorised to participate in the front line in the wars which the Baruya wage with their neighbours, for fear that he might be killed in combat before having transmitted the whole of his ritual formulae to one of his sons or nephews. Finally, despite the fact that his function raises him above ordinary men, the *kwaimatnie* man cannot transform his prestige into a true power of general command over the rest of society. In no way can he make a claim on it in order to require material advantages as the price of his services. On the contrary, he declares unceasingly that what he does he does in order to respond to the appeal of fathers and mothers, who wish their sons to change as fast as possible into true men, in order to defend them and accomplish their duty. In the course of initiation ceremonies orators therefore constantly remind them that it is not they alone who create initiates, and that everyone has worked hard to supply the grass skirts, headdresses and necessary foods to celebrate the ceremonies. Thus the emphasis is placed on the contribution of all lineages and all generations to the common task, and silence is maintained about the monopoly which certain lineages have over the use of sacred objects.

In conclusion, with the *kwaimatnie* men we are faced with a sort of stable social framework of the Baruya tribe, a framework of functions and institutions which escapes competition. Beyond this, a vast domain opens up — that of war, of shamanism and of hunting — in which someone or other is bound to succeed.

### Warriors, shamans, cassowary hunters: statuses for appropriation

This heading, like all stylistic devices, calls for commentaries and qualifications. In effect, every Baruya man is, and must be, a warrior and a hunter, but only a few will become *aoulatta*, the 'great warriors' or cassowary hunters or shamans. When I write of statuses for appropriation this is what I mean.

### 1. The *aoulatta*: the great warriors
*Aoulatta*, in Baruya, means three things: a certain type of arrow, used to

18

kill birds; a variety of pandanus, in which the trunk is so covered with hard, spiny leaves that it is difficult to climb; and certain warriors — the greatest — who confront the enemy directly, body to body, club in hand, or stop an enemy attack with arrows, sheltering alone behind a shield. The greatest feat of the *aoulatta* is to issue a challenge to enemies on the field of battle and to advance alone towards their lines, followed by a few aides, called his 'dogs'; these will cover him when he has knocked down his adversary and is dispatching him. The *aoulatta* is therefore a man of individual exploits, who nevertheless gives victory to his tribe or protects it from defeat. His exploits are in all memories, in the form of recitations and chants which have withstood the test of time, carrying with them names and prestigious deeds. Bakitchatche was one of these and, until the Whites arrived, the fingers which allowed him to fire so many deadly arrows at his enemies were preserved, dried in a Baruya village. This relic disappeared when an administration officer set the village on fire, in order to punish its inhabitants for participating in a feud.

Admittedly, these exploits are explained by a supernatural power, rather than by exceptional physical capacities. The *aoulatta* is described as inhabited by a power which discloses to him the presence of the enemy, anticipates his movements, and fixes him in a position where he will fall in ambush. The very weapon which the *aoulatta* prefers, the stone club, is considered to be a magic weapon, because the Baruya did not manufacture in stone and claimed that these clubs had been given by benevolent spirits to their ancestors. However, this type of individual can be fully understood only if one bears in mind the role of war in Baruya society and history. The Baruya themselves emerged from an unfortunate war and a fortunate conquest. In doing so, they threw their neighbours into other groups, overturning the political relations of a whole region. But all these groups were constantly under strain from internal dissensions, which led more or less rapidly to their splitting and their disruption. It is in this context that one can appreciate the importance of the *aoulatta*, who maintains the territorial integrity of his group, or who helps to seize a part of the neighbouring territory.

One thus easily guesses what prestige and glory the *aoulatta* carried because of his exploits. His name was known far and wide, among enemies as well as allies. When an *aoulatta* enemy was killed in single combat, his hand was often cut off and exhibited, nailed on a stand, on which was also hung the club of the *aoulatta* victor.

But did the *aoulatta* not accumulate power and wealth in addition to honour and glory? Certainly not wealth. An *aoulatta*, say the Baruya, thinks of nothing but war, he has few wives, few children, and he leaves behind for his descendants little land cleared by his hand. Today certain clans renowned for the number of their warriors still have little land, because their ancestors were preoccupied with fighting, in order to conquer land for all. As to power, the *aoulatta* enjoy a privilege in which no other partakes. In case of conflict between brothers or between brothers-in-law, conflict which threatens the unity of village or tribe, he has sufficient authority to stand up between the antagonists, and demand that they make peace. His prestige thus allows him to surmount the limits and constraints which the normal working of kinship obligations imposes on everyone among the Baruya. However, occasionally the *aoulatta* abuses his authority and the dread in which he is held.

Examples of *aoulatta* who transformed themselves little by little into despots or petty local tyrants are not uncommon among the Baruya. They killed their neighbours' pigs, forced their wives to have intercourse with them and beat them in front of their husbands if they refused. In general, sanction was not long in coming and the death of the tyrant was the punishment for his despotism. Perhaps an arrow went astray in combat; perhaps, in the same way, some were not reluctant to forewarn enemies of the movements of a great-man who then fell in ambush. This recalled to everyone that, among the Baruya, social differences are not sought unless they serve the general interest. Furthermore this is the major lesson of all initiations: to be strong, but to put one's strength at the service of others.

Yet, behind the warriors, and behind the greatest among them, stand some men who do not go, or seldom go, to war and who, far from being scorned by the Baruya, are, like *kwaimatnie* men, called by two terms which also indicate the importance which is attached to their functions: *tannaka* or *tsimie*.

*Tannaka* means a 'protrusion' which gives a handle for pulling oneself up a rock face or the trunk of a tree. *Tsimie* denotes the central post of a great ceremonial house. Who are these *tannaka*, or *tsimie*, whose existence I had not even imagined for years? These are the men who are strong at agricultural work, who make large gardens and with whose help the warriors and the *aoulatta* make war without having to be preoccupied with their subsistence. One or two or these men, upon whom everyone could count, exist in all villages. They mobilise their women and receive the aid of other women of the village and sometimes even of the youths of the men's house to clear the forest.

In times of peace, the *tannaka* put their gardens at everyone's disposal, when it is necessary to organise initiations, or assemblies, or discussions on general points of interest. By their ability to pool the male and female work-force around them, the *tannaka* strongly resemble big-men. But the difference from big-men, who finally raise themselves above all others, is that the *tannaka* do not pursue personal enrichment. They produce in order to redistribute, and they redistribute in circumstances of wars and initiations where they gain stature with others, the *aoulatta*, who also appear as indispensable as themselves to the general interest.

## 2.   The *koulaka*: the shaman

In all Baruya villages one comes across some individuals, men and women, to whom frequent appeal is made to cure an illness, to prevent or get rid of an epidemic, etc. These are the shamans (see Herdt 1977). The analysis of shamanism is very complex and I shall restrict myself here to pointing out some essential aspects. Immediately, two of these aspects must be under-lined. On the one hand, there is the fact that shamanism is the only status-producing activity in which men and women participate directly: and, on the other, there is the fact that this activity is the object of a process of particular initiations, which develop in a separate way from the big male and female initiations. Of course, we shall see that, in this domain also, male domination is reproduced both in the difference between magical tasks which men and women can perform and in the symbolic ornaments which each sex is allowed to wear.

What are the functions of shamans? In a general way, they have the task of protecting the Baruya against illness and death. In this task, men and women shamans participate, in distinct but complementary ways. Shaman men assume an additional function, which is to wage a magical war, by sorcery, against neighbouring enemy tribes. Shamans do not attend to every kind of illness. Excluded from the practice are, for example, open wounds, fractures and chills. They concentrate on the treatment of internal illnesses: stomach pains, general weakness. They are called in by the patient, and it is their duty to respond to this appeal. They examine, then seek, the 'cause' of the ill, by creating a state of communication with the world of spirits through smoking large quantities of green tobacco. They enter into a sort of secondary state which allows them to see the cause of the ill. Often they discover the cause at night, in dreams, when their spirits detach themselves from their bodies and travel over Baruya territory. Once the cause of the ill is identified, they set about extracting the poisons and objects which bad spirits have introduced into the patient's body, and they send them in the direction of enemy territory. Thus each cure is at the same time an act of aggression against the health and integrity of hostile neighbouring tribes. Besides this, the shaman furnishes an interpretation of illness; he explains to the patient what he has discovered in his dream and, most of the time, the explanation comes down to accusing the patient of having violated, involuntarily or not, some important taboo. For example, he explains to a patient that he is a victim of the dealings of a spirit which lives in a mountain, where it is forbidden to till the soil, and that this spirit has punished him because he has transgressed the prohibition by clearing a garden in this area. The shaman thus interprets the illness of men in a way which reinforces the social order. One must nevertheless state that a shaman is powerless to save the victim of an act of sorcery perpetrated by another Baruya. Only he who has cast an evil spell can lift it. The shaman therefore does not intervene in reciprocal acts of sorcery in which Baruya individuals and lineages are opposed. His fundamental mission is to protect the group as such, to keep it in existence. Indeed, the shamans maintain that each night their spirits assemble on the boundaries of Baruya territory, to prevent the spirits of sleeping Baruya from crossing these boundaries and losing themselves in enemy territories. Such a boundary crossing means death, and when it happens, the next morning they will find the corpse of a Baruya in his house, a body without its spirit. The Baruya believe therefore that each night the shamans, men and women, are occupied in taking care that each person's spirit finds its body again with the dawn.

The Baruya claim not to know the way shamans operate to maintain life. This is in fact a secret which is only revealed to future shamans at the moment of their initiation. Then they learn that their spirit is transformed into a bird if they are men, a frog if they are women, and that under this metamorphosis they are deployed all along the tribal boundaries. The bird-spirits of men fly right to the top of mountains and search there for the presence of enemy sorcerers or evils invisible to common mortals. Thus shamans are credited with two types of action beneficial for the tribe. One is visible and temporary — these are the ceremonies for attending individually or collectively to patients — the other invisible and permanent — for maintaining the whole of the population in existence whether sick or in good health.

On the part of male shamans, a final activity is added. This is an individual or collective practice of sorcery directed against enemies, and designed to paralyse the great enemy warriors, to provoke unforeseen landslides that will engulf men and women at work in their fields or on a hunting expedition, etc. However, it is absolutely forbidden, on pain of death, or public disgrace, for a shaman to practise sorcery against another Baruya.

How does one become a shaman? The term for shaman in Baruya is *koulaka*, which also means 'spiritual power'. All individuals have these powers. It may be that they have acquired them in the course of their existence, by chance, through events or meetings, or it may be that they have inherited them from their ancestors. At the end of a track in the forest a hunter suddenly perceives that a leaf quivers, alone among all those on a tree. This unwonted movement attracts his gaze, and it is thus that the spirit of the tree enters him. Or, again, a woman sees a pig of a certain colour in a dream, and concludes from this that she is henceforth prohibited from eating this type of pig, and that she possesses within herself a little of its power. However, if all Baruya accumulate powers, not all become shamans. It is the shaman who has the power of prescience, the power to divine the cause of others' sickness, and who acquires the capacity to combat this evil, to cure by magic. The initiated shaman foresees future shamans among children, youths and young women, by a gleam which is in their gaze, by the accounts they give of their dreams or by their encounters. Yet it is not only shamans who discover future shamans. Various masters of ritual, as we have seen, have this power of prescience, but only temporarily, at the moment when they celebrate the initiation rites. They also divine the future shaman in the gaze of a young initiate, and they divine the future great warriors. The selection of shamans is thus a complex process, which only comes about at the end of a long period of collective observation and testing. This selection is not made totally by chance. Certain clans are reputed to produce more shamans than others, and people expect that the children of these clans will show the qualities of a future shaman. The female shamans are often the wives or daughters of shamans. Thus shamanism tends to become a quasi-hereditary function, an activity which becomes concentrated within the society much more than fighting activity which promotes the great *aoulatta*. The clearest indication of the closed nature of this is the fact that the master of shaman initiations always comes from the same lineage, the lineage of Andavakia, which seems to form a fixed base of the shamanistic system, the equivalent of which is the *kwaimatnie* men for male initiations.

Despite this fixed base and this very strong tendency for shamanistic activities to be concentrated in certain lineages, the system still remains open. Individuals in each generation, men and women belonging to any lineage, including the autochthonous lineages absorbed by the Baruya, are promoted as shamans on account of the capacities of prescience which they manifest. A proof of the Baruya will to maintain open a domain of

Maurice Godelier

promotion of individuals which has a constant tendency towards closure is
the fact that, during the shaman initiation ceremonies, the man who represents the Baruya clan of the Baruya tribe, the man who possesses the most
powerful *kwaimatnie* (that of the initiation of *tchouwanie*, the young
warriors), is present, and places their headdresses on the heads of the
shamans.

What, therefore, is the social power of shamans? One must recall that
they are distinguished by particular insignia — eagle plumes on the head
and bat bones through the nose for men — and that they move about with
a very guarded bearing — observing silence or speaking very little. In short,
they behave in an almost opposite manner to that of an *aoulatta*, who acts
as a great warrior, sure of himself, a little braggardly and violent. Their
person is surrounded with dread and one does not go into their homes
unless one has been invited. The Baruya think that the spirit of a shaman,
man or woman, feeds upon the raw livers of men. They explain women's
miscarriages by this. Yet this power of doing evil is not sorcery, it is the
involuntary effect of the power of the shaman's spirit. They are thus the
object of ambivalent feelings, of recognition of their good deeds and dread
of their murderous powers. The care that they give is remunerated. The
patients offer salt or, these days, money, sending presents of joints of pork
from time to time. It is not unusual to see a shaman suggest that the gift of
such and such a thing would give him pleasure, and a few days later one
can ascertain that the request has been heard.

In conclusion, I must underline the very great difference in status
between male shamans and female shamans. The latter are not authorised
in collective ceremonies to stand upright like the men and to lead the first
line of combat against the evil spirits. They are initiated in the course of a
ceremony which is separate from that of men, but held immediately afterwards. They thus receive the insignia of their new status from the great
male shamans, and these insignia are male: an arrow given by their husband, then a red forehead band identical to those which are put on the
forehead of initiated boys. Yet, and this is the most hidden secret of this
initiatory practice, the general force, the power which permits men and
women shamans to cure, is supposed to originate in the light of Venus, a
Baruya woman, formerly sacrificed to the thunder god, and metamor-
phosed into a star. Once again, we establish that the power of men has its
origin in the appropriation, the capture, the conversion of a female power.
In daily life it is easy to ascertain that, despite the alleged superiority in
general and in principle of men over women, certain shaman women are
considered to be much greater than a large number of their male colleagues.

24

But to these, as to others, the right of initiating other women is refused. This monopoly is male and belongs to a single Baruya clan, the Andavakia, descended from those refugees who conquered the autochthonous groups two centuries ago.

We are going to find this same ambivalence of masculine power again in the last great personage officially celebrated in initiations: the *kayareumala*, the cassowary hunter.

### 3.  The *kayareumala*: the cassowary hunter

*Kayareumala* denotes at the same time the hunt for the cassowary and the hunter. *Mala* means 'to make war' and 'to kill'; *kayarie* is the term for cassowary. The hunting of cassowary occupies a place entirely apart from the many other forms of hunting practised by the Baruya. The reason for this is found fundamentally in the world picture of the Baruya. For them the cassowary is not a bird, because it does not know how to fly and does not perch. This terrestrial animal is a biped like a man. A unique animal, it is considered by them to be the wild woman of the forest. Admittedly the Baruya distinguish very well between the male and the female of the cassowary, but they describe all cassowaries, whatever their sex, by the terms which they apply to women. According to the size of the animal, they call it 'little girl', 'pubertal girl', 'grandmother', or 'old woman'. The cassowary-wild-woman is considered to have supernatural powers. The Baruya say that it is not unusual, when a cassowary is entangled in the trap which the great hunter has laid for it, for violent winds to blow up and for thunder to begin to rumble over the valley.

The cassowary is caught in a trap. Its flesh is consumed exclusively by men, with the exception of the hunter himself and the first-stage initiates, who are still in the intermediary world between the female world and the male world. The women cannot eat it — to the Baruya that would be like eating themselves. The cassowary hunt thus immediately takes on the significance of a struggle against the female world, and of a proof which demonstrates, in another and particularly spectacular way, the superiority of men over women.

While all the Baruya know how to construct traps to snare game, only some of them will become cassowary hunters. This is not for reasons of technique, but for reasons of magic. The cassowary hunter has been possessed sometime during his life by the spirit of a cassowary and it is this spirit which allows him to attract the game into his trap. The cassowary hunters sometimes reveal themselves during the male initiations when the women bring in the thatch for constructing the roof of the ceremonial hut.

Then they go into a trance and foam at the mouth, possessed by the spirit of a cassowary-woman.

Trances, possession and dreams make the cassowary hunt an activity situated between war and shamanism, one which contributes in a particularly explicit way to the production and exaltation of the domination of men over women. Yet, despite this importance, the activity does not confer a very great status on its practitioners. It adds to the renown of those who are already great warriors or great shamans by another route, but it is not sufficient to push the individual to the first rank.

Finally, I must say a few words about an activity which confers a certain status on those who practise it, but which has never found its place in the great Baruya ideological machinery of male initiations. This is the activity of *tsaimaye*: the salt maker.

## 4. The *tsaimaye*: the salt maker

We have seen how important salt is for the Baruya and how its manufacture calls attention to an extremely complex technique which is also exclusively in the hands of men (Godelier 1971). Baruya salt, which is extracted from the stems of a cultivated plant (*Coix gigantea* Koenig), contains potassium and not sodium, gives a very salty taste to the food with which it is mixed and in strong doses is a fierce poison. This salt is used on all the special occasions of Baruya life. It serves to make the sauces which are spat out and spread on the ceremonial food. According to the Baruya it has the capacity to cool the liver, seat of the vital force of the individual. It is at the same time a good produced for exchange, which functions as money in the economic exchanges between the Baruya and their neighbours. The salt maker is a man who has received from his father or an affine the technical and magical knowledge which allows him to crystallise the salt. He knows how to build an immense oven of fireproof clay and he watches over the slow crystallisation of the salt for five days and five nights. During this time he abstains from all sexual relations and all contact with women — otherwise the salt retains water or weighs too light. In each village one finds two or three salt workshops, each of which belongs to a specialist. When the various families of the village cut their fields of *Coix*, they ask one or other of the salt makers to make them some salt and they repay his trouble by making him a present of one or two bars from the fifteen or so which he has produced. But in no way does this remuneration allow a salt maker to live exclusively on his skill and to cease being an agriculturalist, a hunter, or a warrior, like everyone else. Furthermore, like everyone, he has to procure stone adzes, bark capes, and feathers which allow for his material and social reproduction. Certainly he never lacks the salt necessary to procure them, but at the same time he is never in a position to accumulate them so as to redistribute them to those who lack them, and thus to create the obligations entailing help in work or in acquisition of products, exempting him from work himself. Another important point is that the salt maker is at the service of a 'client' who remains the owner of the raw material and also of the final product of his work, the salt. Following the intralineage struggles and the fissions that came after these, there now exist lineages among the Baruya which do not have salt land. But they receive salt from their brothers-in-law, and one sees here once again the obligations connected with the direct exchange of women which creates a redistribution of resources that compensates for, or in part annuls, inequality of access to the means of production.

It is perhaps for these reasons that the activities of *tsaimaye* on the one hand contribute to distinguish him, to raise him above ordinary men who have no particular competence, but on the other hand are not sufficient to make him the object of a more elaborate ideological significance, to cause him to appear on that Baruya ideological scene represented by male initiations. It is a fact that the salt maker does not struggle either like the warrior, against enemies, or, like the shaman, against evil spirits and death. His practice, if it implies magical knowledge and seclusion from women, like all serious male activities, does not imply the power of prescience, does not entail any possession, any trance or any secondary state, and does not lead to any exploit. The good manufacturer is he who makes the heaviest salt, but the good manufacturer is not necessarily he who goes among enemies to exchange it at the risk of his life. Certainly, his activity distinguishes him and adds a little more to the material, political and symbolic dependence of women on men; but it never allows him truly to transform his prestige into authority over others, into power. In some ways he resembles the *tannaka*, the hard-working agriculturalist, whose activity, more than the salt maker's, is directly linked to the material necessities entailed by war and initiations — the two highest moments of Baruya life — but is not in any way the object of a supernatural significance. Perhaps this is because the exploits of the *tannaka* and *tsaimaye* are not brought about by a direct struggle against enemies, human or supernatural, but against nature, even though this concept does not belong to Baruya thought.

To sum up, we have already found several systems of differentiation which constitute an intricate social hierarchy. These are, first, the general domination of men over women, a domination instituted in a spectacular fashion by the passage of each individual through collective initiations. In this way the collective domination of men over women is imposed. Second, within each sex another principle works, and adds its effects to the general subordination of women to men. This is the principle of superiority of seniors over juniors. The non-initiated owe respect to initiates, the first-stage initiates to those in other stages, and so on, until the moment when a man, having four or five children and still able to fight, is a great-man, *apmwenangelo*. Similarly, a non-initiated young girl owes respect to a female initiate and she will become a great-woman when she has given three or four living children to her husband and has demonstrated that she is hard-working and long-suffering. But the principle of superiority of elders is itself put to the service of male domination because, as we have seen, once a boy is initiated, all his older sisters (genealogically) become his juniors (socially).

This inequality between the sexes is the fundamental basis of the social order. It is on this basis that other differences are produced which add to it. Among men, it is the difference between those who possess the necessary sacred objects for male initiations or the initiations of shamans and the remaining men who do not possess them. This distinction reflects a political distinction between conquering Baruya lineages, to which one must add the autochthonous lineage which facilitated their conquest, and the local, absorbed lineages, which have rallied to Baruya power. This series of individuals who celebrate the rituals for the benefit of all constitutes a social framework, the permanent base of the institutional production of male domination. They exercise their function, not in their personal name, but in the name of their lineage, and they are always surrounded, when they perform, by brothers and parallel cousins, who help them and take part in their responsibility. They certainly have their own prestige if they show exceptional talents in fulfilling their role well, but the essence of their prestige is created more from their usefulness to others than from themselves. Whatever may be their function in the ritual cycle, and whatever may be their special aptitude to fulfill it, this function and this aptitude are never the point of departure for accumulating wealth and material difference between individuals or of distinguishing in this way their lineage from others.

There is another source of differentiation between individuals, a differentiation acquired, this time, by their own merit and no longer, as in the preceding case, inherited or transmitted through the kinship system: the difference between the warrior, the shaman and the cassowary hunter. Here we are faced with distinct functions, and also a domain which is partially open to competition and individual initiative. Here a certain hierarchy is drawn up; the great warrior, *aoulatta*, seems to carry prestige over others. His name is on all lips and he is known in all enemy tribes. He is the object of wonder and recognition, he has his partisans and, in order to suggest the nature of the sentiments which the Baruya can have for their great warriors, I will point out that it is common to see an aged informant begin to cry when he recounts the great deeds of an *aoulatta* who died in war. Always an individual in the first line of combat, the *aoulatta* is much better known to neighbours than the shaman, who himself leads the combat at the interior of the tribe, in the shadow of rituals of sorcery directed against enemies. Yet it would be incorrect to imagine that one is dealing with a hierarchy descending from the *aoulatta* at the top down to the cassowary hunter, because it would never occur to a Baruya to ask a warrior to do the work of a shaman, and vice versa. The two functions are complementary, and they tend to separate individuals even in their style of existence. Nevertheless I do know of examples of several great *aoulatta* who were at the same time great shamans. The judgement on them makes them appear like exceptional heroes, exceptional also in the sense that Baruya social logic tends to separate social functions, much more than it assembles and reunites them in the same man. One can say without question that the status of cassowary hunter remains minor, compared to those of warrior and shaman. Moreover it is an activity which, far from excluding the others, as war and shamanism do, can be combined with them. One frequently sees great shamans who are at the same time great cassowary hunters, for they are predisposed to it by their gift of trance and possession.

More minor again, and more open to individual initiative, we find the status of salt maker. Such are the systems of functions and status which differentiate between men and women among men. And one must not forget that behind these visible distinctions there are others, less apparent; that behind the *aoulatta* there is the *tannaka* who partially shares his prestige and his war-linked authority.

Women themselves are also subject to differentiation. If Baruya men are reluctant to admit there are great-women, they recognise without difficulty that some women are greater than others: the wives of *tannaka* for example, who labour hard in their gardens to help their husbands to redistribute the means of making war, or to celebrate an initiation. But although there is a word in the Baruya language for the *tannaka*, there is none to distinguish his wife from other women. There are also women shamans, some of whom are much more dreaded and admired than most of the male

Maurice Godelier

shamans. There are, finally, women called *aoulatta*, not at all because they are warriors and because they struggle against men of enemy tribes, but because, in internal struggles which set lineages and villages against one another, they are without pity in giving blows of their digging sticks to women of the opposing clan or village. They receive blows without faltering, know how to give them and have no fear of the blood which flows. An essential fact which contributes to the subordination of women is that they are excluded from the possession or use of sacred objects. Yet, paradoxically, these draw much of their force from supernatural female powers.

Finally we see that all roles of general interest — warriorhood, shamanism, the production of means of exchange, the creation of force which is turned as much towards the exterior as towards the interior of society — are satisfied without the support and promotion of a big-man, without the accumulation and spectacular redistribution of wealth. The rule is entirely otherwise — it plays on the promotion not of big-men but of great-men.

CONCLUSION

Now we can return to the problem which I posed at the start and compare the great-man and the big-man. One must note, that this comparison is only possible at the level of domains of activity which are actually open to a degree of competition between individuals. The *kwaimatnie* men and the masters of shamans do not belong to this domain and remain outside competition. They are thus not in any way comparable to a big-man. On the contrary, if one compares the *aoulatta* and the big-man, of whom Sahlins has drawn a stereotyped portrait from the work of A. Strathern (1971) and other authors, the contrast speaks for itself. The *aoulatta* is a man with red eyes, say the Baruya, animated by a deadly force and a supernatural power. Frequently he does not listen to advice, but proceeds in front and unleashes wars with the enemies, to some extent forcing the rest of the tribe to embark on his adventure. He spends most of his time in ambush, or on the track of war, or in the men's house. He has few wives, few children and few gardens. He does not accumulate wealth and, if necessary, he is helped materially by others who do not demand anything in exchange, because he pays for everything with his person. He is surrounded by devoted partisans and he leads the combat with a group of warriors, who are like the 'dogs' of a great hunter, beating game towards him. In contrast with this personage, there is that mass of Baruya who are not distinguished by any exceptional quality, who are good agriculturalists, good hunters, honest warriors. The Baruya have a word for them: a little scornfully they call them 'sweet potatoes'. But there are worse, there are those who are *worianie*, the good-for-nothing men, not fit for war, agriculture or hunting.

If we turn to Sahlins' big-man, we discover a discerning man, a calculator, a great orator, who accumulates wives in order to have wealth and wealth to have wives, who is surrounded by dependants, who creates around him networks of obligations by paying for the bridewealth of young people too poor to marry. His name is known far and wide, because it is carried as far as his ceremonial participation in intertribal exchanges. More than war between tribes, it is exchange and competition in wealth between tribes which become the basis and privileged channel of establishing his renown.

Without wanting to exaggerate the differences between these two types of power and these two types of society, we can already conclude that societies in New Guinea cannot be simplistically reduced to big-men societies, as a certain current tendency in the literature tries to maintain. Many models of organisation coexist there, and one must seek their foundations and eventually discover the laws of transformation from one into another. Having arrived at this point, I shall suggest a theoretical explanation for the contrast between these two types of global social logic, represented by great-men societies and big-men societies.

I think that the sources of many aspects of these social systems are found in the nature of their kinship systems, systems which have *raisons d'être* and conditions of reproduction into which I have not been enquiring here, but which one should analyse elsewhere. The Baruya practise restricted exchange; most big-men societies practise generalised exchange of women for wealth. Among the Baruya, fundamentally, a woman is equivalent to another women and only the gift of a woman can annul or, better, counterbalance one gift against another. It seems to me that the principle of direct exchange of women simultaneously entails a whole series of social effects which determine and comprise a sort of global social logic. I am going to suggest certain aspects of it. The fact that a woman is worth a woman has the direct consequence that one has no need to accumulate wealth in order to reproduce life and kinship relations. There is thus no internal articulation or *direct* connection between material production and the reproduction of kinship relations. In this logic, the production of pigs, like subsistence activities, remains of relatively low value. Another consequence is that the direct exchange of women implies not only a particular control of men over women at the heart of each family, but a general, collective control of all women by all men in all generations.

This exigency seems to be satisfied by the institution of the great male and female initiation rites. Also, in a society like that of the Baruya, where more pigs certainly could be produced, it seems to me that the importance of hunting and game is linked above all to the mechanisms of masculine domination. Men must hunt to give game to women and to young initiates at the various critical moments of their social existence (puberty, child-birth, initiations). Now, game is a resource which cannot be 'produced' by the work of men or, above all, by women. Game reproduces itself in the bush in contrast with pigs which are reproduced with the work of men and, mainly, of women. The importance and social role of the hunt seems to me to proceed from the fact that, among the Baruya, this activity is a privileged field of exercise and celebration of male domination.

The last characteristic of social organisation ties in, perhaps, to this logic of restricted exchange and the absence of large intertribal ceremonial exchanges. War and a form of trade which rests on the production of salt as a kind of currency interweave in a way which is alternately negative and positive, producing a closely woven network of exchanges between the Baruya and neighbouring tribes. By contrast, the big-man appears to emerge in a situation where restricted exchange of women is not practised as the dominant principle, where the generalised exchange of a woman for wealth is carried out and where the accumulation of wealth becomes a direct condition for the reproduction of kinship relations. It seems to me that, in this context, other variations operate which also outline a global social logic. Male and female cults tend to prevail over great systems of male and female initiations (see A. Strathern 1970b). The production of pigs and the intensification of agriculture, which is a condition of this, prevail over the hunt and upon the role of game in exchange between the sexes, generations and kinship groups. Finally, in relations between tribes, in war or in trade, complex systems of ceremonial exchange are added.

Furthermore, it is striking to see that the opposite of the big-man is the rubbish-man; that is to say, the man without wealth, without support, the orphan, the political refugee, the abandoned junior who needs someone to lend him pigs which will allow him to marry and acquire the status of a complete man. This personage does not exist among the Baruya, any more than the big-man exists. It seems that, for him to appear, one would need some very special social conditions: the existence of unequal capacities of accumulation of material wealth between groups which comprise the same tribe, in other words: more intensive agriculture. It seems also that there must be a deep erosion of the collective links which bind men to the earth, a partial dissolution of the communal forms of land ownership. The question thus arises, on the theoretical plane, if one wishes to compare the forms of social hierarchy which exist in New Guinea, under what conditions has the basic equivalence between women ceased to exist, and under what conditions has exploitation, not only of women by men but also of men by men, appeared? More generally again (and this does not only concern New Guinea) the question arises whether one knows under what conditions the principle of equivalence of life for life (for example, the life of a warrior killed in war against life of an enemy; or the life of a woman against the life of another woman) is substituted by the equivalence of life or death against labour or against the product of labour.

It goes without saying that the Baruya society which I have just described and analysed belongs already to the past. I would not wish to give the impression that this world survives intact. Since 1960, the date of the beginning of the colonial period in this part of Papua New Guinea, and since 1975, the date of national independence, profound transformations have been fracturing and overturning the various hierarchical systems which comprised the Baruya social order. The 'White peace' has suppressed war. With the disappearance of the war function, the rites which were directly attached to putting enemies to death have rapidly disappeared from the ceremonies of initiation. In this enforced peace, new political alliances have been established, including their historical enemies, the Andje, who had massacred the first Baruya. The arrival of missionaries has marked the beginning of a questioning of the power of shamans and, in the sphere of ideas, the value of Baruya myths, which explained and legitimated the cosmic and social order. The missionaries likewise attacked polygamy and began the education of boys and girls, in other words the institution of a system of education parallel to and opposed to the world of initiations.

With the development of wage labour and the production of cash crops, the production of salt has lost its purpose little by little, while it still remains necessary in order to keep existing rites functioning. The Australian Administration nominated its own representatives, the *Luluai* and *Tultul*, whom it wished by preference to choose from among the ancient fight-leaders. Most of the time these stepped down, and put in their place young people without authority or prestige, even sometimes the buffoons of the group. On the other hand, in a general way this period, with the cessation of war and the introduction of a new law, has brought certain advantages to women (the possibility of divorce, or recourse to the law, in cases of a husband's brutality, and the beginnings of education for women). But male domination remains the primordial basis of social organisation and cultural identity. Finally, after 1975 and independence, the tribe has obtained the right to elect its own representatives to various echelons of regional and national power, a transformation which was already taking place during the colonial period among the most acculturated tribes of Highland New Guinea (the neighbouring tribes of Goroka and Hagen, for example). But the period of independence, by its political summons to rediscover the fundamental roots of Papua New Guinea societies, has encouraged the Baruya to recommence their great initiations. The *kwaimatnie* men are recovering a large part of their power. The *aoulatta* are, little by little, being replaced by young men, who leave university and occupy different positions in the state or in one of the churches. The *tsaimaye* continue to produce salt for ceremonies, but from now on the principal means of exchange is money, which is earned by working in plantations or selling coffee. Finally, the basis of an individual accumulation of riches from coffee production and other commercial cultivation is gradually being laid, and this will perhaps cause the emergence, before long, in Baruya society of people very similar to big-men, such as existed well before colonisation among the Melpa of Mount Hagen and elsewhere, and who seem also to have been maintained in power afterwards.

# 2 Two waves of African models in the New Guinea Highlands*

*Andrew Strathern*

It is perhaps the fate of recently discovered parts of the world that their societies tend to be understood in terms of analytical models derived from established studies made elsewhere. In the case of the Highlands societies of Papua New Guinea, this happened not so much because of a real lack of earlier studies in Melanesia as a whole, but because of two circumstantial factors: first, the Highlands societies do stand out by comparison with other societies of Melanesia, in terms of their scale, population density, agricultural intensity, and group structure. Second, those anthropologists who made the initial studies of the Highlands were well versed in the range of propositions and tenets deriving from classic accounts of segmentary lineage systems in the Sudan, Ghana, and Nigeria (Evans-Pritchard 1940; Fortes 1945, 1949; Bohannan 1957).

From the start, however, Highlands anthropologists were aware of problems in this approach. Marie Reay, for example, emphasised the themes of expediency and flexibility in Kuma society, showing how these features undermined the significance of apparently rigid segmentary structures (Reay 1959). Langness later protested against 'unilineal bias' in descriptions, arguing, after Leach, that investigators were too influenced by the 'principles first stressed by Radcliffe-Brown' (Langness 1964: 164), and that it would be better to forget about African systems and instead concentrate fully on the 'Highlands structures themselves' (*ibid.*: 162). It was Barnes who definitively began this debate, which has never been fully settled, by speaking directly of an 'Africanist mirage' in Highlands studies (Barnes 1962). Interestingly, Barnes himself never did detailed fieldwork in the Highlands, and he was by training an Africanist. Yet it was he who pointed most clearly to the emergent difficulties of analysis in ethnographies available at that time. With hindsight, one can see which of his

*The substance of this chapter was first delivered as a Royal Anthropological Institute Lecture on 13.12.78. It should be read in parallel with Modjeska's longer essay (Chapter 3, this volume)

points were the strongest, and also which have still not been adequately explored. Taken as a whole, however, his brief contribution has acted, in negative form, as powerfully as did Radcliffe-Brown's early synthesising discussion of Australian marriage systems or Fortes' elegant exposition of the structure of unilineal descent groups (Fortes 1953; Radcliffe-Brown 1930–1). Again, it is a curious paradox that this most noted article on the Highlands is one which essentially still uses the 'African model' as its chief backdrop by pointing out ways in which Highlands societies do *not* fit that model. This is because the focus is still largely on descent and filiation, though Barnes also stresses warfare and exchange as guiding factors to consider.

Barnes argued that, if we take descent as a rule of recruitment to groups, then in the Highlands either there are no such rules or the rules are often not followed; that non-agnatic members of local groups not only abound in some cases, but may provide, because of flexibility of access to positions of influence, leaders of such groups; that the position of women is complicated, since they are neither fully incorporated into their husbands' groups nor do they retain full status in their natal groups; that local groups are not to be described as agnatic 'cores' surrounded by other members; that in some instances, notably the Huli, the picture is influenced by multi-residence and the possibility of multi-affiliation; that warfare and the incidence of refuging must be considered, and that warfare does not necessarily proceed along segmentary lines; that long genealogies are not maintained and that adherence to agnatic forms in genealogies is unimportant; that 'social mitosis' does not proceed along orderly genealogical lines but, rather, segmentation is 'catastrophic'; and finally that the dependence on root crops and pigs contrasts with African cases of dependence on grain or cattle.[1]

All of these can be seen simply as empirical matters, and indeed they are subject to empirical variation in different cases, a point which Meggitt took up when he proposed that effective patrilineality and patrivirilocality depended on 'the pressure on available agrarian resources' in Highlands societies (Meggitt 1965: 279).[2] They cohere, however, in terms of divergence from a generalised model of African polysegmentary systems, in which (1) a single principle is dominant throughout the whole social structure and this principle is one of unilineal descent; (2) the descent principle orders both the allocation of individuals to groups and the corporate nature of group norms; (3) the segmentary or nesting structure of groups defines the processes of opposition and combination between them in political terms; and (4) the prime calculus of all these relationships is genealogical.[3]

In such a model the phenomena of marriage and interpersonal kin ties crossing group boundaries became somewhat problematical, since the model itself does not encompass them. To account for some of these aspects of kinship Fortes used the notion of 'complementary filiation' and was promptly accused by Edmund Leach of hiding under this concept the separate matters of marriage and alliance (Leach 1962). Leach thus implied that even for African cases marriage might be of greater significance than the descent model, however modified, could allow. For Highlands societies, the point regarding marriage has to be made even more strongly, although it is also the case that the special relationship with mother's brother, discussed by Radcliffe-Brown for the Ba-Thonga and elaborated on by Fortes, is present in Highlands societies and in a classic form. The African mirage, if only mirage, sometimes appears persistent. Everything depends, in fact, on which particular feature of a society ethnographers choose to emphasise.

One overall way to handle the problem is to note that the rigidity of the general descent model simply fails to account adequately for the Highlands data. That is, descent may operate as a rule of recruitment, but, as Barnes points out, it does so only weakly or in conjunction with other criteria: groups are variably corporate; there is an emphasis on cross-group ties maintained and often created by individuals and sometimes extending to non-kin friends and partners as well as extra-clan kin; while some political processes reduce to a segmentary rule, warfare is usually more complicated than this or else allies are drawn in on an entirely different basis, perhaps through individual kin and affinal ties; and, finally, genealogy itself is by no means the only way of conceptualising group membership and intergroup relations, as expressions relating to locality and the importance of individual leaders also abound.

Yet it is not in fact possible to dispense entirely with 'descent' as a relevant factor. Its 'total model' significance undercut, it returns as a metaphor used rhetorically by people themselves to justify action or to give an impression of stability where empirical events suggest flux. Most notably, it is male leaders, the 'big-men', who use descent 'talk' in this way. So one moves from a perception of descent as a guiding principle within a structural–functional matrix to a realisation that it is a way of speaking about groups used by actors themselves with their own aims and purposes in mind. The move is thus from holism to individualism, from systems analysis to intentionality, and from function to semantics – all analytical moves which also correspond to more general shifts within the approaches used by social anthropologists of the 1960s and 1970s. Along the way, a good deal of evidence has been gathered to enable us to question whether it is really descent, in any strict genealogical sense, that operates as a rule at the recruitment level. Having argued myself for a re-shaping of the concepts of descent and filiation in order to allow for data which emerged from a study of Melpa (Mount Hagen) society in 1964—5, I would now suggest: (1) that 'descent' always refers to representational models of group structure; people are not directly recruited into groups by descent, but by filiation, adoption, absorption, and other means; (2) operationally, all group members, whether by filiation or otherwise, must justify their membership by continuing support for and action in group causes; (3) when, collectively, men wish to stress their in-group solidarity, their differentiation from other groups, or their category opposition to and superiority over women, then they speak in 'dogmas of descent' or in ways which are at least analogous to these. Such a re-formulation places descent as a means of stating opposition and difference across group boundaries, or of intensifying in-group support and asserting homogeneity. These constructs are also to be seen analytically as in a relationship of continual tension with further themes in which individual free-will, autonomy and heterogeneity are asserted. Big-men, again, use both sets of ideas, according to their purposes.

This way of putting the argument builds on the now-familiar conceptual distinctions proposed by Keesing (1971) and Scheffler (1966). Keesing separates culture, as 'shared codes', from society, as 'events and transactions' (1971: 125). He places emphasis on both codes and transactions in his own analyses and shows how for the Kwaio 'descent' may or may not be relevant, depending on what role or role-set is activated for a particular purpose. The analytical distinction he proposes is crucial, although it sets a hard problem in determining the relationship of code to transaction (cf. A.J. Strathern 1979c). I suggest here that the corresponding distinction between representational and operational models is inadequate because representational models are themselves used or 'operated with' to influence situations. Thus, when a Melpa leader stresses a historical tie or division between groups and uses 'descent' images in pressing his point he is not just 'simplifying' his system, and certainly not just explaining it to outsiders (though he may do this also); he means, rather, to achieve an end he has in mind. Intentionality is thus the bridge between code and transaction, and indeed without it the idea of 'transaction' itself becomes meaningless. The question then becomes 'what kind of intentions are we referring to?' and this brings us to the general problem posed by the discussion on leadership in Melanesian societies. Having dismantled the structural—

functional viewpoint, and lacking here any obvious Africanist models, are we left with a picture of the Melanesian big-man as an individual entirely out for his own interests?

I have previously objected to such a simple view, and the problem is echoed also in Hau'ofa's objection to Sahlins' original formulation in his 'Big-man versus chief' article (Hau'ofa 1975; Sahline 1962–3). Hau'ofa was concerned to stress that there are genuine systems of chiefship in Melanesia, for example among the Mekeo whom he studied (see Chowning 1977: 42–6), and he was quite right; but this is not the point I wish to address here in empirical detail, since Hau'ofa has already marshalled enough data to make the case. The problem of leadership as a form of action really cross-cuts the purely typological division between 'chiefs' and 'big-men'. Whether as chief or big-man, do we assert that the Melanesian leader is 'out for himself' in the main, and that it is the actions of such self-interested individuals that determine the effective social structure of local communities? Do we have in such a notion the pragmatic key to those patterns which fall so persistently to one side of the descent model in the realm of group structure (see Sillitoe 1978; Standish 1978)?

An answer to this question must distinguish between heuristic and more general levels of reply. As a heuristic device, the idea is useful. In Hagen, for example, the forming of sub-groups, the timing of exchanges, and the outcome of court cases can often be related convincingly to the aims of individual leaders, or of individuals whether leaders or not. Social process is thus seen properly as subject to personal innovation, preference and competition. But does this amount to a simple 'own interests' argument? The problem with the notion of 'own interests' is that it cannot be defined at all outside the realm of culturally based cognition. If one's 'own interests' include an aim of gaining prestige, and such prestige can only be gained effectively by securing the approbation of others, then 'own interests' will lead to action which in fact coincides with the wishes of followers or at least a public; and in that case the straightforward opposition between individual interests and collective interests will not apply. Obviously, my point here is one which has been exhaustively dealt with by political philosophers, and my proposition itself contains a number of catches. It is, nevertheless, sufficient to show that defining a category of 'own interests' entirely (a) outside a particular set of cultural values and (b) in exact opposition to the interests of others besides ego, is not a simple or self-evident operation. My conclusion is therefore that we cannot at once label the Melanesian big-man in such a way, even though in western terms these leaders often appear very clearly as 'egoists'. The

Andrew Strathern

psychological category of egoist does not equate with the social category of 'self-seeking', though I do not deny that true self-seeking occurs (see A.J. Strathern 1979a).

I have stressed this point as a way of leading into the next, and thence also on to the topic of social change. Big-men are often presented as self-made, and indeed in essence they are so. However, it has also often been pointed out that some 'family advantages' can be very useful to an able contender. This is as true in Mount Hagen as in the Trobriands, although the overall structure of these societies is quite different (see Brunton 1975). There has not been enough analysis of what may comprise 'advantages' here (e.g. in terms of land, wives, exchange ties), but the general case is clear; Highlands and other Melanesian systems contain a possible germ of further transformation in terms of the intergenerational play of advantage. From the point of view of our first theme of 'own interests', however, this fact indicates the poverty of the notion of 'own interests' itself. Big-men do think of others: in the first place, their own children, particularly their sons. 'Own interests' must be extended at least to 'family interests'. A second set of African models now begins to loom on the horizons of this point. Is there, in fact, 'succession' in these systems (Standish 1978)?

First, it would be interesting to have more extensive information than we possess on detailed family histories of leaders. One thing we are likely to find is that, within a given society, there are variations in the extent to which big-men attempt to build up their sons into big-men to follow them, as well as further differences in the extent to which a big-man's sons do in fact succeed. This point can be illustrated by considering the circumstances and strategies of two Melpa big-men whose family affairs I have followed since 1964: Ndamba and Ongka.

Ndamba is very much a 'family man'; dignified, squarely built and hard-working, he has been an 'elder' figure since at least 1964. Though well over sixty now, he still works regularly in his gardens, especially when new land is to be cleared and apportioned to the women of his own household and to his sons' wives. He talks rather sadly of his sons' failure recently to help him with the work, but he continues to look after their wives and to plan for the future. He has led his sub-group through a number of ceremonial exchanges involving money (A.J. Strathern 1979b) and during August–September 1978 he built a new men's house to stand at the head of a fresh ceremonial ground which he and his close relatives were levelling out. His plan was to use this ground for the next bout of *moka* exchanges and to bypass the use of the clan's main ground as a means of boosting the

40

prestige of his own sub-group, within which he hoped to see one of his own sons take over his position before he died. He had fixed on Nikint, his second eldest, who for many years was also associated with me in my field-work, and his new house and ceremonial clearing was strategically placed very close to Nikint's own settlement. His eldest son, Pangk, was in Ndamba's estimation too mild, and lately had neglected one of his two wives in order to follow his first wife back to her own place. Such an assumption of voluntary uxorilocality was taken as a sign of weakness and irresponsibility. Pepa, the third son, is known as a fiery and energetic speaker, but a little unreliable. Nikint, Ndamba thought, had more knowl-edge of the outside world and a more measured judgement. But Nikint gambled and drank beer also, and Ndamba realised that he might in fact have no successor, especially as Nikint would not buckle to and work in the fields to assist and encourage his wives. Ndamba had endowed all three sons with two wives apiece from early manhood, and Nikint was adept at collecting temporary wives as well. Yet his habits of concentrating on travel in vehicles and on winning money at cards did not endear him to his fellow sub-clansmen, who saw themselves as his equal, but without his unearned advantages. Ndamba's plans, then, were at risk, a circumstance which brought out even more clearly the fact that he did have such plans and that they carried meaning for him (see for a full account of this pro-cess, up to 1980, A.J. Strathern forthcoming).

Ongka is not many years junior to Ndamba. He is, however, Ndamba's son-in-law, his third wife being the daughter of Ndamba's third wife, whom Ndamba inherited originally as a widow plus children from a senior kinsman. Ongka is mercurial, brilliant, loquacious, and very much a 'loner' in his transactional activities. He often repeats that he can make *moka* by himself. Unlike Ndamba, he does not have a big family of sons with him, nor does he belong to a flourishing sub-clan. He has made a virtue out of a certain isolation in his group and is adept at setting up partnerships and friendships outside it. Correspondingly, he does not even expect that any-one will succeed him as a leader or big-man. With his eldest surviving son, Namba, he has had a stormy relationship, which erupted into fierce quarrels and physical combat in Namba's adolescence, but has now settled into a certain symbiotic degree of indifference and effective residential separation. Namba also plays cards and drinks, drives and crashes vehicles, and one wife has left him, causing Ongka much expense to obtain a replacement.[4] Ongka accepts this state of affairs, though he obviously regrets it, and is able to rationalise it through his general attitude that his own achievements have been unique anyway. It is obvious that he will not

41

leave an immediate political successor, although, in contrast, Ndamba's sons probably will continue to have influence after his death.

The contrast between these two men indicates that there can be variations in aim and viewpoint within a particular culture or group. On the one hand, there is the big-man whose status is rooted in the management of a large family-style enterprise: such a big-man seeks and may find a successor or successors. On the other hand is the big-man who picks up a variety of partnerships, visits widely, transacts with an eye to advantage, and thinks less of cultivating his own family's prospects. Hagen ideology accommodates both of these types.

Clearly, the situation nowadays is also affected deeply by change. Ndamba gently chides Nikint for not working. Without the modern distractions of cards, beer and gambling, Nikint would be more likely to work; and without the ability to travel widely and pick up people in the sub-clan truck, he could not spend so much time away from home. Further, there are now numerous offices of introduced leadership: local-government councillor positions, membership of the national parliament, and of provincial government assemblies also. Nikint has aspired to some of these, yet tends to draw back, uncertain of their significance or scope and having seen others fail at them or becoming open to criticism. The opportunities and limitations of leadership are no longer entirely clear.

My sketch of two individual leaders and their sons brings us directly, then, to the general question of change in the Mount Hagen social system. Change cannot be seen from an internal viewpoint only; it is largely precipitated by outside events which Hageners cannot control, and of these the most significant have been: initial pacification, the influx of shell wealth, mission influence, local-government councils, the cultivation of coffee as a cash crop, and the creation of a national parliament followed by political independence for Papua New Guinea. Each of these changes has had its impact, and all contribute to the contemporary social formation. Cash-cropping may be identified as particularly significant, and it is important to consider whether it is leading to a hardening of inequalities in society. Specifically, has cash-cropping, the introduction of which is a part of the general intrusion of capitalism into Melanesia, resulted in capitalist relations of production between people at local levels? Answers to this question depend initially on the way in which the indigenous societies are conceptualised. Just as, when social anthropologists first began to work in Highlands societies of Papua New Guinea, they consciously or unconsciously took over terms derived from the segmentary lineage model of Africanists, so now, in facing questions of social change, some writers have begun to borrow concepts and themes developed earlier by Africanist scholars who were themselves re-analysing the internal dynamics of African lineage systems, using marxist rather than structural—functional ideas (see Lawrence 1975: 262–4). But is this just another example of inappropriate African models? To answer that point, we have to review the marxist re-analyses of African systems themselves. This is done in greater detail by Modjeska (this volume), basing his review mainly on analyses of the Guro and the Mbum peoples.

Here, I am not so interested in the question whether there is an 'African' or a 'lineage' mode of production. Some marxist writers themselves have progressively tended to abandon the overall notion of a 'mode of production', informed as it is by Althusserian structuralist concepts of 'levels' and 'instances', and instead have directed their attention more to empirical problems in the analysis of relations of production. Specifically, they have argued about whether there is a pattern of inequality masked by ideologies of equality in lineage-based agrarian societies. Ethnographically, the major areas of disagreement have to do with relations between the sexes and relations between senior and junior males. Most of the 'facts' about these relationships were already presented in the earlier, structural—functional monographs. For example, who would dispute that the principle of paternal authority is enshrined firmly in Tallensi society? What did give rise to dispute, between Fortes and Worsley, in a precursor phase of present debates, was the degree and significance of overall economic inequality between ordinary men, elders and chiefs in Tale society (Worsley 1956). Such a discussion is in fact crucial for comparisons with Melanesia, but discussions between Terray, Meillassoux, and Rey have centred primarily on the general relationship between senior and junior males, and controversy enters the field when formulations in terms of 'piety', 'authority', or 'reciprocity' are replaced by the assertion that these relationships are in fact exploitative, and hence that elders constitute a class *vis-à-vis* juniors. Meillassoux argues, against Rey, that this is not so, since juniors in their turn become seniors, whereas in a class society those exploited (the working class) do not become the exploiters, but reproduce after their social kind, a pattern modified only by individual mobility (Meillassoux 1975: 123–4). Nevertheless, even if this point is granted in typological and definitional terms, the issue of the seniors' dominance remains important. Meillassoux suggested here that it is based on technical knowledge, since it is certainly not based on physical force, simple kinship status, exclusive land rights, or monopoly of the instruments of labour (Terray 1972a: 129–30). Technical knowledge may be further 'mystified'

by the artificial creation of initiation rituals, which delay the stages by
which men gain access to effective property rights and marital status.
Tallensi rules regarding fathers and sons do the same thing, backed up by
the ancestor cult and notions of sickness and retribution. Terray, in com-
menting, says that so far 'it appears that it would be very difficult for the
elders to transform their functional authority into the power to exploit'
(*ibid.*: 132). Terray buttresses this point by referring to the view that
classes appear directly only in the capitalist mode of production, since in
other systems the economic base may be determinant but not dominant,
whereas in the capitalist system it is both. He then (*ibid.*: 163) passes on
to reconsider the elder:junior relationship. To technical knowledge as the
elders' prerogative he adds control over marriage exchanges, linking these
in turn to the reproduction of essential labour power. Where the goods
used in bridewealth are also scarce goods obtained by trade or by local
production but appropriated by the elders, their ability to control
marriages is clear. Dupré and Rey sharpened up Meillassoux's original
formulation of this statement into the general argument that 'the circulation of this surplus product ensures the reproduction of relations of
dependence between the direct producers and this particular group'
(quoted in Terray 1972a: 169).

Terray notes the identical objections of Meillassoux and Godelier to
this proposition, and pushes further on the matter of ethnographic facts.
Are we talking about goods produced by juniors and appropriated by
elders? For the Guro, if this referred to animal husbandry, the exploitation
would be marginal, as 'the expenditure of social labour in this branch is
very small'. Another item is loincloths; these are made by heads of families
and experienced weavers, not by juniors as a category. Kola nuts are also
used. These are collected by women and children, not male juniors. It is
correct that the juniors' agricultural work frees the elders and allows them
to spend time in weaving, but woven goods are used in bridewealth payments, so that 'this labour of the juniors will be returned to them in the
form of wives', and hence the juniors in turn will be able to become elders.
If an elder delays a junior's marriage too long, the latter may leave him and
go to his maternal uncle instead, and greedy or self-seeking elders can
indeed lose dependants in this way and so fall from effective incumbency
of office.

Several aspects of this argument are highly relevant to the analysis of
Melanesian systems. Terray furnishes also some remarks which take us
from the pre-colonial to the colonial phase. First, he notes that, where
foodstuffs can be traded for prestige goods, juniors can emancipate them-

selves faster from elders (*ibid.*: 171), since they can use the goods to obtain wives on their own account: although their aim is likely to be simply to make themselves into elders in their turn, so that structural changes do not occur automatically. Second, he recognises that: 'In some circumstances the articulation of trade relations introduced by colonisation upon "lineage-type" relations of production might change the elders into agents of the colonial bourgeoisie. Conflicts between the generations might then become the focus of certain "class" conflicts' (*ibid.*: 172). Terray at once qualifies this second proposition by arguing that in such developing economies the real relations of exploitation oppose the mass of the peasants to the administrative personnel and industrialists; and also that conflict between seniors and juniors is not a universal or necessary matter.

Several further discussions of Terray's and Meillassoux's arguments have appeared. Scattered references in articles by O'Laughlin, Moore, and Hindess and Hirst (*Critique of Anthropology*, no. 8, 1977) were followed by more determined assaults in the 'Women's issue' of *Critique*, particularly in the essay by Maxine Molyneux on 'Androcentrism in marxist anthropology'. Molyneux's main aim is to replace the picture of junior males as the exploited class with that of women as the permanent subordinates of men as a whole, and it is Terray's failure sufficiently to stress this that she criticises as 'androcentrism' (Molyneux 1977: 57ff.; see also Bonte 1979).

Molyneux's main point can be applied with good effect to the Mount Hagen ethnography; indeed, in substance the bulk of recent feminist arguments of this type were anticipated in Marilyn Strathern's earlier distinction between women as 'producers' and men as 'transactors' in Hagen society (M. Strathern 1972). However, the ethnography of male:female and senior:junior relations is not always pursued in sufficient depth in these Africanist discussions for the question of exploitation to be properly settled. For example, the term senior:junior can refer to a number of different structural domains: to immediate fathers and sons, to lineage relations of varying span, to senior lines versus junior lines, to eldest sons versus other sons, to elders as a category across lineages versus juniors as a similar category, or to prominent versus not-so-prominent elders. Where there is a ranking or primogenitural principle, an argument about structural inequality is likely to stick much better than in systems where there is not. Correspondingly, the application of the debate to Melanesian cases must be done with care.[5]

Some comparative questions raised by this set of African materials are: (1) to what extent was inequality between social categories developed in the apparently egalitarian and competitive Melanesian societies? (2) were the mechanisms of reproducing such inequalities the same as those identified for the Guro and other cases discussed by Meillassoux and Terray? (3) if there were structural relations of inequality in these pre-capitalist formations, how have these been diverted or accentuated by the introduction of new capitalist relations of production, primarily through cash-cropping (see Bourdieu 1977: 171–97)?

The first two topics were broached, as it happens, in the original German literature on Hagen society, and my first ethnographic efforts were directed towards dismantling a too simplistic 'class' picture of this society suggested by Vicedom, a Lutheran missionary—anthropologist who worked at Ogelbeng near to Hagen town from 1934 to 1939 (Vicedom and Tischner 1943–8). Vicedom's work is exceptionally valuable, and it is impossible for a later worker such as myself to controvert what he says for that early period, immediately following the first discovery of the Highlands by European explorers. One reason why a 'class' view can be plausibly erected for the indigenous Hagen system is that, as often in Melanesia, we are not simply dealing with a senior:junior opposition of the Guro type, but with a system of big-manship based on the prestigious circulation of valuables encapsulated in a sphere of their own, the *moka* exchange system. It is a mistake to isolate the *moka* in analysis from bridewealth, warfare, intermarriage patterns, domestic production and residence. Nevertheless, it is true that it is because of *moka* and its rules that big-manship has to be achieved, separately from the inheritance of family advantages, and that such advantages are neither necessary nor sufficient for the emergence of a big-man. This does set the Hagen system off from the Guro case: elders are an ascribed category among the Guro, whereas big-men in Hagen are emergent individuals. Considering, then, the category of big-men across a set of groups it is plausible enough, in terms of certain criteria, to see them as a kind of class, whose interests lie together and are to some extent opposed to those of other categories. Three points stand out: that big-men are polygynists and depend heavily on the productive and reproductive work of their wives; that they tend to monopolise the circulation of valuable shells; and that there is a corresponding set of men who work directly for big-men and are usually unmarried, called *kintmant*. Significantly, women as a category may also be referred to as the *kintmant* of men, although such linguistic identification should not be taken to imply a definite social identity.[6]

It is still, in my judgement, incorrect to label this original system as one of 'class'. Much depends, however, on exactly what one means by

'class'. A crucial aspect here is the way in which inequality in relationships
is reproduced. To label the system as one of 'class' might imply that big-
men ensure the direct reproduction of their status within their own
families, and this is untrue, though some big-men try to encourage at least
one of their sons to aspire to big-manship, starting by endowing them with
wives and encouraging their entry into *moka*, and hoping that they will
learn the arts of finance and oratorical skill which are needed for success.
The system is also different from one marked by an overall senior:junior
opposition, in that it encourages young men to move into *moka* and
establish themselves as soon as possible. Fathers are more likely to hasten
than to delay marriages, and there is no stress on the father retaining
productive forms of property until his death. Hence severe holder:heir
conflicts do not arise. The possibility of switching group affiliation is
explicitly recognised, and it is a built-in feature of flexibility. Pigs, a major
wealth item, can be reared quickly, and they breed in multiple fashion.
Crops are not stored and, in Hagen, there is little emphasis on garden
magic or other forms of knowledge exclusive to elders as such. In such
conditions, any picture of domination based on a senior:junior contrast is
likely to be illusory. It would seem as though we have identified an
'African mirage' again.

Yet, *contra* this conclusion, there are other points:

(1) The elements are not the same in all Melanesian cases. In some,
there were definite systems of rank and chiefship, and headmen were
definitely singled out and given the prerogative of polygamy (Hogbin
1978); in some, fathers had strong authority over sons (Meggitt 1965), or
the institution of age grades, accompanied by male initiation, did stress
the collective superiority of elders in addition to the ethic of big-manship
itself (Allen 1967); and in some, too, small lineages were structured
according to relations of seniority which at least resemble African cases
(Salisbury 1962).

(2) Just as the influence of elders among the Guro does appear to have
depended on women's work to a greater extent than Terray emphasises, so
in Melanesian systems it is important to assess the predominant sexual
division of labour in terms of the actual relative inputs of men and women
(Modjeska 1977; also this volume), and to examine the relationship of the
division of labour to patterns of inequality between the sexes.

(3) The second point is particularly significant in the colonial and post-
colonial phases of development when cash and cash-cropping are introduced. Terray's two opposite suggestions need to be tested: does cash-
cropping lead to the emancipation of juniors or to the consolidation of

power in the hands of seniors? Re-fashioning this for the Hagen case, and more widely for Melanesia, we have to ask: has cash-cropping thrown open big-manship to new categories of people? Has it altered the big-man structure? Has it further emancipated or tied down women? Has it converted these pre-capitalist societies overall into 'peasant societies', with rural capitalists appearing as 'big peasants' rather than big-men in the old style?

Answers to some of these questions have already been offered. Meggitt, for example, writing of the Enga argued some years ago that Enga society had moved from the 'tribal' to the 'peasant' stage in which the Enga were dependent on the outside world (Meggitt 1971). His later work on the resurgence of Enga warfare in the 1970s in many ways reveals the powerful political 'backlash' against this situation (Meggitt 1977), and this has been repeated in the Chimbu and Western Highlands Provinces also (A.J. Strathern 1977; W. Standish 1973).[7] Finney (1973) identified the emergence of entrepreneurs in Goroka, in the Eastern Highlands, and since then businessmen have become more obviously rural capitalists, some concerned to protect their property by erecting barbed-wire fences around their homes (Good and Donaldson 1980; see Amarshi, Good and Mortimer 1979). The potential end-points of development and the growth of a landless proletariat have been identified by Howlett (1980). Women's changing roles have been less discussed, but evidence is now emerging that cash does significantly affect their positions (e.g. Sexton 1980). I note for Hagen that women can individually earn cash from vegetable sales at markets and that they also take a (less-than-equal) share of the cash from the sale of coffee. Overall, however, their work-load is probably increased, since they still have to raise their children, tend the pigs, and make subsistence gardens, while also contributing work to the production of coffee. Moreover, Hagen men claim significantly large amounts of cash for use in *moka* transactions, now based on money rather than shell valuables, and women have so far gained only a limited right to appear as genuinely independent transactors on these occasions. Established big-men also promote the use of money in this way, to bring it into their sphere of control and to pay for killings which result from new enmities and tensions, notably stemming from motor-vehicle accidents (A.J. Strathern 1979b). Some big-men employ others, particularly young men from less-developed regions, as workers, in imitation of the plantation system, paying them wages; and some have opted completely out of the *moka*, but these latter are in a minority. New forms of ostentatious gift-giving may also replace the old: beer and food parties are common (see Ploeg 1973). Immigrants from areas shorter of land or from cold places where coffee does not grow well are taken in, and either earn cash along with their hosts or become in some respects subordinate to them. A mixed set of strategies and outcomes is in evidence. But central to the question of directions for change is the persistence of ceremonial exchange; and, so long as it persists, Hagen society will not become simply capitalist in structure.[8] My proposition, in fact, is that Hagen men are committed to the ideology of exchange partly because of their perceived need to maintain a relationship of superiority over women, which the *moka* system enables them to do. Business, on the other hand, isolates men from men and, if open to women, can give them status equal to men. The intervening variables here between the latent possibilities of transformation from pre-capitalist to capitalist forms of internal inequality in the society are the exchange system and the ideology of male:female relations maintained by men. These variables also appear to me to distinguish Hagen and other Melanesian cases from the Guro, both in the pre-capitalist and in the contemporary periods. The second application of African models to Melanesian societies must also, then, like the first, be corrected by the recognition of features specific to Melanesia itself.[9] Meanwhile there remains the real work of recording, analysing and reflecting on diachronic processes of development and change in areas such as the Highlands, where so much initial ethnographic work in the synchronic idiom has been done.

# 3 Production and inequality: perspectives from central New Guinea

*Nicholas Modjeska*

## INTRODUCTION

This chapter derives from a thesis (Modjeska 1977) in which I explored the ethnography of the Duna and surrounding peoples of central New Guinea from the point of view of the production process and the social relations of production. The project envisaged in that study was a comparative political economy of a series of tribes, beginning with production rather than exchange as the key integrative concept. While not denying the importance of exchange, I argued that a close examination of the relations of production might offer new insights and posed a logically prior problem.

I began with observations and enquiries made during fieldwork with Duna-speaking people in the Lake Kopiago area of the Southern Highlands of Papua New Guinea.[1] By 1969 the pre-colonial superstructure of cultural and social relations was nearly unrecognisable after a decade of post-contact changes. Warfare had ceased and mission activities had effected a rapid replacement of tribal beliefs and rituals by Christian practices. In place of inter- and intragroup fighting, ceremonial prestations and tribal rituals, there was a new, perhaps somewhat uncertain, construction of relations with government, national economy, and organised religion. But the roots of economic life in production were still firmly intact. The basic social relations by which people produced their livelihood and wealth in pre-colonial times could be readily observed in the gardening and pig husbandry of small domestic groups, and this despite the introduction of steel axes, bush knives and shovels (Steensberg 1980).

I had an interest in the past and made enquiries about the time spoken of as the 'time before Government' or the 'time of Aiyurana' (an ancestor of perhaps seven or eight generations ago). In response to the investigations and speculations of prehistorians and geographers working in the Highlands, I proposed that both past and present, and comparative ethnography, could be usefully organised about a continuum of 'intensifications'. These were developments in economic production, increases in output and developments in technology and work relations. There had been a historical development of the productive potentials of environment and society through a development of social and cultural relations. Although I was ineluctably led into a persistent confusion about time frames, it did not seem too much of a fallacy to interpret ethnographic instances as empirical examples of so many stages in the development of such a process.

Approaching social life from the perspective of production clarified familiar problems concerning relations between men and women and the wider integument of domestic and lineage relations, since these — rather than relations of wage labour, ownership and class — were and are the direct relations of production.

Since production is responsible for wealth or economic value as well as for people's material needs, my findings are pertinent to questions about social inequalities. Rousseau was perhaps correct in reasoning that inequality was accentuated by, but did not originate in, differences in wealth. In any case, among the Duna, ownership and access to wealth has much to do with social position, although one could not say that it is the most important thing in life. (Given pre-colonial conditions of existence, one might say that life itself and the means of securing its continuance and increase were the paramount consideration.)

Here I explore dimensions of inequality, both between men and between men and women, in relation to involvement in pig production, exchange and sacrifice. I see production, circulation and consumption as consecutive moments in a process constituting an area of political—economic practice (Marx 1857) and delineating if not determining the character and extent of inequality. Like other anthropologists concerned with neo-marxist problematics, I am led to conclude that production and its relations do not constitute an autonomous economic level dominating the totality of social relations, since the relations of production are relations of kinship. To pursue the relations of production to their heart only to find structures of kinship is by now predictable, if disappointing (Hamilton 1981). What is perhaps new here is the attempt to pursue the concept and social reality of value to its core, to pursue value's subject, here principally the pig, to its basis in human labour and life. I am led to argue that social practices concerning the pig derive their impetus from a 'cross-over' of values such that one is confronted not with a system of commodity production but rather with a system for the 'production' (or social reproduction) of persons as lineage and family members. The 'inner secret' of the pig in such a system lies in its mediative capacity, its exchangeability both against more purely economic commodities and against those values of human life which we summarise under the notion of 'kinship'.

Some 13,000 Duna-speakers live in the valleys of the Tumbudu and Auwi-Pori rivers, east of the Strickland river and south of the Lagaip. Their immediate neighbours are the Huli of the Tari-Koroba region to the southeast and the fringe Enga of Ipili-Paiela to the east. Like their Highlands neighbours, they live by sweet-potato cultivation and pig production. Gardens are cleared in forest or in areas of secondary regrowth, and sweet potato is cultivated in labour-intensive, mulched mounds called *mondo*. More than half the sweet-potato production supports a pig population of around one pig per person. By comparison with the dense populations of central Enga and Tari, population densities are relatively low, ranging from 20 to 30 persons per square kilometre near Huli country to a sparse 5 to 8 per square kilometre near the Strickland river and toward Lagaip country.

To the north live scattered populations of Hewa, to the west Oksapmin and Mountain Ok peoples, and southwards lie the small tribes of the Papuan Plateau. Production among these linguistically non-Highlands peoples is based upon extensive land use with gardens shifted every year or two. Taro, bananas, yams and sago are important staples, sometimes predominating over sweet potato.[2] Few domestic pigs are kept and there is a strong emphasis upon hunting as a vital male contribution to subsistence. The Duna are situated at a geographical and production-intensity midpoint between these systems and those of the Highlands proper (Table 1). By comparison with Enga and Hageners they produce relatively few pigs, although their production is carried out by means of labour-intensive garden techniques similar to those in high-production systems supporting much larger populations of people and pigs.

By situating the Duna example in a comparative perspective encompassing neighbouring high- and low-production systems, certain dynamic factors involved in the determination of inequality throughout a range of New Guinea societies are brought into focus. The ethnography of central New Guinea reveals a broad correlation between population size of linguistic units, local population densities, levels of horticultural intensification, pig production, and the elaboration of systems of ceremonial exchange — with all the implications of the latter for social control, leadership and inequality. These interrelations would appear causally entailed in the development of densely populated, high-production social formations out of small, sparse populations relying primarily upon hunting

Table 1. *Population and production characteristics of some central New Guinea peoples (sources: Townsend 1971, Hatanaka and Bragge 1973, Steadman 1971, Barth 1975, Glasse 1968, Waddell 1972, Feacham 1973. See also Brown and Podolefsky 1976)*

| People | Population (linguistic unit) | Population density | Pigs per person | Zone of occupation (altitude) | Subsistence technology |
|---|---|---|---|---|---|
| Hiowe Sanio | 234 | ? | ? | 150–300m | wild sago; hunting and gathering, minimal gardening |
| Saiyolof | 250 | 0.9/km$^2$ | ? | 460–1,000m | shifting cultivation of taro; hunting and gathering |
| Hewa | 1,500 | 1.8/km$^2$ | 0.2 | 700–800m | shifting cultivation of sweet potato; hunting, some gathering |
| Faiwolmin | 3,000 | 0.75/km$^2$ | 0.2–0.35 | 500–1,000m | shifting cultivation of taro; hunting and gathering |
| Oksapmin | 6,000 | 8–25/km$^2$ (est.) | 0.4 (est.) | 1,000–1,500(?)m | shifting cultivation of taro and sweet potato; casuarina fallowing |
| Duna | 15,000 | 10–40/km$^2$ | 1.1 | 950–2,000m | mounded sweet potato; intensive shifting cultivation – gardens cropped for 3 to 12 years |
| Huli | 60,000 | 10–100/km$^2$ | ? | 1,600m | mounded sweet potato; fixed field system |
| Enga | 100,000+ | 40–140/km$^2$ | 2–3 | 1,600–2,400m | mounded sweet potato; fixed field system |

for their supply of animal protein. Leaving aside questions of the revolutionary impact of the sweet potato and the rapidity of the Ipomoean transformation, it seems otherwise reasonable to suppose that these correlations have generally obtained in the past.

In my thesis I suggested that the mechanism of such developments may be understood as an engagement of two sets of self-amplifying feedback loops: a use-value cycle (of ecological causations) in which a growing human population offsets declining wild food resources by increasing garden and pig production, and an exchange-value cycle (of social causalities) in which increasing potentials for violent social conflict are mediated by the substitution of pigs as compensation for loss of life and, ultimately, by the mutual incompatibility of large-scale ceremonial exchange and warfare. Beginning with Watson's earlier suggestions (1965a and b) and the critique of Brookfield and White (1968), and working through a consideration of central New Guinea ethnographic evidence, I arrived at conclusions similar to those published by Watson in the same year (1977) concerning the ecological cycle of population growth and protein imbalance. The interactions of the principal elements of this cycle are shown in Figure 1. As human populations grow, wild food resources decline — owing to over-hunting and the destruction of natural forest habitats by the spread of shifting cultivation. Escape from serious protein shortage and an ecological and demographic dead-end is effected by the cultivation of sweet-potato fodder and increased pig production. Increased cultivation may however lead to a further deterioration in the productivity

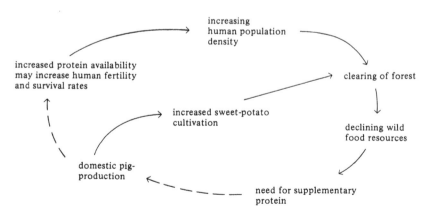

Figure 1 The ecological use-value cycle of increasing population and pig-production (after Watson 1977: 62)

of hunting and foraging. And to the extent that pig production actually produces more protein than hunting there is also a likelihood that improved fertility and decreasing mortality rates will result in further population growth, thus intensifying the causalities of the cycle.

Pigs, however, are not for consumption alone. Indeed, in low-production societies (e.g. Mountain Arapesh, Mead 1940; Garia, Lawrence 1967) there are often explicit prohibitions against the consumption of one's own pigs (cf. Rubel and Rosman 1978). Among the Duna, men say 'pigs are for killing when people are sick, for marrying women, and for *damba* [compensation payments]'. Pigs killed as sacrifices when people are sick tend to be consumed by those who have mixed their labours in production, but even this consumption without exchange is represented as an exchange — between the living and the (imaginary) beings of the spirit world. Sacrifice and bridewealth and the paying and accepting of *damba* in compensation for injuries and loss of life are the central pre-colonial social practices in the circulation of pigs among the Duna. *Damba* is the responsibility of the lineage; bridewealth is the responsibility of the individual and his personal network of friends and relations. Sacrifices were organised at all levels in society from the individual and his immediate family through lineage-level sacrifices to massive affairs involving all the lineages of a parish, together with invited non-residential descent-group members.

The central role of pigs as indemnity payments for the ordering of social life has led me to formulate a second positive feedback cycle engaging or operating simultaneously with the use-value cycle. In this cycle (Figure 2), increasing complexities of social relations within expanding groups and increasing competition between local groups lead to increasing potentials for conflict. In the absence of effective means of mediating and resolving conflict the outcome is likely to be conflict-escalation following the typical Melanesian 'pay-back' pattern (often with gratuitous increments) first identified by Bateson (1936) as 'symmetrical schismogenesis'. More recently Schieffelin (1976) has described the same cultural pattern from a cognitive perspective as 'the opposition scenario'. As Schieffelin makes clear (*ibid.*: 144–7), the difficulty experienced by people in avoiding an escalation of conflict lies in the absence of recognised and acceptable alternative courses of action. Among the Duna and Huli the practice of accepting large numbers of live pigs in compensation for death or injury provides such an alternative.[3]

It may be that the pig, as the only valuable truly capable of reproduction, is particularly suited for the role of mediative substitute for lost

Nicholas Modjeska

human life. Once the substitution of pig-values for human life-values becomes both acceptable and technologically possible a further escalation of pig production would be expected on the assumptions of the model. Pigs are produced as exchange-valuables to match the current level of conflict and to sustain peaceful relations within and between groups. As this can have further consequences for group size and population levels, further conflicts and mediations may again be brought into play.

This social exchange-value of the pig is not the same as the economist's exchange-value of commodities — unless we choose to regard human lives and rights in people *qua* social persons as simply 'commodities' exchanged in market-like fashion for pigs. Perhaps this is only a matter of semantics, but my suggestion is that for societies of the type under examination a major insight follows from the premise that the notion of a 'kinship system' consists largely in the articulation of rights in people with values deriving from the system of economic production.[4] Compensation payments provide one such articulation. Marriage payments, child payments and death payments provide others, and should be understood as operating within a generalised cycle interweaving the values of economic production with the social construction of people as occupants of kinship positions (see Rossi-Landi 1979).

Nor is this social exchange-value cycle of the pig quite the same thing as Watson's (1977) 'Jones Effect'. For Watson, as for Veblen, social order appears as an almost ethological response to prestige and the ability to

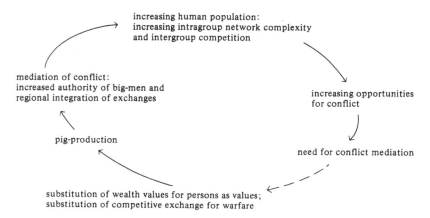

Figure 2 The exchange-value cycle of increasing social integration

impress. Watson emphasises 'the prestige of owning and exchanging pigs' where I would stress the transactional creation of social and political power through pig exchange. Where I would see the construction and enhancement of political order as a consequence of an increased capacity to mediate conflict via production and exchange, Watson sees increased production and the coordination of massive pig-slaughters as creating a need for the growth of polities (1977: 61, 63). Such a formulation seems to imply a crude techno-environmental determinism in which Highlanders have a certain level of social organisation because they have many pigs, whereas the converse is more nearly correct. I would also question Watson's emphasis upon the 'escalation of production resulting from competition . . . for limited goods and benefits' (*ibid.*: 64). Watson notes that pigs are exchanged 'for brides; for children; for death payments; . . . for personal prestige-seeking and tokens of status; . . . for the maintenance or expansion of security' (*ibid.*) – but are these really limited values? By emphasising competitive 'inflation' Watson implies that the values of social order are largely fixed quantities, incapable of expanding together with the expansion of production and exchange.

Watson's Jones Effect takes the exchange of pigs for kinship-values ('brides and affines, partners and allies' viewed as 'commodities', *ibid.*) as an unanalysed given, assuming this relationship prior to the expansion of production. Ethnographically this is perhaps so, since people like the Kaluli with little pig production nevertheless have definite notions of accepting compensation payments in lieu of the direct exchange of equivalents (as for example a life for a life). But it is also clear from Schieffelin's account (1980) that the Kaluli regard such substitutions as less satisfying than the exchange of precisely equivalent identities. Killings in retaliation for witchcraft/sorcery rather than compensation payments to resolve conflicts apparently predominated in pre-colonial society. Likewise, the direct exchange of women in marriage rather than a generalised exchange based on bridewealth suggests a preference for reciprocal identical actions rather than mediative substitutions. Among the Duna these circumstances are reversed. A reliance upon pig production for the accumulation of social capital rather than upon trade in non-reproductive valuables (axe heads, plumes, cosmetic oils, dogs' teeth) would seem to go hand in hand with an increased tolerance for mediated responses in social behaviour. I would see the achievement of pig production as the achievement of new forms of social integration, rather than being the automatic consequence of some universal social law. Pig production and exchange creatively develop a new and more 'economic' version of social control

Nicholas Modjeska

and social order. I will suggest below that in doing so they also bring social inequalities to rest upon more economically 'rational' grounds.

Unlike the Hagen and Enga areas, post-colonial Duna country has experienced a decline rather than an efflorescence of exchange activity. Since the cessation of warfare there are no longer occasions for large compensation payments between lineages. Traditional cult activities ceased in the early contact period and major sacrifices uniting lineage members and groups of lineages have not been held in 25 years. As Duna country is remote from regional centres there has been little economic development, and post-contact changes have provided few new involvements to replace what has been lost. Older men complain that young men are no longer concerned with the land and pigs but instead 'think only of work and money' as migrant labourers. Rather than causing a transformation of traditional forms under the impetus of new economic opportunities, development since 1960 has resulted in an abrupt termination of major social patterns characteristic of the pre-colonial lineage formation. That is another story. My focus here is on forms of production, exchange, sacrifice, and inequality in the recent pre-contact period. Necessarily this requires recourse to a reconstructed and sometimes speculative account based on informants' recollections and ethnographic interpolations.

## AFRICAN MODES OF PRODUCTION IN THE NEW GUINEA HIGHLANDS?

Over the past twenty years a number of studies based largely on African materials have developed analyses of inequalities between age and sex categories of tribal societies in terms of their forces and relations of production. There has been debate over the interpretation of relations between these categories as class (or class-like) relations founded in exploitation (Bonte 1977, 1979), but there is general agreement that the domination of women and junior men by the elders in African societies has a double aspect. Older men dominate both through control of the material production of subsistence staples and surplus wealth, and through control of the reproduction of the conditions of production. This latter control is achieved through the circulation of surplus wealth in exchange for a counter-circulation of rights in women and children, i.e. through the institution of bridewealth.

The debate over exploitation follows largely from differing theoretical premises. Meillassoux (1964, 1979) focuses on the cycle of production and human reproduction ('the continuous conversion of subsistence into labour power, of labour power into productive agents and producers of subsistence'). He defines exploitation in terms of differential constraints upon the potential of 'productive domestic cells' to reproduce themselves from generation to generation. In a 'domestic community' (the Guro are the implicit empirical example), the acknowledgement of kinship entails that kin cannot be deprived of the means of reproducing themselves: subsistence and a spouse. Since the elders arrange that juniors eventually marry, there is in this perspective no exploitation. Terray (1972b, 1975, 1979), however, re-interprets this same material while emphasising the primacy of production. In his analysis exploitation is a concept proper to the economic level and occurs whenever direct producers are unable to determine the appropriation of their surplus. The elders are exploiters since they direct women and juniors in agricultural work and appropriate the product for their own management and distribution. While agreeing that the elders dominate the mode of production through their control of the conditions of reproduction, Meillassoux and Terray reach different conclusions because they start from different concepts of exploitation and of the totality of the object of analysis.

Little use has so far been made of these perspectives in the interpretation of New Guinea social formations. Obviously the notion of a generalised African 'lineage mode of production' cannot simply be exported to New Guinea without a close examination of the similarities and differences in the forces and relations of production. Before I enter this comparison there is another point, an apparent empirical difference between two African examples, the Guro and the Mbum of Chad, which require further attention.

O'Laughlin's (1974) analysis of male dominance among the Mbum, like the analyses of the Guro, proposes that authority is based upon control of the means of reproduction. Surplus is concentrated in the form of livestock and cash managed by the elders to assure the continuing availability of brides, seed-stock and agricultural implements for the men of the lineage. By controlling bridewealth the elders control the destinies of women in marriage as well as the obedience of the juniors, who must contribute unreciprocated labour to the elders if they hope to marry. But how are the elders able to control the surplus that grants them control of social relations? In the final analysis it is the structural practices of exogamy, patrilineality and virilocal residence, made possible by male-controlled bridewealth, which together construct the conditions for male appropriation of the surplus. Bridewealth separates a woman from her kin through patrivirilocal marriage, thus permitting the co-residence of patrilineally related men. Labour recruitment to granary groups is based on family and lineage membership, with the consequence that men can recruit more surplus labour than women (who may also head granary groups).

But Meillassoux and Terray posit a different final condition for the dominance of the Guro elders. Their argument is that a position of authority is necessary as a technical condition of the requirement for agricultural planning and continuous provisioning. The elders occupy this position due to their, 'in a sense, "natural" ' (Terray 1972b: 130) possession of technical knowledge. In simple agricultural communities this technical knowledge is limited, and the elders' control of production is correspondingly limited. Yet, the argument runs, this small advantage is sufficient to gain complete control of the surplus, thereby assuring final control at the level of the conditions of reproduction. Based as it is on a technical rather than a social condition of production, this explanation is less satisfying than O'Laughlin's. Moreover, it overlooks the point that a large component of 'technical knowledge' in these societies usually turns out to be magical/sacred knowledge — and, hence, mystification. But perhaps there is no other recourse, since it appears that there is considerable local endogamy among the lineages of Guro villages, and without local exogamy O'Laughlin's explanation does not work. One is here confronted with either an empirical difference or an analytical error. If the former, then the specific circumstances upon which domination ultimately rests may vary substantially in different cases. In considering the applicability of African lineage-mode-of-production concepts to New Guinea Highlands societies similar questions need to be asked. Is dominance based on control of the means of reproducing the conditions of production (i.e. the circulation of rights in women)? And how, specifically, is control of surplus production achieved at the lineage level, since production takes place within separate family/homestead units rather than lineage-based units?

There are important similarities between the African examples and the New Guinea examples considered here: a low level of development of the productive forces, the authority of older men over women and juniors, the global organisation of social relations under lineage formats, and the institution of bridewealth, which in both sets of examples serves to link production to the circulation of women and children via rights in their persons. But there are also significant differences in the relations of production. These concern access to the product, and the ways in which this circulation determines access to the means of demographic reproduction: women.

The productive forces in pre-colonial central New Guinea were those of simple horticulture, hunting and pig husbandry, requiring stone axes and bows obtained in trade and locally manufactured wooden implements. Even in the high-production systems the level of development of the productive forces was probably lower than in the African examples, although objective empirical determination would pose difficult problems.

Extended units of production in hoe cultivation and net hunting are a characteristic feature of African modes of production. Labour is recruited to production units on the basis of village residence or lineage kinship ties extending beyond the family or domestic unit.[5] Garden production in New Guinea is carried out by smaller groups, with domestic groups usually functioning as the primary units of production. Although close affines may exchange labour, throughout much of central New Guinea there is no seasonal cultivation cycle and hence no technical requirement for large labour forces at particular times of the year. Clearing, planting and harvesting continue throughout the year, and it is possible for single men successfully to garden and raise pigs on their own.

The importance of extended production units in Africa has a counterpart in the factor of technical knowledge. Although there is no demonstration that extended production units form the only technically feasible basis for the organisation of production under African conditions, once the existence of extended production units is assumed, the complexities of agricultural production on such a scale imply (as Meillassoux and Terray argue) a position of technical or managerial expert. But although the technical conditions of grain production in a seasonal regime may require more expertise than sweet potato in an aseasonal regime, peasant producers the world over nevertheless manage similar problems within domestic production units and without lineage organisation. It is doubtful, then, if the existence of a position of authority outside the domestic unit can be inferred on the basis of self-sustaining agricultural production alone.

Whatever the basis of the managerial function of Guro and Mbum elders, it is evident that in New Guinea Highlands horticulture the requirements for both technical knowledge and the coordination of labour are slight. Among the Duna men frequently clear gardens on their own, although several men may join together to construct a common fence around their plots.[6] Women work alone, or close by one another but without any coordination of their activities. Men allocate separate sub-plots to each woman of their household, and women individually decide when and where within the plot to mound, weed and harvest. Each woman must break up and re-mound an average or two to three mounds each day to

61

maintain required levels of sweet-potato production throughout the year. The mounding system creates a series of easily managed gardens in miniature, with women making most of the production decisions in the garden by themselves — taking into account the requirements of their families and pigs and the urgings and coercions of their husbands or male kin.

With minimal coordination of labour and no storage of sweet potato there is little argument for the existence of a position of communal authority based either on the technical conditions of cultivation or on any functional necessity of managing reserves against periods of scarcity. The appropriation and re-distribution of grain by African elders has no counterpart in Highlands sweet-potato production — and this sets limits on the possibilities for appropriating surplus within the production process.

The sexual division of labour in subsistence production is clearly emphasised in central New Guinea societies, compared with its apparently slight and socially unmarked manifestations in Africa. No specific sexual division of labour is mentioned by either Meillassoux or O'Laughlin for Guro and Mbum extended production groups. Among the Mbum, women may own axes as well as hoes and both sexes clear and cultivate their own plots. In contrast, among the Duna and elsewhere in the Highlands only men fell trees and construct garden fences and houses, while women do the mounding of garden plots and planting, weeding and harvesting. Although Duna men harvest and cook for themselves and can perform all other tasks necessary for their existence and comfort, women are considered incapable of clearing gardens, building houses, killing pigs, and making fire. Nor can they defend themselves in warfare or enter into relations with the supernatural. The social division of labour thus effectively defines men as potentially independent and women as necessarily dependent.

In the Highlands, particularly in the Duna example, pigs are the chief form of wealth. Since their circulation establishes the distribution of power and prestige as well as control over women and children, pigs occupy a structural position analogous to prestige goods in the African examples. Like prestige goods, pigs are in a sense the surplus economic product, although with a number of significant differences. Pigs are 'surplus' in the sense that they are ordinarily produced for exchange rather than immediate consumption. Although social life among the Duna would be inconceivable without pigs, there are nonetheless men who own no pigs and choose not to raise them. Pigs are not a necessity of life as sweet potato is, and so pig production can be seen as an embodiment of surplus labour capacity remaining after essential garden production has

been realised.[7] But unlike certain African prestige goods, which take the
form of useful objects rendered useless by the over-embodiment of surplus
labour in their embellished manufacture, pigs are always finally destined
to be used, to be eaten.[8] There is also the difference that as a store of
surplus value pigs require constant expenditures of labour for their upkeep.
And if they are to be regarded as the surplus product of the lineage or
community, it is notable that pigs are produced in separate and largely
independent homesteads. In Africa, prestige goods are obtained by trade
or produced by artisan specialists whose labour is subsidised by the elders
out of the communal or lineage granaries. Since the elders control the
granaries they are able to control the production and circulation of prestige goods. But no comparable concentration of power occurs in Highlands
pig production. Unless shells or other monopolisable tokens are introduced, the possession of wealth is open to all producers, thus undermining
inegalitarian control of juniors by elders or of lesser men by big-men.

The appropriation of the labour of junior males which figures so
prominently in the African examples is problematic in central New Guinea.
Where young men are isolated for considerable periods of time in bachelors' hunting lodges (Papuan Plateau, Duna, Huli), their product is mainly
destined for their own consumption.[9] Where young men engage in gardening they may do so in partnership with others of their age and without
supervision by elders.

The authority of elders over juniors is further muted in New Guinea by
emphasis upon the economic, political and ceremonial achievements of
big-men. Differences among mature men may overshadow differences
between elders and juniors, although there is still an expectation that
young men will ordinarily have little standing in the community. Even
men 25 or 30 years old may be referred to among the Duna as *nana yao*,
'nothing boys'.

West of the Strickland river graded initiation hierarchies provide the
social framework for dominance and deference among men. Male initiation
is also universal in the Plateau area, although graded hierarchies are absent.
Homosexual relations between initiates (who become wife-receivers) and
initiators (wife-givers) are here an important feature of the subordination
of juniors. Among the Duna and Huli there was voluntary participation in
bachelors' cults, emphasising hunting, male purity, and masculine growth
— much as in the non-voluntary cults, although overt homosexual elements
were absent. Among the Enga similar themes of purity and growth, with
an added heterosexual twist, are bent to the purpose of emphasising clan
strength and military prowess while at the same time preparing youths for

Nicholas Modjeska

marriage. Participation is again universal (Meggitt 1964; Gray 1973). Finally, some of these same motifs appear in the Hagen area in fertility cults without initiation or emphasis upon bachelorhood (Strathern 1970a and b). Variations in male cults are thus suggestive of a continuum from low-production formations in which men are 'made' by male society (as represented by the ritual powers of the cult and by homosexual activity) to high-production formations in which men make themselves (as it were) through participation in production and exchange and through acceptance of marriage.[10]

Duna myths provide an intriguing paradigm of relations between elders and juniors, suggesting some of the ambiguities involved by contrast with the one-dimensionality of the relationship portrayed in the African examples. Rivalries between fathers and sons (covertly expressed in Enga stories — Meggitt 1976) are largely absent. There is actually little conflict in this relationship, probably due to the late age of marriage for men. In pre-colonial times men did not marry and establish themselves in production and exchange until past 30, by which time their fathers were either deceased or prepared to retire. Both actual events and myth reveal instead a pervasive rivalry and antagonism between elder and younger brothers. Myths associate elder brothers with hunting and the control of magical powers, while younger brothers are portrayed as mundane characters engaged in gardening and family life. Elder brothers possess secret knowledge and the rituals necessary for the reproduction of the fertility of lineage land, wild animals, pigs and people, but unlike younger brothers they are aloof from women and do not reproduce themselves. (Perhaps one may see in this a parable of the succession of modes of subsistence from hunting to horticulture?)

As a model of the relations of domination between elders and juniors, Duna myths establish elder brothers as 'owners' of the magical means of reproducing the conditions of production. The elder brother is a non-labourer who issues imperative ritual instructions while the younger brother expends his vital juices in the 'hard work' of gardening and sexual procreation. Periodically it is necessary for the younger brother and his descendants to renew the fertility of the land by sacrificing pigs to the elder brother's *auwi* (a black spherical cult stone believed to be a petrified soul). A charter for a form of appropriation under the form of sacrifice is thus established. Elders possess magical knowledge, issue commands and receive a portion of the product as sacrifice. Juniors labour in ignorance, depending upon the elders for the continuity of fertility.

Antagonisms between elder and junior are thus situated within the sibling group rather than between generations. To some extent Duna myths provide a model of what actually happens between siblings. But the mythic elder brother dies without descendants and the myth is charter for the lineage. In relation to the lineage there are no elders and juniors; all are equally younger brothers, following the instructions of the absent ancestral elder brother and depending upon his power. The authority of the African elders – apparent in ritual, in production relations within the lineage, and in family relations between fathers and sons – is displaced laterally with the Duna. They conceive of a comparable authority but they negate its effects in social organisation by a displacement from the direct chain of descent laterally into sibling relations. There are no lineage elders claiming power for themselves as representatives of the ancestors. Elder brothers in separate families within Duna lineages may make similar claims, but there is no genealogical differentiation of a line of descent from ancestral elder brothers. Men expect in any case what the myths portray: younger brothers never have accepted and never will entirely accept their subordination. Relations of siblingship are perhaps always more compatible with egalitarian assumptions than are relations by descent. Duna cosmology and genealogy are thereby incapable of providing a model for routinised authority relations within the lineage.

In the above African examples, access to land is a communal right rather than a right by descent. In central New Guinea rights in land are usually held corporately by clans and lineages. O'Laughlin makes it clear that descent groups have no special claims on land among the Mbum; more generally in the African literature it appears that clans are not autochthonously associated with particular tracts of land (as they are, for example, among the Duna). Local descent groups instead move slowly over the landscape, claiming new land as old farm sites are exhausted or become insufficient (Sahlins 1961). Thus in Africa men and women have symmetrical relations to land rights, equally as members of a community, while in New Guinea men have rights by descent and women, to the extent that they are exogamously married wives, have rights only by usufruct.[11]

Social organisation in central New Guinea varies considerably between low- and high-production societies. As a generalisation, lineages are more clearly patrilineal both in ideal and in actuality among Enga and Hageners, while cognatic lineages with a patrifilial bias are found among the Huli and Duna.[12] Among the Etoro of the Papuan Plateau (Kelly 1977; cf. Modjeska 1980) patrilineally related groups of men conceptualise their unity more in terms of siblingship than in terms of descent, and marriages are arranged to create overlapping matrifilial sibling links within the patri-

lineal group. Social organisation in the Ok region is based on cult organisation rather than lineage structure, and although clans have relevance in
ritual contexts they are otherwise 'weakly conceptualised' (Barth 1975:
25). Craig (1969) reports that descent is largely irrelevant among the
Telefolmin. Descent conceptualisations thus vary from weakly cognatic to
moderately patrilineal, with the structural efficacy of lineage organisation
and the extent of local exogamy increasing roughly with increases in productive capacity.

The authority of men over women is as much a basic condition of
sociality in New Guinea as in Africa, but again there are internal variations
and broad contrasts with Africa. Where local exogamy is weak, women can
have rights of ownership in the land they cultivate, and their control over
staple crops may receive greater recognition. In the extreme case, among
the Telefolmin, crops are separately owned by individual men and women,
while marriage has few consequences for lineage relations. Widows need
not re-marry and Craig notes that among their own kin such women may
become wealthy and respected. Among the Etoro, however, the importance of maintaining lineage relations among men through arranged
exchange marriages would seem to undermine whatever independence
women acquire through tendencies to local endogamy. Here men's control
over women is further assured through the practice of child betrothal.
Where marriages are arranged later in life, as in the Highlands proper,
women are perhaps more likely to assert their own wishes and to have
some chance of compelling men to accommodate them. Then again, it
may be that women's influence in marriage arrangements and the threat
posed for male interests are factors in the propagation of the extreme
ideologies of sexual pollution found among Duna, Huli, and Enga.[13]
Women's status and degree of subjugation, interdependence or autonomy
is complexly determined in each case by their position in economic production, marriage arrangements, ritual activity and their influence in the
formation of gender ideologies. At present it does not seem possible to
formulate general propositions relating male authority over women to the
level of production taken as a global dimension of societal variation. It is
possible to emphasise that by comparison with women in the African
examples, women in central New Guinea are more clearly jurally disadvantaged, that ideological denigration of their gender and sexuality is
far more extreme, and that this seems to correlate with the emphasis upon
the false appropriation of women's labour in the Highlands as compared
with the exploitation of junior males in Africa.

In both Africa and New Guinea bridewealth separates women from rights in their reproduction, from rights in their children; but in central New Guinea sexuality and reproduction are less differentiated. Women are then in a sense doubly alienated. Pre-marital sexual relations are not seriously regarded among the Guro and Mbum, and women retain a large measure of control over access to their sexuality. In the Highlands (particularly with the Enga and Duna) rights of sexual access to women are among the rights totally alienated in the marriage transaction. Among the Duna sexual morality is severe, and a man accused of 'stealing intercourse' (i.e. without legitimation by marriage payment) may be beaten and have his pigs killed. Women who engage in extra-marital affairs are occasionally killed, but usually they are beaten by their husband or brothers and sometimes sexually maimed with firesticks or thorn canes. Significantly, men who 'steal intercourse' are not mutilated. A man may even elicit sympathy by pleading 'my penis stood up; what was I to do?'. This and other affirmations of phallic sexuality, and the aggression directed at women's sexuality, are evidence of deeper assumptions about human nature and morality completely at variance with the matrifocal values found in many African societies (Tanner 1974; James 1978). James has argued that matrifocal values are widespread (although presumably not universal) in Africa as an underlying foundation in both jurally matrilineal and patrilineal systems. This seems consistent with O'Laughlin's finding that women in patrilineal Mbum society have jural equality with men although they lack *de facto* equality.

In addition to marriage payments there is an emphasis upon the exchange of brides in the area west of the Strickland river and on the Papuan Plateau. This emphasis can be understood in relation to the small size of local and tribal groups, the people's vulnerability to demographic extinction and their awareness of the realities of demographic competition (Barth 1975: 167). As Craig (1969: n. 14) points out, bride-exchange ensures the status quo of groups while bridewealth serves the different function of defining rights in women and children. It would seem an indication of the demographic success (as well as the success in pig production) of the large groups east of the Strickland river that men are there able to forego the direct exchange of women.

A further point of variation concerns the restricted or generalised availability of the valuables required in marriage payments. Although such payments are everywhere larger than a single individual can ordinarily amass by his own effort (Meggitt 1969), in Hagen (and Tambul: Bowers 1965) the inclusion of pearl shells as well as pigs in bridewealth gives greater control over marriage arrangements to financier big-men who are able to monopolise the circulation of these valuables. To the extent that they are not able to acquire bridewealth by their own productive efforts, prospective grooms in New Guinea find themselves in much the same position as African juniors. However, unless the control over valuables exercised by the African elders has been exaggerated to suit the requirements of a theory, it would seem that juniors in central New Guinea societies are never so completely dependent upon the goodwill of their elders. Pigs cannot be monopolised to the extent suggested for marriage valuables in the African examples. Duna men are usually able to count on friends and relations of their own generation to provide much of their marriage payment. Bridewealth is conventionally set at 4 or 5 large pigs and 14 to 16 smaller ones and, as one informant pointed out, a man without pigs can always force a marriage by 'stealing intercourse' and obliging his lineage mates to find the pigs to avoid further trouble. Still, the circumstances of marriage have been affected by post-contact changes, and it is difficult to assess what degree of freedom young men may have had in pre-colonial times.

To summarise: women's subordination appears as a primary fact of society in central New Guinea and encompasses not only their productive activities and child-rearing but their very being as sexual persons. In the African cases women enjoy a larger degree of jural equality. Their actual inequality appears almost as a by-product of the control of bridewealth by the elders. The control of bridewealth is crucial to the subordination of junior males and the primary jural cleavage in production is between elders and juniors. In central New Guinea women have neither factual nor jural equality and the primary social distinction in the production process concerns the sexes rather than elder and junior males. Among men the subordination of juniors to seniors and of lesser men to big-men has a less certain institutional base. The inequality of women can perhaps best be understood in relation to this relative equality of men (Strathern 1979b: 535ff.).

African lineage modes of production involve extended production units in which the labour of community members is combined and the managerial position of the elder is assured by the requirements of redistribution — an arrangement with a perhaps serendipitous correspondence to traditional marxist notions of the primitive communal mode of production (see Dunn 1979). But in New Guinea the relative autonomy of production within domestic units from the control of lineage or communal authority poses a problem. Sahlins' (1972) notion of the Domestic Mode of Production (DMP) would seem more appropriate than an African model, but as Sahlins points out, the DMP is a prescription for social anarchy. As a societal mode of production it is an impossibility; of itself it specifies no mechanism for the re-distribution of surplus among domestic units. Each family operates for itself, yet without an appropriation of surplus the lineage or community cannot come into being as the practice of any wider sociality, as a community for itself. How, then, in central New Guinean societies are men as representatives of the interests of lineages able to extract surplus from men and women as representatives of individual domestic units? The importance of domestic pig production suggests Engels' (1884) prognosis of an increasing power of families against the collectivity through differential accumulation of private property. Yet the collectivity persists. Unequal accumulation between domestic units is kept in check by practices that construct the lineage as a collectivity not only in itself but for itself, by exchange, sacrifice and especially warfare.[14]

## PRODUCTION WITHIN DOMESTIC UNITS

As opposed to the extended production units of African societies, production in central New Guinea is primarily domestic production. Pig production depends on sweet-potato fodder, produced through women's garden labour in combination with men's labour in preparing garden sites. There is no question of men being thought of as non-labourers. The domination and presumably exploitation of women by men must be understood in terms of the relations of two classes of labourers, exchanging products and services. Although both men's and women's labour are required in combination to produce sweet potato and pigs (and in that sense both men and women are direct producers), it is to be noted that men are the producers of garden plots, the necessary pre-condition for women's more immediately productive labour in gardening and tending pigs. Within this gender-based division of labour men are the direct producers of the means of production while women are the direct producers of subsistence and wealth in the form of pigs.

An evolutionary perspective might suggest that while women in food-gathering systems have relatively direct access to their means of production, the shift to horticulture has effected a strategic male technological intervention in women's conditions of production. Instead of nature as the subject of their labour, garden work places women within a domesticated production site. The cleared and fenced garden becomes the instrument of labour for the production of sweet potato.[15] Women have access to land only through men, both because they require male labour to prepare the site, and because exogamic patrivirilocal marriage separates them from their natal clan land and accordingly modifies their jural and ideological attachments.

A fragment of Duna mythology relates that in primeval times the land was constantly in motion. Whole parish territories changed their positions. Social order began when the tracts of land were fixed in relation to one another and to their human occupants by supernatural intervention and male ritual. Monocarpellary territorial organisation further fixes ownership of land upon the lineage or clan, and the labour of individual men in clearing forest and building fences confers individual ownership of garden sites and fallow plots. The land as subject of labour and garden sites as instruments of production are as much the property of men as raw materials and factories are the property of capitalists – the difference being that Duna ownership is conferred by labour, direct labour in the case of garden clearings and indirect and mystified ritual labour in the case of lineage and clan estates.

Since labour confers rights of ownership the question arises of men's and women's shares in the labour of pig production. If the embodiment of 'hard work' is recognised by Duna as the condition of being *aua*, 'father', of a garden site, a house or a net-bag, how are rights of ownership recognised in domestic production when different qualities and quantities of men's and women's labour are combined? Unless rights in pigs are directly proportional to differential labour investments, it would be here – in the movement from the organisation of production to the allocation of rights – that the primary moment of false appropriation would lie.

There seems to be a basic disagreement between outside observers – administrators, missionaries, and even anthropologists (e.g. Maracek 1977) – and the opinion of Duna men themselves on the question of labour inputs. Outsiders see women doing the greater part of subsistence labour and are inclined to cast men in the role of lazy and arrogant overseers. Duna men insist to the contrary that their work is greater than ('truly big', 'goes above') women's work. Data summarised in Table 2 suggest that there may be some truth in both points of view. Consistent with the view of outside observers, women spend considerably more time than men working in gardens and tending pigs, while men spend more time visiting and in other social activities.[16] Moreover, women's spare time (not a Duna concept!) is spent for the most part close to home, attending church and infants' health clinics, and caring for sick children. Men attend church less often and their visiting includes trips to other parishes in the pursuit of 'business'. But, consistent with the men's point of view, a large part of the

Table 2. *Activities reported and estimated hours in 35 man-days and 35 woman-days, Horailenda, Jan.–Feb. 1979 (note that women rarely mention child-minding, nor does it seem possible to assign a time value to this task)*

|  | Men | | Women | |
|---|---|---|---|---|
|  | hours | % | hours | % |
| Heavy garden work: clearing, ditching and fencing | 55 | 13% | 12.75 | 3% |
| Mounding, planting, harvesting, weeding, burning, feeding pigs and walking to and from gardens | 41 | 10% | 123.25 | 29% |
| Care and harvest of nut pandanus and fruit pandanus | 17 | 4% | – | – |
| Looking for lost pigs | 6.5 | 1.5% | – | – |
| Gathering | 11 | 2.5% | 3 | 0.5% |
| Hunting | 3 | 0.5% | – | – |
| Craft manufacture | 14.5 | 3.5% | 19.5 | 4.5% |
| Obtaining water and firewood | 5.5 | 1% | 15.75 | 4% |
| Carrying construction materials | – | – | 12 | 3% |
| Cooking | 8 | 2% | 16.5 | 4% |
| Work for local enterprises, missions and schools | 12.75 | 3% | 6.5 | 1.5% |
| Visiting, attending church, caring for sick, mourning | 91.5 | 22% | 62.5 | 15% |
| Sickness | 41 | 10% | 32 | 7.5% |
| Hours unaccounted for in 35 twelve-hour days | 113.25 | 27% | 116.25 | 27.5% |
| Totals | 420 hrs | 100% | 420 hrs | 99.5% |

time they spend in garden work is devoted to the especially hard labour of felling trees, fencing and ditching. Another 8.5 per cent of men's reported labour time is taken up with such tasks as searching for lost pigs and checking on scattered holdings of nut pandanus and fruit pandanus trees, i.e. productive work that involves considerable travelling time and absents them from the gardens. As well, the 'business' trips tabulated here as visiting are of course seen by men as part of their necessary 'work'. Men spend many hours in travelling to and fro, particularly before an exchange payment or a pork distribution, holding whispered, secret confabulations to arrange that suitable pigs will be available on the day. A division of labour that assigns to men tasks involving spatial mobility and the arrangement of transactions makes much of their 'work' less visible to outside observers who tend to equate garden work with the sum of necessary labour. Yet it must also be recognised that men's work is by these same considerations more interesting and adventurous, less repetitive and confining than women's work. In any case, excluding cooking, time spent in getting water and firewood, and time spent in visiting or being ill, it appears that men contribute just under 50 per cent, and women just over 50 per cent, of the total time invested in productive labour. If time spent in cooking and obtaining firewood and water is included in the necessary labour of subsistence, the contributions of men and women become 44.3 per cent and 55.7 per cent respectively, not including work for mission and school, or 45.4 per cent and 54.6 per cent including this external sector work.

Although precise comparison of these data with published data for other Highlands societies is not possible, it is nonetheless apparent that there is considerable variation in the proportions of male and female labour involved in different production systems. As Table 3 indicates, these differences are consistent with the level of surplus labour realised as pig production. The higher the level of pig production, the more the division of labour tips the balance toward a heavier work-load for women. Pospisil's (1963a) data for the Wissel Lakes villagers of Botukebo, who operate a low-production system, show men doing more work in direct horticultural production than women.[17] Pospisil does not provide information on the hours of labour required for tending pigs and other subsistence tasks, but there are few pigs and the imbalance in garden labour in the Duna and Enga examples falls clearly on the other side. As well, given the Kapauku emphasis on economic individualism (to the extent that even family relations may be overridden by relations of credit and debt — Pospisil 1963b: 90),[18] it seems unlikely that imbalances in other subsistence tasks performed as surplus labour for the opposite sex (cooking, house building, child minding, etc.) could greatly offset the imbalance in garden labour. Among the Duna, with pig production in the middle range, the balance of time spent in horticultural production and tending pigs has shifted decisively against women, although their position improves slightly when other subsistence tasks and work in the external sector are con-

Table 3. *Mean hours of work per week and proportional contribution by sex in three Highlands production systems (sources: Pospisil 1963a, Waddell 1972)*

| | Men | | Women | | Total hours for both sexes |
|---|---|---|---|---|---|
| | hours | % | hours | % | |
| Botukebo Ekari ('Kapauku') (0.17 pig per person) gardening and harvesting only | 14.0 | 54.5% | 11.7 | 45.5% | 25.7 |
| Duna (1.1 pig per person) gardening, harvesting, and tending pigs | 19.2 | 41.4% | 27.2 | 58.6% | 46.4 |
| other subsistence work | 13.1 | | 13.4 | | |
| Total | 32.3 | 44.3% | 40.6 | 55.7% | 72.9 |
| Raiapu Enga (2.3 pigs per person) gardening, harvesting, and tending pigs | 15.6 | 37% | 26.3 | 63% | 41.9 |
| other subsistence work | 6.1 | | 4.9 | | |
| Subtotal | 21.7 | 41% | 31.2 | 59% | 52.9 |
| cash crops and other commercial activities | 5.1 | | 4.7 | | |
| Total | 26.8 | 42.7% | 35.9 | 57.3% | 62.7 |

sidered as well. Finally, in the Enga example the same imbalance in men's favour appears again, but in slightly greater proportion.

How are these differences to be accounted for? According to theory, imbalances in labour inputs are referable to the relations of production (just as is the crude dichotomy between labourers and non-labourers). All of the circumstances noted here as situating men and women in relation to the production process (lineage organisation and ownership of land, local exogamy, marriage payments, alienation of rights in women and children, the sexual division of labour) are involved. But one factor in particular stands out at the level of direct production: variation in the horticultural technologies by which sweet potato is produced. Among Botukebo villagers, despite the development of labour-intensive cultivation techniques utilising raised and ditched beds (*bedamai*), the bulk of sweet-potato production comes from simple, land-extensive shifting cultivations.

Nicholas Modjeska

The proportion of male labour to female labour is much greater in extensive shifting cultivation than in labour-intensive methods, since the work of felling trees and building fences must be repeated for each crop cycle. In intensive cultivation, by contrast, the total proportion of women's labour increases in relation to men's contribution with each successive re-cycling of the garden plot. Among the Duna, men begin the clearing of new garden sites every 3.2 years on average, although with repeated mounding and composting a garden may continue in production for 12 years or more. Men say that new gardens produce 'soft' tubers which are best for pigs, while older gardens produce the 'hard' tubers preferred by people. Since it is men who do the clearing and fencing, their labour contribution per garden decreases with each successive *mondo* (mound) cycle. Enga *mondo* cultivations are even more labour-intensive than Duna *mondo* and permit the permanent field cultivation of sweet potato without the clearing of new gardens. Waddell (1972) finds that 92 per cent of the labour time in field cultivation is contributed by women. Men devote most of their garden labour to the clearing and fencing of mixed and kitchen gardens in which yams are the predominant crop. Yams are planted by men only, as a luxury food for consumption on ceremonial occasions. Compared with sweet potato their yield is low in relation to labour inputs. If yam cultivation is seen as a male prestige activity more than a contribution to subsistence, then women's involvement in the non-prestigious direct production of the staple crop and pig fodder is almost total under the Enga system of cultivation.

The development of increasingly labour-intensive techniques of cultivation in the Highlands, by increasing the period of continuous cultivation in relation to the time required for clearing and fencing, has resulted in an increasing appropriation of women's labour in direct production. Correspondingly, there has been an increased embodiment of women's labour in the pigs supported by this production. Horticultural intensification has meant increased appropriation of women's labour in relation to the values produced. But this increasing appropriation presupposes that the sexual division of labour is relatively constant in relation to changes in production techniques. Empirically this is so; whatever the factors supporting the division of labour (socialisation, ideology, the distinctive physiological adaptations of markedly dimorphic Highlands populations), it is evident that task assignments have changed more slowly than cultivation techniques. Moreover, it looks as if men have exploited the advantages of technological innovation to further their dominance within the social formation.[19]

Returning to the Duna example, the division of labour together with the particular combination of garden cycles and mounding techniques characteristic of Duna production arrangements have been shown to result in a slight but not decisive inequality in labour inputs to the disadvantage of women. However, the above analysis takes no account of the possibility that one sex's labour may be more productive or efficient than the other's, nor is it clear that hours of labour are an appropriate measure of contributions to production in a system without wage labour. Indeed, Duna notions of time in relation to work are necessarily imprecise and their estimates of the magnitude of production tasks as 'big work' or 'little work' convey an appreciation of effort as much as of time. In view of these uncertainties an alternative approach to the empirical question of men's and women's contributions to pig production can be considered. In this approach the male and female labour forces resident in each homestead are correlated with their associated pig-production levels.[20]

The sample comprises 63 of the homestead production units of Horailenda parish in the lower Tumbudu valley, 7 remaining units having evaded my attentions in the field. The histogram of male labour per homestead (Figure 3) shows the preponderance of the typical one-man homestead. The homesteads with less than one male labour unit each are those occupied by elderly men, their contributions being reckoned as 50 per cent to 25 per cent of that of an able-bodied adult, depending on age. Homesteads with more than one male unit are occupied by a father and his son(s) in 11 cases, or by two or three men working together in partnership. Men with joint homestead arrangements, e.g. sharing a common women's house and gardening within a common fence, are considered to be 'friends'; adult brothers rarely share a homestead together.

The histogram of female labour per homestead in Figure 4 shows a

```
Workers —
middle of         Number of
interval          homesteads

0.0               0
0.5               5       *****
1.0               31      *******************************
1.5               12      ************
2.0               7       *******
2.5               3       ***
3.0               4       ****
3.5               1       *
```

Figure 3  Histogram of male worker units resident in 63 Horailenda homesteads, 1970–1

similar preponderance of one-woman homesteads. However, there are 6 homesteads without any female occupants and by comparison with males there is considerably more spread in the distribution of women among the homesteads. (A range of 0 to 5.25 women with a standard deviation of 1.02 compares with a range of 0.25 to 3.5 men with a standard deviation of 0.69.) The correlation between male and female worker units is only 0.21, so the greater spread indicates the extent to which some men are successful in accumulating and holding a female work-force. However, only two men in the sample maintain enlarged female work-forces on the basis of polygynous marriages. Most homesteads with above-average female labour are composed of a single wife together with unmarried daughters, widowed or separated sisters and their daughters, and/or an aged mother. Men are well aware of the contribution that women make to pig production and it is not unusual for a man to refuse to allow a sister or daughter to marry on the grounds that he would be unable to care for his pigs without a replacement. Men sometimes demand an exchange of 'sisters' for the same reason, although actual exchange marriages are virtually unknown. The low rate of polygyny is due partly to mission influences, but it also reveals the difficulty that men experience in raising more than one marriage payment, as well as their preference for accumulating women by means other than marriage. (There are some men in the Tumbudu valley area with as many as 12 wives, but none of them were well-known or influential at Horailenda.)

The measure of pigs adopted here is a composite statistic, the average of two verbal enquiries made of homestead heads at the beginning and end

| Workers – middle of interval | Number of homesteads | |
|---|---|---|
| 0.0 | 6 | ****** |
| 0.5 | 1 | * |
| 1.0 | 24 | ************************ |
| 1.5 | 14 | ************** |
| 2.0 | 6 | ****** |
| 2.5 | 4 | **** |
| 3.0 | 3 | *** |
| 3.5 | 3 | *** |
| 4.0 | 1 | * |
| 4.5 | 0 | |
| 5.0 | 0 | |
| 5.5 | 1 | * |

Figure 4  Histogram of female worker units resident in 63 Horailenda homesteads, 1970–1

of a year, plus half the number of pigs reported killed or given to others during the year. Piglets are further counted as fractional pigs (the 1.1 pig: person overall figure counts piglets as whole pigs). By this measure the distribution of pigs per homestead in Figure 5 shows a slight positive skew, with a range of 0.10 to 12.20 pigs per homestead, a mean of 5.14 and a median of 4.4. Most homesteads maintain only a few pigs, while a few homesteads maintain pigs in considerable numbers.

It is commonly assumed that women in the Highlands are the sole direct producers of pigs, so that big-men are motivated to marry more wives in order to increase their pig herds. However, this assumption overlooks the mixing of distinctively different male and female labour activities in production, particularly the necessity for male labour in preparing garden sites before female sweet-potato cultivation and pig tending can begin. A man with a large female labour force must either over-extend himself in clearing and fencing gardens, or appropriate the labour of other men (perhaps as dependants of his household), or run the risk of under-utilising his available female labour. These considerations appear to be well borne out in the data assembled here. The contributions of available male and female labour taken separately are not significant in predicting pigs per homestead, and the best-fitting linear model (pigs = 3.24 + 0.87 of the product of male and female units) relies on interaction alone in predicting homestead production levels (Figure 6). In other words, male and female labour are combinatory and not additive in their contributions. A homestead with one man and three women is likely to produce no more pigs than a homestead with three men and one woman, while either com-

| Pigs — middle of interval | Number of homesteads | |
|---|---|---|
| 0. | 2 | ** |
| 1. | 4 | **** |
| 2. | 5 | ***** |
| 3. | 13 | ************* |
| 4. | 8 | ******** |
| 5. | 8 | ******** |
| 6. | 3 | *** |
| 7. | 6 | ****** |
| 8. | 4 | **** |
| 9. | 3 | *** |
| 10. | 2 | ** |
| 11. | 2 | ** |
| 12. | 3 | *** |

Figure 5  Histogram of pigs per homestead, Horailenda data, 1970—1

bination is likely to produce more than a homestead with four men only, or less than a homestead with two men and two women. The question whether women's labour contributes more to pig production than men's labour or vice versa thus seems to be meaningless.

The strength of the linear relationship in the data as measured by $r^2$ is 40.1 per cent, leaving 59.9 per cent of the total sum of squares of variance in homestead pig production unexplained by regression on male and female labour interaction. Other unidentified factors are responsible for this larger part of the variability in the data. Examination of the cases departing most from the predicted pig values suggests what may be involved. Considering first the five homesteads with pig production most in excess of that predicted by the model, all five are headed by dynamic and influential men with reputations of the first order for wealth, gener-

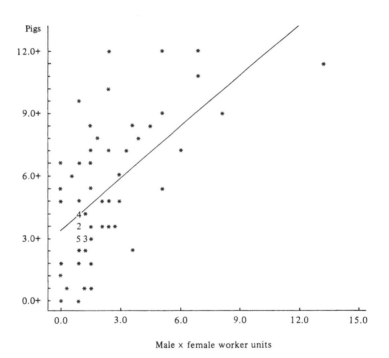

Figure 6  Scatter plot of pigs and product of male multiplied by female worker units for 63 Horailenda homesteads with the regression line predicting pig-production: pigs = 3.24 + 0.87 male × female worker units. Numbers in plot refer to multiple instances with the same values

osity, and oratorical ability (see next section below).[21] It would seem likely that the energy and capability that these men display in public affairs also find expression in their management of domestic production activities, just as their success in production contributes to their public influence. Four of these men manage homesteads with labour forces larger than the average and with a balanced combination of male and female labour in each case. However, the particular domestic relations involved vary. Two homesteads comprise husband, wife, adolescent son and adolescent daughter. One man is aided by his wife and mother together with part-time help from three adopted sons and an adolescent girl, a visiting friend of the family. The fourth homestead with above-average labour resources comprises husband and wife, adolescent son and daughter, together with a second man, his wife, and an elderly male friend all joined in partnership.

By comparison the five homesteads with pig-production levels furthest below model predictions are all headed by men with lesser public reputations. Two homesteads comprise husband and wife together with children too young to contribute to productive activities. In another the homestead head is an old and decrepit man unable to clear new gardens. The remaining two homesteads are headed by unmarried men together with their mothers, widowed sisters and sisters' children. One man was generally regarded as a ne'er-do-well who made little use of his available female labour force. The other man had some ambition but seemed thwarted by the adverse sex ratio of his work-force. His two male partners were often absent from the parish and the homestead's 5.25 female workers were inadequately employed in too small a garden area. Both of the unmarried homestead heads had discipline problems with the adolescent girls in their charge, and one of these men offered a further insight into the difficulties of his domestic relations by relating that he had dreams in which he was persecuted by *pamuk meri* (prostitutes). These traces of evidence point to the consideration that homestead production is always and necessarily a matter of domestic relationships. The quality of relationship between husband and wife, between parent and child, and between brother and sister must bear heavily upon the success or otherwise of the domestic enterprise. Some men drive themselves and their families to achieve high levels of production without many workers, while other men with more than adequate labour forces complain that their pigs die and they have given up trying. Were the data available the analysis might be furthered by a correlation of pig production with the frequency of domestic disputes and wife-beatings. And there is certainly enough room in these largely unchartable dimensions of domestic variation for a belief in magic as a factor in production as well.[22]

If women and men inextricably mix their different labours in producing pigs, then who controls the circulation of the product? On the face of it men do, and by their own intent. Men declare that they are 'boss': 'Men clear gardens, build houses, think, and go to fight; women can listen and do as they are told; women can mound sweet potato and look after pigs.' But men grant that women have rights in pigs too: 'their hard work is there'. And men recognise that women have lineage and kinship attachments and obligations of their own which require pigs for sacrifice and occasionally exchange. Perhaps 20 per cent of the pigs in mortuary distributions and a lesser number in compensation payments and marriage payments are *ima loma*, pigs contributed by men to 'help' their wives. (A man's contribution to the affairs of his wife's kin is of course also a contribution in his relations with his affines.)

But the lineage structure, notwithstanding the availability of membership rights to all cognatic descendants of the ancestors, is a strongly patriarchal structure.[23] Relations between in-laws are very much secondary to relations among 'brothers', and men emphasise that belonging to a lineage means following the instructions of the ancestors and acting in concert with 'brothers'. The lineage structure channels the flow of major compensation payments and sacrifices, and it is largely from within the lineage that men draw support in raising the bridewealth necessary for marriages. As the major financial blocs in the circulation of pigs and in decision-taking for sacrifices and internal distributions, lineages (or, rather, men in their capacity as lineage members) act primarily and predictably in male interests.

How do men arrange that the circulation of pigs is in their interests, under their control and ideologically justifiable as well?[24] It must be admitted that the justifications work well, since women for the most part relinquish their control over pigs without dispute. The following instances illustrate the general trend of Duna discourse concerning ownership/control over pigs, the persistent ambiguity of women's rights, and the impossibility of separating their rights from male involvements:

(1) In the contexts of tending pigs both husband and wife may say that the woman is *aua*, 'father', of the pig. But in the contexts of decisions concerning allocation only the man is *aua*: 'Women don't argue. Why? Because a woman knows it's not her pig; it's my pig. Where did she get it from after all? That's right, I gave it to her to look after. There's no argument; the woman does what the man says.'[25]

(2) Idiomatically it is often said that pigs belong 'half—half' to husband and wife or to a man and another woman with whom a pig is agisted. But apart from the 'halves' being understood in the Melanesian sense of an indeterminate part of a whole, the idiom actually concerns only rights in consumption and not rights of allocation. Being half-owner of a pig does not confer any rights on a woman to make decisions concerning circulation but only the right to receive a customary share of pork or other compensation in return for labour invested.

(3) Almost the only circumstance in which a woman might try to assert her interests in allocation would be where the pig was originally acquired by her, usually as an inheritance from a deceased father without surviving sons. But even here there are contradictions. When a man is asked about pigs his lineage-mates have given to out-married sisters and daughters he will say: 'If we give a pig to one of our women married elsewhere, later when we're killing pigs we'll ask her: "What became of the pig we gave you?".' But when a man is asked about a pig his wife has received from her kin the reply is different: 'Oh, my wife can't say anything; it's our pig. I did the hard work of making the gardens; she will get to eat it too.'

(4) If a man donates a pig to a friend's bridewealth payment it is expected that the donor's wife (or other pig-caretaker) is also a mutual friend. The final justification for a woman to relinquish a pig for bride-wealth, beyond considerations of friendship with the prospective groom, is that daughters of the marriage will bring pigs back when they marry in turn. Bridewealth pigs are distributed to all who contributed to the bride's mother's marriage, so that a woman who helps her husband's friends will eventually receive a share of the return pigs, or her children will inherit rights to any return. But usually it is only male children who inherit.

(5) As to pigs allocated by husbands for lineage compensation payments: 'women know there will be no end of fighting without *damba* [compensation]'. Fighting usually originates from disputes concerning the interests of the men of the lineage and not their wives, but women are expected to contribute their share of jointly produced pigs as the necessary cost of maintaining peace and security without which production is impossible.

(6) If a woman tending another man's pig wants to use the pig for her own and/or her husband's purposes, she will arrange with the other man as co-owner to replace the pig with a substitute. Sometimes this may be a payment (cowrie shells, salt, or nowadays cash), but the preferred arrangement is to replace a large pig with two small pigs, one of which the woman continues to tend. (Notice how mediating money-forms terminate the relationship, while the exchange of pigs for pigs continues it.)

(7) If a man wants to send an agisted pig elsewhere in exchange, he will compensate the caretaker for her interest with shells, money, or a small pig. When a small pig is given in compensation for a woman's half-interest in a large pig, the giver is no longer considered a co-owner. And yet, 'when she [i.e., her husband] kills this pig she'll tell me and I'll go and eat pork too, because I was the "father" of this pig before and we're partners'.

Generally, it seems clear that pigs cared for by women other than wives and sisters cannot be put into exchanges not involving the kinship interests of the woman without some tangible recompense, but at the same time there is a tendency for all agistment relations to take on the qualities of an on-going relationship as between spouses. That small pigs are given in compensation for half-interests in large pigs and yet the giver still comes to eat when the compensatory pig is killed may seem an unjustified appropriation. To Duna however it is intelligible on other grounds — the connection between the original 'father' and his pig is never completely dissolvable. The division of labour assures this, since men arrange for the servicing of sows. Men also search in the forest to find the litter and bring it to the house, and in this way men are always the original 'fathers' of pigs. Men's role in arranging all pig transactions is further reinforced by their monopoly, again granted by the division of labour, over the killing and butchering of pigs. Finally, not only is a man's garden work inextricably embodied in each pig, but there is also the ultimate ideological justification (for all but the uxorilocally married man) that the ground itself from which all welfare comes is the ground of his lineage. This claim was formerly reinforced by the belief that only men were able to maintain the fertility of the ground and the health of pigs and people through sacrifices in the cult of the elder brother and the cults of lineage founders. And within the context of their Christian beliefs men are still able to maintain that women's gossip and talking behind men's backs causes pigs to sicken and die.

The appropriation of women's labour in pig production thus takes place at two points. In the first instance the interactive and social character of domestic production is not matched by equal rights in determining the allocation of pigs. Women are granted equal rights in consumption, but their rights in determining circulation are flatly denied. This denial is mediated by ideological justifications: in controlling the breeding of pigs men become the ultimate owners, just as by their ritual activities and through the perpetuation of virilocal marriage they become the ultimate owners of land. The identification of the owner as *aua*, the 'father', completes the patriarchal construction. By their labour men become the fathers/owners of houses and gardens, by their strategic intervention they become fathers/owners of women and children, and by the metaphorical analogies of ritual they become the fathers/owners of land and the mysterious powers of fertility. And finally, 'in the last analysis' and beyond all ideological mediations, there is simple coercive force. Men have no need to conceal the fact that women must either do as they are told or be whipped and beaten.

Yet women seldom find reason to oppose male decisions, and this — the rationality of the structures of exchange — is the second point of appropriation. The agenda for the circulation of pigs is set by the modalities of exchange, bridewealth and sacrifice within the structures of the global lineage formation.[26] Lineages are structures made and perpetuated by the circulation of pigs under male control. Bridewealth initiates the construction by separating women from their natal groups while aligning the men who pay bridewealth together in universal condemnation of uxorilocal residence. Once separated from their natal kin women find that their immediate interests in the circulation of pigs are largely congruent with the interests of their husbands. By contributing their interests in pigs to the marriage payments of their husbands' friends, women improve their standing as outsiders within the group and assure their children of an inheritance as well. By contributing to compensation payments they help to assure peace and security for the parish as their own place of residence. And by contributing their interests together with their husbands' to lineage and parish sacrifices they receive back for consumption a share of pork largely equivalent to the share they have surrendered.

This last point bears further consideration. Marilyn Strathern (1972: 137) reports of Hagen women the complaint that: 'Men only think of shells and money (i.e. things to be obtained with the pigs), but women think they rear the animals to eat them later.' This complaint (which I have not heard echoed among the Duna) raises questions concerning the relationship between exchange and final consumption. All pigs, however circulated through exchange, must have consumption as their final destination. Thus, although pigs are transferred from homestead to homestead and from one lineage or clan to another by exchange, on an aggregate basis at some regional level production is ultimately balanced by consumption. Perhaps Hagen women are really complaining that they do not get to consume the particular pigs they have reared and cared for, but it seems more likely that their complaint stems from local imbalances such that some women consistently receive back for consumption less than they have put out in production. (While it is not clear exactly what happens to Hagen pigs at the end of their careers in *moka* exchange, it would seem that someone, somewhere in the system, must receive for consumption a share correspondingly larger than their local production.)

Among the Duna almost all pork consumption is publicly regulated through events that may be broadly conceptualised as sacrificial distributions. In former times small sacrifices were usually made to appease malign non-ancestral spirits thought responsible for sickness; larger sacrifices were directed to parish founders and lineage and stock ancestors, represented in the material form of an *auwi* stone. Memorial feasts on occasions of secondary burial were also important events for the killing of pigs and distribution of pork and have been continued in the post-colonial period, although burial practices have changed. People now deny that there is any sacrificial intent in memorial distributions, although their place in the structure of circulation is much the same. Church and community events provide other contexts for slaughter and distribution, replacing the ancestral and spirit-based sacrifices of former times.

It could be argued that Duna women do not complain about the appropriation of their pigs for exchange because of effective ideological mystification, but I think it more likely that they accept men's pig transactions because they do receive on average as much for consumption as they lose in exchange. In the post-colonial period there has been a drastic reduction in *damba* payments, so that the circulation of pigs between production units is largely confined to marriage payments. The flow of women and pigs between localities tends to balance out, and in any case mortuary distributions, church festivals and other events have now assumed such prominence that most pigs are locally killed and distributed without ever being exchanged. In the past this was probably not the case, and it may be that women did sometimes complain when men appropriated their pigs to finance warfare and make good its consequences. But even under those circumstances a balanced flow of pigs into the lineage for consumption and out of the lineage for compensation could have prevailed. A lineage sponsoring a fight would accumulate large compensation debts to allies, but lineage members were more frequently engaged as allies in the fights of other groups. In any case there appears to be a difference in predictable outcomes between a system of exchange based on compensation payments and a system based on a principle of increment as in the *moka*. If the participants in *moka* succeed in their aim of surpassing their rivals in generosity, the outcome of such inegalitarian practice should be that the women of a successful big-man's group will indeed be deprived. The pigs they might have eaten have been appropriated and transformed into inedible male prestige. Duna warfare required that pigs be given away and also generated a kind of prestige, but there was no principle of increment. The aim was to inflict retribution for injury or, if attacked, to even the score. When casualties on both sides were about equal fight leaders would counsel withdrawal, since an excess of killings could only lead to further attacks.

There is little evidence in the literature concerning differential consumption of pork by men and women. Among the Duna it appears that consumption is both subjectively and objectively approximately equal. Whenever pigs are killed great emphasis is placed upon the public butchering and distribution of the meat such that the apportionment of shares should be 'straight', i.e. equitable and equivalent. In formal distributions first men and then women are called, locality by locality, to receive shares of lean meat strips. The remainder of the carcasses are then divided in a second round of distributions. Men may receive slightly more lean meat than women, but women's share of fatty meat and offal is considerably larger than men's. Men facing each other in two lines, separated by a row of carcasses to be butchered, represent for Duna the epitome of harmonious cooperation. Another ideal model for distribution, as one informant explained it, is that of the mother, exactly dividing morsels of pork to prevent quarrels among her children. Lacking any evidence to the contrary I must suppose that people take these ideals seriously, and that the shares in formal distributions are indeed seen as equal by both men and women. Occasionally men are accused of trying to favour their own families at the expense of the wider interests of communal distribution, but I have never heard of women complaining about their shares. A final corroborative point: on other occasions when men secretly eat small game animals on their own, they emphasise that to be seen denying meat to women and children is to risk sickness and witchcraft. Given this sanction, I doubt that men would think of practising any discrimination or deception against women in the distribution of pork.

This evident equality of women's shares in consumption emphasises the significance of the mode of appropriation involved. At the level of use-values there is little evidence of exploitation since approximately equal labour inputs are rewarded by approximately equal shares in consumption. But at the level of exchange-values men are clearly the appropriators of the prestige and power created by the exchange of pigs against rights in human lives. Women find themselves labouring within a structure of social relations created by a flow of pigs in circulation, produced at least half by their own labour, and yet it is a world they never made. The surplus

Nicholas Modjeska

product can be returned completely to its producers without altering the alienations of a social edifice constructed by male-dominated circulation.[27]

## PRE-EMINENCE, PIGS, AND POWER

Leadership, and the inequality implied by it, among Enga and Hageners is based upon pre-eminence in the ceremonial exchange of *tee* or *moka*. Among the Ok and Papuan Plateau peoples leadership is based upon participation in hierarchies of ritual initiation, or upon shamanistic spirit-mediumship (Barth 1975; Schieffelin 1976; Kelly 1977). An obvious point emerges: lacking pigs, these latter peoples have not developed forms of domination and influence based upon the production and circulation of material wealth. Pre-colonial Duna society lacked an elaborated ceremonial exchange system and maintained little more than the sketchy outlines of an all-encompassing ritual hierarchy. Contact with the spirit world, although periodically necessary, was more often avoided than cultivated. Participation in both exchange and ritual was important in the exercise of leadership, but neither amounted to a self-sufficient arena of power. Leadership was, and to a degree still is, based upon pre-eminence in several practices, none of which constitute an unequivocal cultural focus. Positioned at a mid-point between low- and high-production systems, Duna society seems also balanced between ritual and political—economic modes of domination.

In discussing pre-eminence, the Duna focus attention on several qualities or attributes: oratorical skill, knowledge, wealth, participation in exchange, personal assertiveness, independence of mind, and readiness to engage in violence. Some men are outstanding in some respects, others in other respects; only a few can be outstanding overall.[28] More often what matters is not so much that a man is outstanding but rather what he is outstanding in. Duna ideas about pre-eminence thus appear as a decomposition (or, rather, a pre-totalisation) of the more unitary ideal of the big-man in high-production societies.[29]

The truly pre-eminent man (*anoa yaga puko*, 'man with a big name'; *anoa yaga 'ro*, 'man with a name') of pre-colonial times was a man with a reputation for influential oratory, for wealth and hospitality, for willingness to fight. Such men were frequent contributors of pigs to marriage payments, blood compensation payments, sacrifices and mortuary distributions, both within their own residential groups and among neighbouring and more distant groups where they maintained active ties with kin and affines. They acted as group spokesmen on these occasions as well as

86

coordinating the contributions of their supporters in the case of compensation payments. They were redoubtable warriors and dangerous adversaries, quick to escalate an affront or trespass into armed conflict. How many men in the past truly combined such qualities cannot be said; from the perspective of the present, 'men with names' have taken on heroic proportions unmatchable by the men of today. Judgements are in any case difficult. There was no single public criterion of achievement such as participation in *tee* or *moka* provides for Enga and Hagen men. 'Men with names' were not distinguished by any insignia such as the Hagen *omak* or the Kewa red hat (Strathern 1971; LeRoy 1979), nor did they enjoy acknowledged privileges by which occupancy of their position might be recognised.

'Men with names' had regional reputations. At the levels of the parish and the lineage-neighbourhoods within parishes, pre-eminence is regarded more in terms of qualities taken separately, as individual or personal specialities. Men are seen not as generalised big-men, but rather as 'men with talk', or as 'wealthy men'; as men who are quick to fight, or men who devote themselves to pig husbandry and gardening. Duna place emphasis upon the separateness of these activities and the differences among men: 'some men "have talk" but haven't many pigs; some men "help" everywhere but have little talk'. These varieties of pre-eminence might be seen as corresponding to a potentially limitless variety of forms of power strategically available in the social environment (cf. Foucault 1979): power comes from the mastery of language and knowledge, from the production and ownership of pigs, from the creation of networks of indebtedness and mutual aid, from the ability to influence, coerce or terrify through personal assertiveness, sorcery, and violence. Alternatively, these many modes of power could be seen as aspects of a small number of basic structures common to all human societies (Lévi-Strauss 1969; Clastres 1977: 28): the exchange of words, the exchange of goods, the exchange of women, and — possibly a fourth modality — the exchange of deaths in the state of war.

An *anoa hakana* is a 'man with talk', a man with knowledge who can express himself forcefully, sometimes poetically and melodically, to persuade his hearers in the frequent moots that continue interminably whenever men gather. There are some men to whom 'everyone comes to listen' while others 'speak only a little in small gatherings, but sit and listen when everybody is there'. A man with nothing to say is an *anoa yao*, a 'nothing man', an uninfluential man or a *tsiri*, an ignoramus, fool or coward. A 'man with talk' is usually also a man with real knowledge, sacred, secular, or both. Some men specialise in secular knowledge such as the histories of past battles, the details of genealogical relationships and the financial accounts of contributions to marriage and compensation payments. Others specialise in the sacred: knowledge of the mythic origins of the cognatic stocks of their descent, knowledge of spells and ritual acts for cult performances and individual magic, secrets of sorcery, the ability to divine for lost pigs or to discover a witch. Most of this magical and mythic knowledge is now said to be lost (if indeed some of it ever really existed) and it is difficult to assess its importance in the past.[30] Secret/sacred knowledge in general seems to have been jealously guarded by old men as a form of almost personal property, to be imparted only in exchange for the care and attention that might be offered by an obedient and interested protégé.[31] Local cult leaders were confirmed in their position by participation in the regional *Kiria Pulu* flagellation cult (*Tege Pulu* in Huli), but there was no compulsory initiation into male adulthood and only a weak sense of ritual hierarchy. Ritual performances seem to have been too infrequent to provide for positions of continuing social power on the basis of esoteric knowledge (contrast Barth's account of the Baktaman). Even the regular transmission of any substantial body of sacred knowledge posed problems, and cult and ritual performances were frequently abandoned for lack of knowledgeable specialists. Individual men might benefit from their knowledge in particular situations, but other situations would require the expertise of other men. It may be concluded, then, that power and pre-eminence in this modality lodged primarily in the ability to induce others to common action through persuasive talk, rather than in the possession and transmission of any particular body of esoteric tradition.

An *anoa gango* or 'wealthy man' is 'a man with many wives and pigs'. (The term is also used in a mildly derisive sense. A man with a new shirt from the trade store may be greeted as 'you wealthy man' by his friends.) Although wealth was formerly accumulated also in salt cakes, 'ropes' of cowrie shells, stone axes and rarer valuables, the pig was considered the cardinal measure and basis of wealth. Marriage and compensation payments, for example, are referred to as so many 'pigs' although some of these 'pigs' are usually other valuables.

Having many pigs is considered to be a result of successful pig husbandry rather than a matter of acumen in exchange or trade. The raising of pigs is seen as an integral part of the developmental cycle of the domestic homestead group. A man's mother and sisters tend his pigs until such time as there are too many pigs or not enough labour, either because the pigs have multiplied or because of the marriage of sisters or the declining strength of an aged mother. Although Duna say that 'some men like their pigs more than they like women', the need for women's labour in domestic pig production makes marriage desirable for most men. Indeed, the requirements of pig production are often presented as a primary justification for marriage. Men scorn the suggestion that they might marry for sexual gratification and they express ambivalence about the desirability of children. The care of children is seen as detracting from a woman's potential as a garden worker and pig producer. The Enga attitude, that early marriage enhances a man's chances of becoming a lineage founder, is entirely foreign to the Duna. A child who looks like a parent is said to be that parent's 'replacement', and look-alike children 'make people think they will soon die'.[32] With ideas such as these, Duna men explain their reluctance to marry and have children.

Sometimes a man's mother arranges his first marriage, since the bride will share her house and work with her in tending gardens and pigs. Men say that it is likewise the first wife who will urge her husband to marry again when the increasing pig herd demands too much labour. But polygyny is not particularly widespread, and many men regarded as wealthy have but one wife. The labour deficit is made up by other kins-women (who may sometimes be prevented from marrying) and by dependent young men attached to the homestead domestic group, or it may otherwise be made up by the increased exploitation of the labours of existing family personnel. For the Duna, however, attention is as often focused not so much on the availability of domestic labour as on the imagined 'true' cause of an expanding pig herd, the magic of *itsia palena* ('pig bog-iris'). In pre-colonial times the *palena* plant (*Acorus calamus*), together with spells and ritual prohibitions requiring long periods of sexual abstinence, was obtained for considerable fees from unrelated wealthy men. (A man could not discuss matters concerning sex, even the pro-hibition of sex, with any of his own kin.) Nowadays men say they have abandoned the *palena* as 'Satan's ways', although they still suspect others of using it.

The antithesis of the wealthy man is the *anoa piaro* or 'stink-bug man', an unattached nomad without pigs, garden or house of his own. His situ-ation is apparently a matter of choice, since even orphans and refugees without rights of descent are able to establish gardens and homesteads. Unlike Hagen or Enga 'rubbish-men', *piaro* are not permanent bachelors or failures at exchange, nor are they men receiving cultivation rights in exchange for labour service. Being a bachelor is no disgrace among the Duna, and minimal participation in exchange and distribution activities is typical of many ordinary 'little men'. Ideals of generosity rather than competition are emphasised in exchange, and unambitious, retiring men are granted a ready tolerance. The stink-bug man is a complete drop-out from the domestic production system as well as from exchange. People say that such men are quick to appear when pigs are being killed, but soon gone when there is work to be done: 'they never stay in one place for long'. No one exemplifying the *piaro* could be pointed out during the period of my fieldwork and the few examples recalled from the past seem to have been deaf mutes, mental defectives, or perhaps sociopathic personalities.

An *anoa hani* is 'a man who is always helping by killing pigs'. Such a man almost always has a pig to spare when compensation and marriage payments are readied by his kinsmen, affines and friends or when pork half-sides are assembled for sacrificial or mortuary distributions. An *anoa hani* contributes pigs and pork to men of other lineages within his parish as well as to kinsmen and affines residing elsewhere. The more frequent and further afield a man makes such contributions the more often he participates in socially significant activity and the wider his range of social contacts becomes. Each contribution creates, as well, an obligation of reciprocal contribution or help in time of need. A generous man thus has a wider support and security circle than other men and he is assured of a large attendance with many contributions when he sponsors a distribution of his own. It is also primarily through these contributions that men maintain their cognatic rights of descent in groups where they are not currently residing. By supporting kin in other parishes men maintain their rights to reside elsewhere, their rights to expect support from allies in their defence and to claim access to land for gardening, hunting or gathering. 'Helping' (*piatsaya*) thus has a double aspect: it creates obligations for reciprocal help and serves as a token of continuing involvement in the affairs of other groups.

Men who help little (*anoa ketse uana*) suffer a disability both in relation to the more generous men of their own group and in terms of the avenues open to them for involvement and residence with other groups. Yet it is characteristic of Duna attitudes that 'middling' and 'nothing' men are readily excused their deficiencies: 'lots of men just don't have pigs. They help when they have pigs and they don't when they don't.' What is not tolerated is selfishness. An *anoa digi daguya* is 'a man who pulls everything to himself'. An informant illustrated this by grabbing everything within his reach and stuffing it into his net-bag, remarking 'a man like that is a real cunt!'[33]

Finally there are the qualities of personal prowess and assertiveness by which men command respect and precipitate conflicts demanding the involvement of others. Such men are *anoa deu*, 'hard men'. In the pre-colonial period they often became *wei tse*, 'war initiators', as well. 'Hard men' were (and are) both admired and feared. They are recalled as heroic figures who could not be deterred from their course: 'they don't retreat when surrounded. Everyone shoots at the *anoa deu* but he just pulls the arrows out and keeps fighting!' An *anoa deu* acts autonomously and with little regard for what others think. Sometimes this isolates him from his kin (as in the case of a man who boasted he was so strong he could not be stopped from marrying his sister), but more often the hard man's actions involved his kin in fights that might otherwise have been avoided. In retrospect men now say 'we were like that; we'd fight first and then think about it later. Really crazy!' It is also said that a boy who is frequently beaten will become hard when he grows up, and older men admit with much mirth that the severe beatings they have administered to young boys were often on groundless pretexts for their own amusement. The almost paranoid sensitivity reported of pre-eminent men in the past, particularly their propensity to make accusations of witchcraft and sorcery which often led to executions and warfare, becomes understandable in these circumstances (see Schwartz 1973).

*Wei tse* (literally 'fight base/origin') were men who initiated battles in defence of their interests (or the usually indistinguishable interests of their lineage) and who carried the responsibility for compensating allies for deaths and injuries as well as rewarding those who killed men on the opposing side. Duna warfare was closely regulated by these financial responsibilities and its successful pursuit required both military and economic strength. The most serious battles were usually planned in advance and required the planting of 'war gardens' to support the pig production required to meet obligations to allies. Unpremeditated battles could only be fought as long as the initiators were confident of obtaining the necessary pigs from the productive resources of their lineage. *Damba*, blood compensation payments, required 30 or more pigs for each death in a fight, and the ceremonial presentation of the payment to allies was marked by celebratory *mali* dancing. Warfare was the pre-condition (and perhaps pretext) for these largest of Duna exchanges, and *wei tse* thus enjoyed a particular pre-eminence. As one man put it: 'A man who is a fight initiator only once, he is a man of intelligence. But if he is *wei tse* two or three times, then he is truly a man. That is strength!' The nexus created by warfare and compensation payments comes closest of all Duna institutions to constituting a socio-cultural focus comparable to the *tee* or *moka* (both can be initiated by blood compensation payments: the word *tee* means blood payment) — an effective arena of power both creating and justifying pre-eminence, dominance and hence a degree of inequality. As major battles were often premeditated and precipitated by mutual accusations of sorcery in circumstances without apparent conflicts of interest, Duna warfare may often have been a subterfuge (either consciously or unconsciously perpetrated) for the mobilisation of men and finances by *wei tse* in the pursuit of power and domination.[34]

Yet, if accusations of sorcery were little more than mystifications of unacknowledged urges to power, there were none the less conditions limiting the expansion of this realm of inequality. When a *wei tse* made repeated claims upon the pig production of his lineage for the finance of successive battles it was open to his followers to exercise their cognatic rights of descent and take up residence elsewhere. Most men change their parish of residence several times during their lives, so an over-demanding *wei tse* had always to consider the risks of losing financial support.

These multiple aspects of pre-eminence as recognised in Duna society, an ethno-catalogue of dimensions of inequality among men, lend themselves to a conceptualisation of power such as proposed by Foucault: power as a multi-faceted, shifting, strategic resource, with dominance and inequality developing according to the points of power available for the manipulation of on-going social arrangements — here ritual mystification, there commodity production, at another point naked coercive force. Yet violence unmediated by legitimating institutions clearly has its limits, and ritual elaborations have not been pursued in the Highlands to the extent found, for example, in the Sepik. The achievement of pig production, like the development of all objective productive forces, represents an attainment of rational control over nature, a surer grasp over the uncertainties of the world (so palpable in an environment of mountains, clouds and jungle, surrounded by unknown and often hostile peoples). The aleatory character of hunting (Meillassoux 1967) as a mode of existence cannot be as conducive to rational calculation in daily life as animal husbandry, particularly when husbandry requires foresight for the provision of fodder, requiring in turn the organisation of production relations between men and women. And, while pig production lends assurance as to where one's next protein is coming from, it at the same time generates the exchange-values by which social relations themselves become potentially more controllable and predictable. With pigs one can (*pace* Watson) obtain wives, children and allies, placate enemies, and perhaps influence the unseen and uncertain spirit world. Duna men have emphasised to me that the making of gardens is hard and dirty work, that the smell of pig excreta nauseates them. They would rather go hunting, but they haven't the time. Their commitment to pig production has sentenced them to their Highlands ethos of Protestant practicality. To generalise in a historical perspective, the development and intensification of pig husbandry has been an exercise in the increasing rationalisation of both self and society.

And so I single out pig production and the social relations of production, circulation and consumption as the important strategic points for understanding inequality in the Highlands. Here Strathern's suggestions (1979b) concerning the importance of pearl shells in the Hagen exchange system provide an opportunity to further the analysis. Strathern suggests that the dominant position of Hagen big-men depended in the past upon their control over the circulation of pearl-shell valuables:

> Everyone could rear pigs, and everyone had access to rights of land use. The overall scarcity of shells, by contrast, enabled a 'purer' version of prestige economy to be built on them. Ordinary men were drawn into the network of exchanges managed by big-men, and less fortunate men . . . would actually have to work directly for big-men . . . to raise a bridewealth payment. Big-men were thus in a commanding position, not so much as owners of ground or tools . . . but as transactors in shells. Control over these gave them an extra edge over other men who had similar resources in terms of land and pigs.
>
> (Strathern 1979b: 533)

The argument here is not that equality would prevail on the basis of pig exchange alone: power distortions cannot be simply an effect of control over shells, since shells are obtained in trade exchanges for pigs. Strathern's characterisation of Hagen political economy as 'a "purer" version of prestige economy' can be elucidated by a comparison with Enga political economy, where pigs and not shells are the cardinal values in exchange. As in Hagen society, the pre-eminence of Enga big-men rests on participation in large-scale ceremonial exchanges. Everyone could rear pigs, and pearl shells were not so important, but this did not make all men equal in exchange. As Feil (1978a — following Strathern 1969) points out, Enga big-men are prominent in exchange by virtue of the financed pigs which they are able to control through their skills in arranging transactions. Lesser men depend upon their own home-reared pigs for their participation in the *tee*. The big-man, like a capitalist financier, risks other people's wealth more than his own. Inequality is not then simply an effect of shell manipulation, although shell manipulation may well be a refinement of financial manipulation directly in terms of pigs.

Pearl shells were too rare in Duna country to serve as significant tokens of exchange, and participation in the salt trade linking Ipili-Paiela with the trans-Strickland and Ok regions was diffuse and apparently uncontrolled. Other valuables, particularly ropes of cowrie shells, might have served as monopolisable tokens of value surpassing the pig, but for whatever reasons they did not. The role of cowrie shells and salt as 'money' cannot be examined in detail here. However, as the examples of Duna pig-agistment transactions indicate, their function was unique in that they were completely abstractable from particular social relationships in a way that pigs were not. Duna cowrie shells and salt were much more like money then, for example, the Baruya 'salt currency' which Godelier (1971) has shown to be involved in a dual system of significations, as abstract exchange-values and as tokens of particular social relationships. Duna do not sentimentalise over cowrie shell 'ropes' in the way that Baruya do over old bars of salt. They recognise and debate over the diverse merits of money-stuffs and pigs — money does not need feeding and will not sicken and die, but unlike pigs neither will it reproduce — but they do not explicitly recognise the crucial analytic point, that money-stuffs free value from the particular social contexts in which it is created. Yet what is not recognised analytically seems nevertheless to announce itself symbolically. Duna say that formerly they did not know that cowrie shells came from the sea, or even from which direction they came in trade. *Cypraea moneta* simply circulated, and like abstracted wealth elsewhere in the world it had its god, the *tsiri dange-ane*, 'mother-of-cowries demon'. This Duna mammon takes the form of a man with shells growing on his skin, wearing the red, horned wig of the bachelors' cult. He haunts underground caverns and low, hot places and exercises dominion over pigs. A Duna tale relates how, Faust-like, a man once entered into a pact with the *tsiri dange-ane* and became fabulously wealthy, only to be ruined by the prying eyes of his wife. Ordinary men greatly fear this demon and formerly offered occasional propitiations in the form of a pig's large intestine — a suitably faecal offering for a god of wealth.[35]

Shells, as Strathern goes on to point out, function in two ways to enhance the big-man's quest for power. Where it is possible for big-men to maintain a monopoly over access through regional collusion and control of trade, lesser men can be shut out from prestigious transactions and compelled to support particular big-men (even to the extent of working for them) in order to acquire shells for marriage payments. And when (or

where) monopoly control is not possible shells continue to serve the
interests of big-men, not so much against lesser men as against women, by
reifying a notion of value apart from pigs and the concrete conditions of
their production. Shells enable men to create an illusion of creating and
controlling exchange-values independently of women's productive
labour.[36] This second function of shell manipulation provides a key for
the interpretation of pig transactions among the Duna. As indicated above,
the circulation of live pigs among the Duna occurs under two forms, as
reciprocal 'helping' in which only approximately equivalent returns are
expected, and as marriage and compensation payments in which pigs are
exchanged directly against values and rights involving human lives. Generosity above the norm is desirable, but neither returns with interest nor
even delayed reciprocity are involved. Thus the Duna lack not only shells
but two even more fundamental financial mechanisms: the enchainment of
exchanges and the 'principle of increment'. Strathern pointed out (in
1969) the importance of these mechanisms in the exchange activities of
big-men; the point here is that the value-reification argument concerning
shells can also apply to pigs when these mechanisms are in operation.

My argument is that the diffuse balanced reciprocity among kin and
affines in Duna 'helping' relationships, and the separation of this form of
circulation from non-reciprocal *damba* and marriage payments to non-kin,
precludes the development of a transactional sphere in which financed pigs
become differentiated from domestically produced pigs. This can be seen
most clearly in enchained exchanges, exemplified by the *tee*, where men
plan on a regional basis to meet their exchange commitments to one set of
partners largely out of their receipts from another set of partners. Feil
notes that Enga clearly distinguish between 'pigs of the house' and 'pigs of
*tee* roads'. Where exchanges are enchained, 'roads' are created, and the pigs
that pass along these roads become separated from identification with the
particular domestic production units whose labour they embody. As with
shells, their value becomes abstracted from the social identities of particular owners and labourers. No such process occurs among the Duna,
although certain pigs in marriage and compensation payments may eventually be passed on in some later payment. This is largely unintentional and
affects only a small number of pigs; it is not a structural effect of an institutionalised arrangement. There is no sphere of pigs in circulation separated from close identification with particular inputs of productive labour,
no structural process abstracting pigs from their particular social contexts
of production and reconstituting them as tokens for financial manipulation.[37]

The separation of pigs from their specific contexts in domestic production permits big-men to manipulate alienated values independently of the claims of producers. One's pig is no longer one's pig once it is entered into an enchained exchange; exchange transforms it into an abstract claim for future reciprocity. As with Hagen pearl shells, Enga *tee*-financed pigs create the impression of men exchanging valuables without depending upon women's productive labour. Feil observed that at least 27 per cent of the pigs entered in a *tee* were house pigs, directly identifiable with women's labour and subject to women's decisions regarding their destinations. But another way of looking at this is to say that 73 per cent of the pigs had been separated from women's control, although 100 per cent of the pigs embodied women's labour in their production. Nor is it only a matter of separating pigs from women's always partial and qualified control, since the structural processes accomplishing this separation are those responsible for the qualitative distinction between big-men and ordinary men. The existence of exchange patterns differentiating financed pigs from home-produced pigs constructs the sphere of transaction that allows Enga and Hagen big-men to function as true transactors.[38]

The 'principle of increment', the expectation that interest will accrue on financial transactions, does not seem to result directly in a detachment of pigs as exchange-values from their identification with particular owners and caretakers. It can however be seen as conducive to much the same end. Whereas the Duna, lacking a notion of increment, 'help' their kin and affines with pigs to maintain balanced reciprocity within their support network — an assurance of support 'in case trouble finds us' — Hageners and Enga look to an advantage beyond mutual support. They expect a profit from their gifts/loans, and so they give pigs with the motive of improving their own position and not simply to assure their security. However it is that the 'principle of increment' has come about in the Highlands, its adoption would seem to betoken a radical shift in the conduct and aims of financial strategy. Marx encapsulated the transformation from simple to capitalist commodity production in his formulae $C -> M -> C$ and $M -> C -> M'$; a similar formulation would seem to apply here. Duna men give pigs to obtain an immaterial security of kinship, which they can later call upon to obtain pigs. The Hagen or Enga big-man uses his debts to call up pigs which he uses to create further indebtedness.

Production and exchange among the Duna are characterised by the absence of mystifying exchange tokens such as pearl shells and the absence of mystifying financial transactions in which exchange rather than production appears to 'produce' pigs. Except possibly in the more densely populated upper valleys, good land is freely available to everyone. Is inequality among the Duna therefore reduced to a simple effect of the differential productivity of individual men in recruiting labour to and managing their domestic production units? To answer this question I first introduce some empirical evidence. Three knowledgeable informants were asked to agree upon a rating for each man of their parish in respect of their public influence in speaking, their reputation for wealth, and their reputation for 'helping' in exchanges and distributions. Assessments in each respect were on a three-point scale with men of the first order being 'truly men with talk', 'truly wealthy men', and 'men who help everywhere'. Men of the second order were 'middling men' (*anoa aroko*), and the third order included 'little men' and 'nothing men'. The results of this enquiry are displayed in Figure 7 and in the Tables 4a–4c. Numbers in parentheses are the distributions expectable on the null hypothesis that each of the three aspects of pre-eminence is randomly distributed throughout the population.[39]

Several points emerge from this exercise: (1) Approximately 75 per cent of all men have some reputation for 'helping'; about 50 per cent have some reputation for wealth, and 25 per cent for wealth of the first rank; about 35 per cent have some reputation for oratorical ability, but only 14 per cent are considered 'truly men with talk'; (2) almost half of the

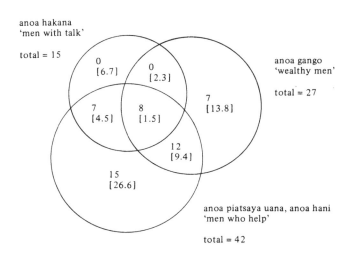

Figure 7  Men of the first order in three aspects of pre-eminence, Horailenda parish, 1971 (total number of men included in survey = 104)

Nicholas Modjeska

Table 4a. *Association between* gango *(wealth) and* piatsaya *('helping')*
*ratings of Horailenda men (N = 104)*

|  | Gango ratings | | | |
|---|---|---|---|---|
|  | 1 | 2 | 3 | Totals |
| Piatsaya ratings | | | | |
| 1 | 20 [10.9] | 13 [8.9] | 9 [22.2] | 42 |
| 2 | 6 [9.6] | 8 [7.8] | 23 [19.6] | 37 |
| 3 | 1 [6.5] | 1 [5.3] | 23 [13.2] | 25 |
| Totals | 27 | 22 | 55 | 104 |

$\chi^2 = 34.7$ $\qquad \varphi' = .41$

Table 4b. *Association between* gango *(wealth) and* hakana *('talk') ratings*
*of Horailanda men (N = 104)*

|  | Gango ratings | | | |
|---|---|---|---|---|
|  | 1 | 2 | 3 | Totals |
| Hakana ratings | | | | |
| 1 | 8 [3.9] | 5 [3.2] | 2 [7.9] | 15 |
| 2 | 3 [5.8] | 10 [4.9] | 10 [12.2] | 23 |
| 3 | 16 [17.1] | 7 [14.0] | 43 [35.0] | 66 |
| Totals | 27 | 22 | 55 | 104 |

$\chi^2 = 22.2$ $\qquad \varphi' = .33$

moderately and truly wealthy men have little or no influence in speaking,
and 60 per cent of the truly wealthy men have little or no influence; (3)
only 30 per cent of the men with some influence in speaking fail to be at
least moderately wealthy; (4) although 12 per cent of all men combine
reputations for wealth and 'helping' generosity of the first order while
having only moderate influence or less in speaking, there is no man who is
both wealthy and skilled in speaking who is not also active in 'helping';
(5) only 8 per cent of the men of the parish are pre-eminent in all three
respects: wealth, generosity, and skill in speaking; although I would not

Table 4c. *Association between* piatsaya *('helping') and* hakana *('talk')*
*ratings of Horailenda men (N = 104)*

|  | *Piatsaya* ratings | | | |
|---|---|---|---|---|
|  | 1 | 2 | 3 | Totals |
| *Hakana* ratings | | | | |
| 1 | 15 [6.1] | 0 [5.3] | 0 [3.6] | 15 |
| 2 | 12 [9.3] | 9 [8.2] | 2 [5.5] | 23 |
| 3 | 15 [26.7] | 28 [23.5] | 23 [15.9] | 66 |
| Totals | 42 | 37 | 25 | 104 |
|  | $\chi^2 = 34.4$ | | $\varphi' = .41$ | |

see these men as quite 'big-men', they were certainly the most influential
and pre-eminent in the group.

There is a strong tendency for wealth, influence in speaking and participation in exchanges and distributions to be associated together rather than
randomly distributed. Few men are pre-eminent in only one of these three
aspects of power and esteem. Associations between the three variables
taken in pairs are highly significant in each case, although the strengths of
the associations are not particularly high, suggesting that wealth, influence
in speaking, and 'helping' are unlikely to be reducible to a single underlying variable. Graphically, the apparent strengths of association might be
represented as:

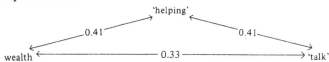

Participation in exchange and distribution is more closely associated
with both wealth and speaking than the latter are associated with each
other. Although it would be unwarranted to place much emphasis upon
small differences in correlation, the indication is that influence in speaking
is more closely linked with 'helping' than with the possession and production of wealth. In part this may be because a reputation as an *anoa
hani* does not require a great amount of wealth by Duna standards, but it
may also be the case that some 'men with talk' are able to 'help every-

where' with pigs not produced in their own homesteads. Although the institutions of exchange are not sufficiently developed to effect a structural differentiation between house pigs and financed pigs, there are nevertheless pigs in circulation which 'men with talk' are probably more successful in appropriating than other men. These pigs could be used to enhance a reputation for 'helping' without a corresponding level of domestic production. (Unfortunately I have little direct evidence on the point.) Different men may thus support their participation in exchange and distribution on the basis of different strategic procedures: either domestic production or the manipulation of exchange relationships external to their domestic economies. Here Strathern's contrast between finance and production appears at the level of individuals rather than as a global contrast between societies: the strategy of manipulating exchange obligations can be seen as an incipient and pre-structural realisation of the societal role of big-man as transactor.

Influential men and not a few lesser men devote considerable energies to the pursuit of outstanding debts and the furtherance of possible claims against others. Marriage and compensation payment distributions are often disrupted by the competing claims of men who have heard of the occasion and arrived on the scene to demand pigs due to them, whether or not these claims have anything to do with the reasons for the distribution. It is not unusual in this situation for marriage arrangements to be called off by the bride's kin when they find themselves unable to agree upon the distribution of the bridewealth. And just as different men will pursue their claims with varying degrees of persistence and persuasion, so too claims themselves vary in their apparent legitimacy. Deaths often prompt demands for compensation on the grounds that old injuries or arrow wounds were the cause (*tse*), and sorcery accusations between influential men of different parishes were in effect demands for heavy compensation backed by the threat of warfare. Since sorcery accusations often took the form of 'your father ensorcelled my father (and now they're both dead)', an accused man is usually unable to judge the truthfulness of such claims. Occasionally, however, a deception is exposed, as in the following case:

> Minima of Haiuwi spoke falsely about my father, Dego. He went to Dela of Yanguane and deceived him, saying: 'Dego ensorcelled your father. Your father didn't die of nothing, Dego ensorcelled him and he died. Pangi [of Horaile] went to Dego and asked him to do it, because of enmity with Yano [Dela's father].' Minima wanted to 'pull' Dela's pigs by deceit [as a reward for revealing the sorcery].

Dela didn't 'have talk' but he was a wealthy man with many pigs. Dela heard this talk and wanted to kill Dego. The Yanguane men armed themselves and went to the *noma* [meeting ground] near Dego's house. Here they waited and sent a man with their accusations . . . Dego replied: 'I didn't do it. They are talking falsely. I won't run away. If I run away everyone will think I did it, but I'm not afraid because it's not true.' . . . When Dela and his kin heard this they repeated what Minima had told them: 'Minima said that Pangi came to your house at night and arranged it. Minima said that after Yano died he saw you going back to Pangi's house and staying with him at night.' Dego said: 'Where is Minima?' Dela answered: 'He's around somewhere, but we called out for him and he didn't come.' . . . Then they called for Pangi, but Pangi called back that they could come and 'shake hands'! [a remark accompanied by an obscene gesture.] Then Dego said 'you have spoken my name for nothing. You can kill a pig for me. I too will kill a pig and we can eat.' . . . Minima heard of this and fled up-valley. [Q. Why should Dela have believed Minima anyway?] It was true; there was enmity between Yano and Pangi, but what it was I didn't hear. Did Yano ensorcel Pangi's brother? or did Pangi's father ensorcel Yano's father or the other way around? (fieldnotes, report of Ambulu of Horaile)

Inequality among Duna men cannot then be reduced to differential pig production, although production is probably more a determinant of inequality than would be the case among Hageners and Enga where finance predominates. The absence of strategic tokens of exchange (pearl shells) and the absence of a sphere of strategic financial manipulation (reciprocal incremental exchange, enchained exchange) condition the pattern of domination in the direction of equality. But although pre-eminent Duna men are not big-men transactors, there are none the less inequalities beyond differences in production alone. Wealthy but unassertive men may be the victims of false claims by the dominant and assertive, who in any case will more often succeed in claiming pigs at distributions following exchanges. The pig producer is not the most powerful man since he lacks the temperament and rhetorical skill of the 'man with talk'. It is the latter who appropriates pigs by his persuasiveness. And it is he as well who precipitates wars, which end by focusing attention and prestige not upon the producer but upon the public distributor, the 'man with talk' in his capacity as *wei tse*, 'war base' or fight leader. Production remains a necessary condition of domination (in a way that it is not in neighbouring low-production societies), but the capacity to produce pigs is more general (and hence conducive to equality) than the capacity to 'produce' domination through persuasive speech. 'Talk' appears as the final determinant, since it is the strategic resource restricted to the fewest men, and since few 'men with talk' fail to acquire reputations in other areas of pre-eminence, while more than a few wealthy men fail to speak.[40]

## THE STRUCTURE OF CIRCULATION AND THE MEANING OF THE PIG: EXCHANGE AND SACRIFICE

Pigs enter into commodity exchanges as well as into marriage and compensation payments and sacrifices for distribution. Pigs, sweet potato, axe blades, net-bags, salt, oil, furs, plumes and cowrie shells can all be directly exchanged against one another, and in the process definite (but nevertheless imprecise and flexible) exchange values are established. But commodity exchanges play a minor role in Duna 'economic' affairs and are not the dominant form of circulation in social life. The main forms of circulation are not exchanges of commodities but, as in the African cases, exchanges of produced goods (pigs, valuables) against rights in human lives. As well, sacrifices in which pigs are distributed and consumed without exchange play an important role in the regulation of production. I designate compensation and marriage payments as Circuit I, and sacrifice as Circuit II. Pigs entered into Circuit I are transferred from one lineage to another in exchange for rights in people. (Compensation payments are concerned with rights in people in that they validate the renunciation of retaliation. *Damba* payments exchange pigs for security from 'pay-back' revenge following the death of an ally.) Pigs entered into Circuit II are sacrificed to lineage ancestors and then distributed and consumed largely within the lineage.

Circuits I and II have an intentional resemblance to Departments I and II in Marx's scheme of expanded economic reproduction (*Capital*, vol. II). Department I comprises goods recirculated as further means of production, the basis of economic growth. This corresponds to the circulation of pigs between lineages as the basis for the demographic perpetuation and growth of the lineage. Compensation secures the lineage against attack by former allies and assures their support in future; bridewealth secures women and children for the men of the lineage and provides the basis for future demographic expansion. On the other hand, Department II comprises goods circulated as consumer commodities, the basis of the worker's subsistence wage. This corresponds to Circuit II, in which pigs that other-

wise could have been exchanged to secure the lineage's demographic
position are instead consumed directly by the producers, albeit under the
guise of a sacrifice to the ancestors necessary for the reproduction of the
(imaginary) conditions of production. Just as the balance between the
capitalists' expansion of the means of production and the workers' expansion of their means of subsistence determines the economic growth or
expanded reproduction of the economic system, so likewise the balance
between Circuits I and II should have a determining effect for the maintenance and demographic growth of individual lineages and the system of
lineages as a whole. Lineage organisation is not simply an effect of the
ideological validation of certain pre-existing genealogical ties and distributions of people. Rather, it is a matter of actively creating certain ties
and securing others through the exchange of pigs against rights in people,
as well as the continuing validation of relations between men within the
lineage through reciprocal 'helping'. The circulation of pigs in 'helping',
compensation payments and bridewealth creatively defines the limits of
the lineage. At the same time, the maintenance of effective lineage organisation requires some balance between the labours of pig production and
the gratifications of pork consumption so that tensions within the lineage
do not lead to breakdowns in cooperation.

The determination of the balance between Circuits I and II must lie
beyond the scope of this enquiry. As in the balance between Departments
I and II, it would appear that exchange and sacrificial consumption come
to be associated with potentially opposed social interests, the interests of
men in their capacity as lineage members, and the interests of women as
residentially separated and alienated from their own lineages. Men tend to
promote the exchange of live pigs between lineages, while women desire
sacrifice and internal consumption. Women can to a very limited extent
participate in the system of exchange, but always within the pre-existing
framework. They must accept that the product of their labour will be
exchanged to perpetuate the system of bridewealth and *damba* compensations for deaths caused by men in warfare. Women cannot take control
of the system to arrange marriages as they might want (e.g. uxorilocally)
or to alter the patriarchal and violent character of lineage relations.

The balance between exchange and sacrificial consumption may then be
seen as a historical outcome of a 'class struggle' based on these competing
interests, in part a 'battle of the sexes' but also a conflict between the
divergent interests of lineages and families. The situation is not a simple
one: however much it may represent a capitulation to the desires of
women and the needs of families, sacrifice is also arranged as an ideological

affirmation of the male ancestral powers of the lineage.[41] Circuit I constructs the lineage through marriage and military alliance, but Circuit II re-affirms the lineage's internal ordering through descent and renewed acknowledgement of ancestral authority.

It can be suggested that pig cycles in the Highlands have some of the features of capitalist business cycles. In 'boom' periods a large part of the product is available for entry into Circuit I, for the expansion of the lineage as a demographic and jural structure. In the lead-up to 'recession', demands for consumption, like demands for higher wages, may curtail further expansion. Among the Duna, periodic sacrifices seem not to have been events planned for in advance. Rather, one must suspect, they were forced upon lineage leaders by the developing exigencies of production. Men relate that a decision for a major sacrifice would be made when people and pigs were hungry and sick. In meetings to discuss this depressing situation some influential man would obliquely suggest that perhaps the ancestors were angry and hungry to eat pork. Supposedly such a suggestion would be greeted by a snap decision to sacrifice almost all local pigs as soon as possible. But although men say that hungry periods are due to an insufficiency of sweet potato, the shortage may itself be brought on by pig population levels outstripping the ability of people to feed their pigs out of current garden production. An over-production of pigs or under-production of sweet potato would then require a cut-back in 'capital stocks', taking the form of a sacrifice in which people eat what they have themselves produced. Conditions invariably improve after the sacrifice, as indeed they should, since fodder consumption levels have been reduced and dietary deficiencies compensated by protein intakes.[42]

A political economic perspective on sacrifice suggests that there is more to the phenomenon than its Maussian unity with exchange, noted by Rubel and Rosman. They come closer to the point in observing: 'Giving pigs to the spirits is designed to influence the spirits to promote the productivity of the female sphere' (1978: 312).[43] Sacrifice is slighted if it is assimilated to a model of exchange as an integrative mechanism. Exchange integrates lineages with one another while integrating men within lineages under the directive coordination of big-men. Sacrifice integrates the men and women of the lineage in their internal relations of production. In the Duna example, sacrifices brought to a conclusion periods of increasingly counter-productive effort. They radically reduced the pig population and the work levels necessary to sustain that population. Sexual relations were tabooed for half-year periods after major sacrifices, so demographic growth was also given a rest. And women were given a rest from the demands of the children who might otherwise have been conceived during the period.

Among the Duna, sacrifice corresponds to a communal mode of appropriation of surplus. Those who have mixed their labours in production partake mutually in consumption. It contrasts with exchange, which is an inegalitarian mode (women's shares appropriated by men and transformed into the conditions for continued oppression, lesser-men's shares appropriated to finance the military adventures of *wei tse*). Sacrifice appears essential to the continued operation of the system, since it resolves at necessary points the conflicting interests of men and women as co-producers of pigs, as well as terminating deadlocks in the global system of production/consumption when pig production for lineage expansion (Circuit I) is blocked. But sacrifice is ambiguous and contradictory, since men believe that the ancestors desire it, whereas in some ways they clearly desire it for themselves.[44] Sacrifice would seem to be a regressive social phenomenon in that: (1) it amounts to a falling away from the optimisation of men's power through exchange, (2) it represents itself as a feeding of pork to the ancestors, thus denying that women require rewards for their efforts in the production of pigs and children, and (3) this denial rests on a more psychologically primitive denial: the pork eaten by men and women as producers has not in truth been eaten, since it has been given to the ancestors in exchange for a renewal of productivity.

As a regressive phenomenon sacrifice displays a conflation or condensation of social functions and symbolic cathexes. In this sense sacrifice (and the pig in sacrifice) are able to mediate between a realm of commodity production and a realm of kinship, between embodied labour and desiring production. Humans and land are the original values. Pigs are values produced by human labour. They embody human labour and are identified with the personality of their owner or caretaker. Like other embodiments of labour they are separable from the self, but unlike purely economic commodities they are invested with an emotional commitment, an energy of the self. Like Nuer cattle and the Australian Dreamtime landscape (Roheim 1945), attachment to pigs has a libidinal tinge. The directness of the libidinal connection is indicated by a dream interpretation common in Duna country: to dream of sexual intercourse means that you will soon eat pork. This investment of a projected human self into the subject of exchange, the pig, makes separation problematic. As the Duna say of reluctant bachelors (above), 'some men like their pigs more than they like women'.

The identity of human life with the life of the pig and the necessity for the two nevertheless to be distinguished and kept separate are expressed in a story widely known in the Tumbudu valley area. The myth explains that the 'madness' of cannibalism (as for example among the nearby Faiwolmin) can be stopped by the correct distinction (i.e. separation) of pigs and people. In the story the hero, carrying salt from the fringe of Enga country, arrives at the half-Duna, half-Bogaia parish of Yerundua, located along the Strickland gorge. He finds the people gathered at a place called Pukuli:

> 'What are you doing?' he asked.
> 'We're eating here because a man has died,' they said.
> 'But where's the pig?'
> 'Right here,' they said, showing him a young boy who was sitting there with tears running down his face.
> 'What? You're going to eat him?'
> 'Yes.'
> 'Well, where is the man who died? Is he here?'
> 'Yes, look in the coffin,' they said to this man who had come carrying salt. He looked — and, oh mother!, there was a big white sow in the coffin. This man was really angry then. He grabbed his axe and chopped down the coffin scaffolding so the pig fell out on the ground. Everyone spat on the ground and fled in disgust!
> Then this man chopped wood and prepared the pig. He got a bamboo knife and butchered it. He baked the joints and roasted the pork strips over the fire. He got a banana leaf and softened it over the flames. He put roasted pork on the leaf and put ginger on it and sprinkled it with the salt. He ate some and it was delicious.
> One Yeru' man came back and this man held out the pork to him and he tried it. Finally everyone came and tried it. Then this man, who came with the salt, said (pointing to the pork):
> 'This is man, is it? This is man who makes houses and gardens, who talks, who fights other men and who thinks?' Then, turning to the boy who was to be eaten: 'And this is pig? Pig, who eats insects in the forest and comes to the house to be given sweet potato?' The Yeru' people said nothing. 'You are really crazy (*inu tsaleys waiya kononia*)! *This* is man, and *this* is pig!'
> He told them this, he really straightened them out.

The precise circumstances in which a production situation necessitating sacrifice could appear in the pre-colonial Duna economy are far from clear, but an important factor would seem to be the absence of large-scale ceremonial exchanges functioning regionally to integrate the production and transfer of pigs. Elsewhere in the Highlands cycles of pig production are articulated with exchanges planned well in advance, an arrangement which should facilitate coordination between gardening activities and pig production at increasingly higher levels. The *moka* and *tee* both require and facilitate forward planning, and peak production is increased as social life comes to revolve around an intensified anticipation of peak periods for the retention and disbursement of pigs.

Such a coordination would optimise exchange and the sociality founded upon it, inequalities and all. In the model suggested here, it is the growth and development of lineage structures which is seen as the historical outcome of increased production.[45] As production increases, so possibilities increase for the realisation of the patrilineal, exogamic lineage form. Women's inequality with men increases as changes in technology shift onto them an increasing part of direct productive labour and as separation from their natal lineage and from rights in their children become more absolute. Inequalities among men also increase. Increasingly complex and reified financial manipulations increase the magnitude of status differences between those with little and those with great political— economic leverage, while decreasing land resources prevent the disadvantaged from readily shifting residence and allegiance in order to undermine the growing power of a regional clique of monopolistic big-men.

But the ethnographic realities of central New Guinea clearly depart from this model in some respects. In this essay I have attempted to model a trajectory by taking the middle-intensity production and social practices of the Duna as a reference point and seeking concomitant variations in systems with lower and higher production. At very low levels of pig production one might say that the trajectory shifts to a qualitatively different scale as ritual hierarchy tends to replace economic inequality. And at high levels of pig production the inequalities and systemic rigidities suggested by the model only partially appear. The fault with the model would seem to be that in abstracting from the real world its logic tends to contradictions which people in practice manage to avoid. The increased exploitation of women implied by increased production seems a case in point. While enchained competitive exchange appears as a concomitant of increased production among the Enga and Melpa, it is a point of major significance that this intensification of exchange is accompanied by an emphasis upon affinal relationships in exchange partnerships — an emphasis that could not have been directly foreseen from the perspective of Duna ethnography. In effect, just at the point where women are exploited as never before, an institutionalised re-alignment of exchange relationships wipes out exploitation by causing men to appropriate pigs from their wives only to present them to their wives' brothers. When women complain that they did not raise their pigs for exchange, men can cleverly reply that pigs sent away in exchange haven't really been given away at all, since it is a woman's brothers (with whom her lineage identification is maintained) who are the benefactors. Moreover, this linkage of brothers-in-law as exchange partners alters the character of bridewealth transactions and may have further effects on the construction of lineality. Marriage payments among the Enga and Melpa feature reciprocal payments emphasising the future of the relationship as an exchange partnership, rather than the one-way transfer of pigs against rights in the bride as practised by the Duna and Huli. Perhaps one could reason that under such arrangements women are not so completely alienated from rights in their children. The Enga and Melpa practice of matrilateral child-growth payments, as on the occasion of a child's first hair-cut, suggests this (such payments are unknown among the Duna). This is not the place to trace out these ramifications. The point is that the contradiction of interests originating in the relations of men and women to the system of production are not necessarily amplified with the intensification of production, and this makes models of the kind proposed here potentially misleading.

A final example may perhaps suffice as a suggestive conclusion. I have reasoned that increased production increases inequality between men, and Strathern (1979b) has suggested that the importance of maintaining a united front in the face of their exploitation of women leads Hagen men to tolerate a degree of inequality among themselves. By a slight twist an equally valid but contrary proposition emerges: inequality among men must be contained at some level and cannot be expanded without limit, lest breakdowns in male solidarity should threaten the lineage's security *vis-à-vis* other lineages and undermine as well the collective exploitation of women. Perhaps, so long as production can be contained within kinship-structured units, there is no ultimate contradiction to these modes of production, no conflict of interests that an inventive adjustment of social practices consistent with the tribal ethos of exchange, sacrifice and equality cannot contain.

# 4 The Ipomoean revolution revisited: society and the sweet potato in the upper Wahgi valley

*Jack Golson*

## INTRODUCTION

The body of literature on the societies of the New Guinea Highlands has tended to support the early characterisation of their political life as a competition for power in which individuals achieved big-man status by their ability, through the manipulation of wealth in the form of pigs and other valuables, to recruit supporters from within their natal groups, clients from outside them and exchange partners in the accessible universe of cognates, affines and non-kin. There has been debate, however, about the specific manifestation of these principles: the extent to which, for example, competition constituted a form of anarchy within the political arena (e.g. Brown 1963: 3—6) or was limited by the segmentary character of the social system (e.g. Sahlins 1962—3: 289; Reay 1964: 243—5; Meggitt 1967: 23—4); the degree to which leadership depended on consensus (e.g. Read 1959) or could take the form of 'serial despotism' (Salisbury 1964: 225—8); and the existence of tendencies towards hereditary succession to leadership and internal stratification of social groups, which is a major concern in the sequel.

It is evident from the literature that there are two factors at work to prevent easy generalisation. One is variation between Highlands societies themselves, so that different propositions may be true for different groups. This is of course so for other dimensions of Highlands society, some of which have received systematic attention (e.g. Meggitt 1964 on male: female relationships; 1965 on descent and group structure). There has been no similar treatment of leadership and its contexts (for a partial study, involving exchange systems, see Strathern 1969) and any such exercise is made difficult by the second of the factors complicating the picture. This concerns the effects of European contact from 1930 onwards on leadership situations throughout the Highlands and the chronological

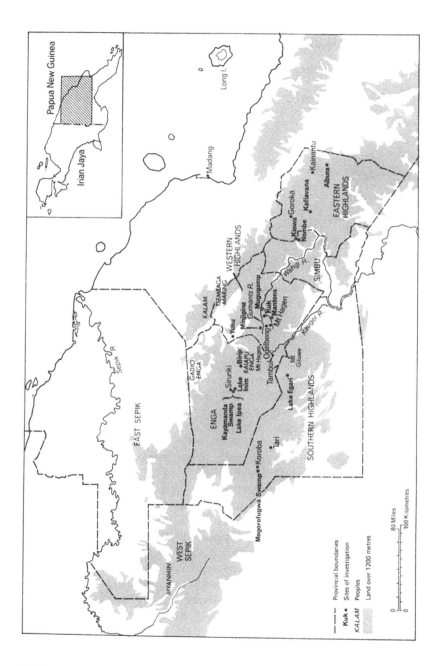

110

relationship of ethnographic description to the point of contact in any particular setting (e.g. A.J. Strathern 1972: 191–2).

We are fortunate in having, for the upper Wahgi in the years following immediately on first contact, extended accounts by German Lutherans who established a mission station in 1934 at Ogelbeng, a few miles north of the present township of Mount Hagen, and worked there through a period when large parts of the Hagen area remained unpacified. In particular the monograph by Vicedom (Vicedom and Tischner 1943–8), who spent four-and-a-half years at Ogelbeng, provides information on big-men, their status and their intra- and extra-clan relationships which, as a number of writers have appreciated, describes a structure considerably less open and egalitarian than we are used to in depictions of Highlands societies. Indeed Vicedom's observations encouraged Salisbury (1962: 136) to see in the upper Wahgi at contact a series of small 'empires' ruled over by dictatorial big-men. The discussion of the issue that follows is based on Strathern (especially 1966 and 1971: 108–10, 204–10), who, from his work with the Hageners since the mid-sixties, in particular with communities in the hills north and northeast of Ogelbeng, has been concerned to see whether, when there are differences between his own and the earlier observations, Vicedom has overdrawn the picture for the 1930s, or there have been genuine changes over the 30 years that have elapsed between the two.

Vicedom gives a long list of named categories within Hagen society, which fall into three broad and exclusive groups: those of big-men, ordinary men and men of low status. Defined in economic terms, the big-men were wealthy individuals, rich in pigs, shell valuables and wives, the ordinary men were economically independent, but the men of low status were poor and the most unfortunate of them provided the labour force for the big-men on whom they were dependent, around the house and in the gardens and pastures. Some are called 'bachelors' and, in so far as bridewealth had to include shell valuables, big-men could control marriages and keep men in debt. There were also exiles and war refugees whom a big-man had attracted into the clan and who for many years had to render service to him.

The big-men were leaders of the clan to which they belonged and the richest of them became the principal leader (Vicedom and Tischner 1943–8 II: 45–6, 60–1), directing the life of the clan with the help and advice of his fellows. These leaders were drawn only from certain families, fathers endowing their sons with the pigs and other valuables by which they could contract the polygynous marriages and enter into the *moka*

111

exchanges through which future wealth and prestige were ensured. The *moka* community was an exclusive one, the wealthy families monopolising pearl-shell valuables and circulating them only amongst themselves. The *moka* became the means and the symbol, however, of differentiation not only within the clan, but also between clans. The wealth of a clan determined the extent to which its leaders could meet the demands of the system (*ibid.*: 455), so that a man could be head of his clan but of little account outside it, because of his unimportance in *moka* exchanges (*ibid.*: 459).

Strathern (1966: 363; 1971: 205–7) has reservations about some of Vicedom's conclusions from his own evidence but allows (1971: 207–8) that the situation which he himself observed in the 1960s could have developed from that described by Vicedom 30 years before, as a result of the arrival of the Europeans and the particular circumstances of their contact with the resident communities. It is not necessary here to review these matters in detail. We should note, however, that, in both immediacy and degree, the impact of the early European miners, missionaries and government officials was out of all proportion to their numbers on the ground and the limited scale of their direct operations. As Hughes (1977: 52–8) vividly describes it, this was because, initially accepted as spirit people, they became indispensable sources of supply for universally desired goods, amongst which steel axes could replace, and marine shells provide in abundance, items which traditionally were valuables in bride-wealth payments and complex networks of ceremonial exchange. In time, however, the newcomers did more than unbalance the systems through which big-men achieved and maintained their positions of prominence. They were able progressively to suppress warfare, which, though it may have been small scale, was nevertheless frequent. As such it afforded abundant opportunity for big-men to exercise their influence in transactions with enemies, allies and refugees and created the conditions for the firmer attachment of clansmen as a whole and dependent groups like bachelor-servants and exiles in particular to their patrons. Finally, as administrative control extended and became more effective, Europeans began increasingly to usurp the 'juridical' authority of traditional leaders over followers in some domains and to prohibit its exercise in others (Vicedom and Tischner 1943–8 II: 104–5).

As Strathern (1971: 207–8) interprets it, all this meant the weakening of the authority of big-men over their dependants, who, if servants, had the opportunity of working for or selling to Europeans and/or of switching their allegiance to another big-man and, if refugees, the possibility of returning to their own territory. Such potential losses in labour power threatened the productive capacity of the big-man's household, by which important festivals were financed. In these circumstances leaders would develop new strategies to hold or attract followers, while widening their support group by increasing the size of their networks of exchange partnerships. The latter could account for the elaboration of the *moka* system observed by Strathern in the 1960s, while both would need the exercise of those qualities of generosity and cajolery, persuasiveness and compromise prominent in contemporary descriptions of big-men (e.g. Sahlins 1962–3: 289–92). These qualities became increasingly necessary as previously scarce shells, brought into the Highlands in vast quantities by the Europeans as payment for goods and services (Hughes 1978), not only stimulated and inflated ceremonial payments but also put valuables into the hands of men who traditionally would have had no direct access to them. The new wealth, in Strathern's words (1966: 364; cf. 1971: 108, 207), 'democratised' a system hitherto dominated by the leading men and laid the basis for the present situation where all adult men can make *moka* and, in order to secure their support, big-men have to extend friendship to those less important than themselves.

We have Vicedom's contemporary witness to the reality of some of the lines of development theoretically proposed. He describes (Vicedom and Tischner 1943–8 II: 49–50) how European presence benefited the poorer members of the population, since these were the ones more willing and able to supply labour and provisions. Not only did work for Europeans provide an alternative to work for big-men, it supplied the means of economic advancement, through the possession of pigs and shells. Some men are said to have become wealthy as a result of their earnings from Europeans but in Vicedom's time they had failed in efforts to challenge the traditional leadership because they were unsuccessful in recruiting followings of their own (*ibid.*: 61) and in entering the *moka* community (*ibid.*: 455–6). By the time Strathern began his work such barriers to self-advancement were not in evidence (Strathern 1966: 364; 1971: 207).

Whatever the real nature of big-man authority in the upper Wahgi at the time of European arrival, it appears to have been appreciably greater and more exclusive than today and to have been diminished and diluted by circumstances attendant on the European presence in the Highlands. In addition it seems, though there is less direct evidence on this point, that such authority was greater in the upper Wahgi than in at least some other areas of the Highlands. It is one purpose of this chapter to propose that there are some historical reasons, based on the practice of agriculture in the Highlands and its long-term ecological effects, why this could have been the case. It is a second purpose to suggest that the lines of authority were once even more firmly drawn in upper Wahgi society than they appear to have been at European arrival and that the recent diminution of that authority associated with the appearance of Europeans with steel and shells had a parallel a few hundred years before when the appearance of the sweet potato made possible for more people the possession of another powerful valuable, the pig.

The evidence on which the proffered reconstructions are based has been accumulated by archaeological and palaeoenvironmental research in the Highlands over the past 20 years, and particularly by a multi-disciplinary project on the history of agriculture in the upper Wahgi valley centred on swampland at Kuk Agricultural (formerly Tea) Research Station at 1,650 m altitude near Mount Hagen, which started in 1972. The fullest most readily available statement of results is Golson (1977). The new thinking evident in the present contribution (and in Golson 1981a, b, c, which set the Kuk investigations in a New Guinea-wide context) owes much to three ethnographers, who have speculated about the New Guinea past in ways which have proved very valuable for the interpretation of the historical evidence now becoming available. J.B. Watson was one of the first to appreciate that the recency of the sweet potato's appearance in New Guinea and the completeness of its take-over of Highlands agriculture pose questions of some importance for Highlands culture history and has been a persistent advocate of the need to keep this point constantly in mind (Watson 1965a, b, 1967, 1977). G.E.B. Morren (1977, 1979) has stressed the dynamic nature of the relationship of agriculture, animal domestication and the exploitation of wild-plant and animal resources in New Guinea economies and explored the links between types of pig husbandry, levels of agricultural intensification and extent of alteration of the natural environment. C.N. Modjeska (1977), in exposing the hidden assumptions of previous treatment of the Kuk data (especially Golson 1977), has suggested that it was amongst the populations practising the prehistoric swamp cultivation systems investigated at Kuk that were developed the distinctive features of the ethnographic cultures of the region, for which current interpretations of the archaeological evidence conspicuously fail to account. The ways in which these propositions have contributed to the argument now to be developed will become clear as we proceed.

## THE HISTORY OF HIGHLANDS AGRICULTURE

In different ways these three ethnographers are addressing the same long-standing problem: the genesis of the distinctive cultures which Europeans found throughout the intermontane basins, valleys, plateaux and slopes of a massive cordillera, long thought to be a single, uninhabited mountain chain, when they first entered the central Highlands in the early 1930s. Here, as we now know, there live, in vast open landscapes of grassland and managed regrowth, mainly at between 1,400 and 2,000 m, what are over-all the biggest and densest populations and the largest speech communities in the entire island, subsisting off the harvest of extensive and orderly food plantations, in which the tropical American sweet potato (*Ipomoea batatas*) is the dominant crop. Many of these populations maintain, to a marked degree out of garden produce, big herds of domesticated pigs, considerable numbers of which are incorporated, together with other valuables like shells, in complex systems of ceremonial exchange.

For Watson (especially 1965a, b) the sweet potato was the crucial factor. Writing before appropriate historical evidence was available, he based his reconstruction of the pre-Ipomoean situation on observations of contemporary agricultural plants and practices. He noted that the intensive techniques of husbandry which supported the entire system were exclusively used in the service of the sweet potato, the other crops receiving, by comparison, almost haphazard attention. These non-Ipomoean procedures were for Watson (1965a: 298) pre-Ipomoean. In the extreme application of his view (*ibid.*: 301–3), Indo-Malesian plants like yam (*Dioscorea* spp.), taro (*Colocasia esculenta*) and banana (*Musa* spp.), which are staples in most of lowland New Guinea and must be prime candidates for pre-Ipomoean agriculture in the Highlands, were so disadvantaged at altitude that they were incapable of providing an agricultural base for stable populations of people and of pigs. In these circumstances the appearance of the sweet potato, with its greater altitudinal tolerance and its unparalleled attractiveness as fodder for pigs (Watson 1977: 60–1), constituted an Ipomoean revolution, responsible for the situation which amazed the first explorers and continued to impress those who followed. In the light of the accepted view (Barrau 1957; Conklin 1963; cf. Yen 1974: 323–4) that the sweet potato cannot have been in New Guinea for more than a few hundred years, having found its way there as a result of its introduction into island Southeast Asia by Iberian voyagers in the early sixteenth century, the changes it wrought were not only sweeping but recent. For Watson

Jack Golson

(1965b: 442) 'the inescapable implication seems to be that the Highlands
... do not, in many fundamental respects, represent a long-established or
stable situation, socially or culturally'.

A number of his contemporaries took a much less radical view of the
effects of the sweet potato on Highlands life (Clarke 1966, 1971: 98–9n;
Brookfield and White 1968). Their conception of the contemporary Highlands situation as the expression of long-term trends older than the sweet
potato, though influenced by it, seemed to gain support from the first
results of historically directed research (see discussion in Golson 1976:
204–9). Subsequent investigations into Highlands prehistory, which have
considerably extended our knowledge of the development of Highlands
agriculture and its environmental context, have produced decisive evidence
on this score and in three main respects.

## Forest clearance

The first point concerns the antiquity of the characteristic open landscapes
of the Highlands. Vegetation histories show that forest cover in the agricultural zone was once complete (Hope and Hope 1976: 46–9; Powell and
Hope 1976). Its partial removal and replacement by grassland is generally
accepted to be the product of clearance for cultivation maintained by fire
(e.g. Brookfield 1964: 32–3; Golson 1981b and references cited). The
total extent of grassland is not large. Hope (1980: 155) calculates that the
non-forested areas total only 12,000 km$^2$ compared with over 180,000 km$^2$
of montane forest still extant in New Guinea, but they are regionally concentrated and where they occur they form extensive tracts, with forest
restricted to isolated patches or to ridgetops. They represent a spectacular
environmental transformation with wide implications, which we shall have
occasion to pursue.

Pollen diagrams for the upper Wahgi valley at between 1,580 and
1,885 m show that by 5000 years B.P.[1] the primary forest cover had been
significantly reduced (Golson 1977: 617 and references cited there). Evidence from the Manton site on the southern margins of the valley bottom
itself suggests that while trees of primary forest like *Nothofagus* and
*Castanopsis* still grew on the slopes adjacent to the site, large areas were
covered by a degraded secondary forest of light-demanding trees and
shrubs (Powell *et al.* 1975: 43). Grasslands, the final result of the process
of retrogression, are not much in evidence at this stage. Indeed it is
impossible to reconstruct the genesis and expansion of the Highlands
grasslands from the available palaeobotanical information: the reasons

include the difficulty of knowing the extent to which the grass pollen in borings at any one collection site reflects the regional or the purely local picture and the inability to differentiate between the pollen of grasses from different environments.

In these circumstances we have to turn to other evidence, specifically to the character of the sediments forming the deposits investigated at the Kuk site. These sediments are erosional products washed into the Kuk basin from the catchments of the swamp, and their varying character, disposition and rate of accumulation are in important respects a reflection of different conditions in the catchments at different times, including different forms of land use. At one point in the sequence there is a marked and widespread change from sediment deposition in the form of clay particles to deposition in the form of soil aggregates. This is interpreted as marking a change in the nature of agricultural land use in dry-land catchments of the swamp, with the appearance of soil tillage in the agricultural technology. As we shall shortly see, soil tillage is thought to be a specific adaptation to cultivation in grassland. If this chain of reasoning is sound, grassland had become established in the upper Wahgi valley by the time of the depositional change in the Kuk sediments, which is dated, not as firmly as could be wished, around 2500 B.P.

**Agricultural technology**

A second result of the historically directed research of recent years has been the demonstration that the intensive techniques of husbandry which Watson saw as characteristically employed in the cultivation of sweet potato in fact appreciably predated its appearance.

Investigations by human geographers in the sixties (summarised by Golson 1976: 203–4) suggested that these techniques were in fact developed out of a need to keep up production in environments reverting from forest to grassland and to make prolonged use of the same plot of land. The most distinctive of the techniques involved are tillage of the soil, its disposition in raised beds of various kinds and the practice of tree-fallowing. We are now able to state that these were quite separate innovations and to suggest the dates at which they made their appearances. The following discussion is taken from Golson (1981b), where full references are provided.

By the evidence of the Kuk stratigraphy discussed above, soil tillage was the earliest, at around 2500 B.P. Soil tillage has no role in agriculture under a forest-fallow regime. Forest regeneration after limited cropping ensures the re-establishment of the nutrient store contained in the biomass, which man has temporarily diverted for the benefit of his crops by way of the ash produced by burning the vegetation, and allows rehabilitation of the structure of the soil, which under cultivation has deteriorated through oxidation and compaction. The replacement of forest by grassland means a drastic loss of biomass, so that burning of grassland is insufficient to restore the nutrient status of the soil. Soils under grassland are also physically poorer than forest soils, being fibrous, compact, greasy and often wet. Tillage of the soil by turning of the grassland sod followed by some form of soil preparation has been developed as the remedy for these deficiencies. An experiment by Clarke and Street (1967) suggests that it results in improved aeration and drainage which correct toxic conditions. Soil tillage represents a substantial increase in labour over the requirements of forest cultivation, which accounts for the fact that people prefer to clear plots in forest rather than in grassland when this is possible.

The deliberate planting of *Casuarina* and the protection of seedlings of this and other fast-growing trees like *Trema* and *Dodonaea* are common practices on grassland cultivations which are being put to long fallow after substantial use. They may have originated in the need to provide a supply of timber in circumstances of deforestation, but their ability to restore soil structure and fertility more quickly and more thoroughly than was by then possible naturally would have recommended their development as fallowing devices. Marked and often spectacular rises in the values particularly of *Casuarina* in pollen diagrams from three Highlands provinces (Enga, Western Highlands, Simbu) register its widespread adoption about 1200 B.P.

We have descriptions (primarily by Brookfield 1961, 1962 and Brookfield with Hart 1971: 111–13) of the various ways in which the soil resulting from the turning of the grassland sod is worked into garden plots for sweet-potato cultivation. These range from the longitudinal beds separated by groove drains of the Eastern Highlands Province, through the chequerboard garden pattern of the Wahgi valley, where the spoil from the close-spaced grid of garden trenches is thrown up to form the garden surface, to the large mulched mounds of the Enga and Southern Highlands Provinces. The differences are in part a response to the requirements of the staple crop under different environmental regimes: moisture conservation in the Eastern Highlands, moisture control in the Wahgi and protection against frost at high altitude in Enga and the Southern Highlands (for frost see Waddell 1975: 252–8). The different versions of raised-bed cultivation are all, however, devices to safeguard agricultural production in degraded environments and bear a marked resemblance to practices widely developed in similar circumstances throughout the Old World tropics (Denevan and Turner 1974).

I have argued elsewhere (e.g. Golson 1977: 629–30) that the grid of flat-bottomed trenches, around 25 cm wide and deep, enclosing garden plots about 2–3 m square, which is the pattern of sweet-potato cultivation characteristic of the Wahgi valley today, was originally developed in swampland agriculture. Intensive ditching for water-table control produced abundant spoil which could be most easily disposed of on the surface of neighbouring gardens. Once it was appreciated that bringing subsoil on to the garden surface in this way, repeated as ditches were cleaned out or redug, had a refertilising effect (see discussion in UNESCO 1962: 60, 95–6, 105, 106–7), the practice could be profitably incorporated in dry-land gardening. The type of garden trenching used in Wahgi dry-land gardens today, and something like its gridded pattern, make an appearance in the Kuk swamp about 400 B.P.

### Agriculture before the sweet potato

The evidence reviewed so far shows that the environmental effects of agricultural activities in the Highlands and the responses to those effects in the sphere of agricultural technology are of some antiquity and older than the sweet potato. It remains to discuss the striking indications in the Kuk swamp, and less completely at other sites, for the scale and intensity of pre-Ipomoean agriculture in the Highlands.

These indications are provided by the structural remains of water-control channels and attendant field systems associated with episodes of use of upper Wahgi swampland for agriculture. These phases of swamp use, the details of which are given elsewhere (Golson 1977, 1981c), do not replace, but supplement the practice of cultivation on dry land, which we argue goes back to 9000 years B.P. in the Highlands, and even further in the lowlands, a claim of some audacity and considerable implications, which it is not relevant to explore here (see Golson and Hughes 1976). What we need to consider is the role of swampland cultivation in both the wider agricultural and the total economic system. The basic evidence for this is to be found in the nature of the different phases of swampland exploitation and the circumstances under which each phase began and finished. Much of the effort in the Kuk project to date has gone into the precise definition of these factors.

Jack Golson

We may now generalise the findings. The phases of swamp use and their approximate dates are tabulated below.

| Phase | Years B.P. |
|-------|------------|
| 1 | 9000 |
| 2 | 6000–5500 |
| 3 | 4000–2500 |
| 4 | 2000–1200 |
| 5 | 400–250 |
| 6 | 250–100 |

The first generalisation to be made is that drainage works became more complex over time. In the early phases a single large channel, 1–2 m wide and deep, was sufficient to canalise the water flowing into the swamp from the main inlet to the south, carry it for at least a kilometre and dispose of it at some unknown point beyond the site. In later phases there were a number of channels operating at the same time, often equipped with large tributary drains. It appears that conditions in the swamp were progressively deteriorating, possibly as a result of man's very interference with it, and that what in the earlier phases had been a question of wet-land management later became a major problem in swamp drainage.

The second point is that over time the drainage works not only became more massive, they also seem to have become more extensive, draining larger areas of land in a coordinated network. This generalisation is true up to phase 5, when possibly 200 hectares and more were involved. Phase 6, for reasons we shall discuss, sees a decrease in the extent of drained land, though what remains is drained in a highly coordinated fashion.

The third generalisation refers to the garden system which the drainage works were undertaken to establish. These change from drainage phase to phase, but the major change occurs between phases 3 and 4. During phases 1–3 the structural evidence associated with gardening is diversified and has been interpreted as representing the simultaneous cultivation of a variety of plants. In contrast the field evidence for phases 4–6 is much more homogeneous and consists basically of garden ditches parallel and at right angles to one another. The suggestion is that these represent the intensive cultivation of a single crop, for which taro is proposed for phases 4 and 5 and sweet potato for phase 6.

The fourth point is the demonstration that the drainage phases at the Kuk swamp are not unique to that site. In the upper Wahgi valley the

120

Manton site, where the former existence of swamp drainage for agriculture was first recognised (Golson *et al.* 1967; Lampert 1967) during limited salvage excavations which were partially re-opened in 1977,[2] has the equivalent of at least Kuk phases 2, 3 and 5, while at the base of Mugamamp Ridge in the huge North Wahgi swamp Harris and Hughes (1978) investigated the precise equivalent of Kuk phase 2. Three hundred metres above the Wahgi floor at the eastern foot of Mount Hagen the Minjigina swamp has evidence of Kuk phase 4, while to the southwest a swamp at 2,170 m altitude in the upper Kaugel valley between Mount Hagen and Mount Giluwe has promising indications of Kuk phase 3.[3] Further afield in the Southern Highlands Province, the Mogorofugwa swamp near Koroba has the equivalents of Kuk phases 5 and 6.[4]

The fifth and final point concerns the close correlation that has been established between certain events in the sequence at Kuk and wider developments in the region as a whole. Thus the beginning of phase 3 around 4000 B.P. appears to coincide with a consistently registered occurrence in the upper Wahgi pollen diagrams where the ratio of forest to woody non-forest taxa reaches its lowest-ever point. After this the forest values quickly recover some of the lost ground, before they enter into a stable relationship with the secondary taxa which persists to about 1000 B.P. or less. We have drawn two conclusions from this evidence. One is that the reclamation of unused swampland for agriculture was a response to severe environmental degradation under the impact of shifting cultivation, due to the failure of forest regeneration on abandoned garden land to run its required course. The second conclusion is that the response met with a measure of success in that some forest regeneration took place on hill slopes in association with their continued agricultural use. There is independent evidence for the claims of stress roughly contemporary with the beginnings of Kuk phase 3. This is provided by indications from pollen analysis at Kayamanda swamp, Sirunki, in Enga Province, of sustained disturbance of the forest at 2,500 m, not far below the ceiling of contemporary agriculture, which is more likely to be associated, if indeed with human activities, then with permanent settlement rather than sporadic or seasonal exploitation (Walker and Flenley 1979: 339). This interpretation receives support from the recent recognition of the equivalent of Kuk phase 3 in the upper Kaugel valley, for at 2,170 m this is towards the upper limit for cultivated plants except taro, mountain pandanus and the as yet unavailable sweet potato (Bowers 1971: 22).

The end of phase 3 at Kuk around 2500 B.P. has another set of correlations. It coincides precisely with the stratigraphic break in the sedimentary sequence at which soil aggregates replace clay particles. As already discussed, this is interpreted as signalling the appearance of soil tillage in the technology of dry-land agriculture, which in its turn is thought to register the establishment of permanent grasslands in the local environment. The success of the agricultural innovation in rehabilitating the agricultural status of degraded dry-land landscapes is not only suggested by the immediate abandonment of swamp drainage at Kuk. Pollen studies in Enga Province provide evidence that might be interpreted in the same way. At an inferred date of 3000 B.P., not too discrepant with the close of phase 3 at Kuk, the high-altitude forest disturbance noted for Sirunki came to an end (Walker and Flenley 1979: 340), while at lower altitude (Birip crater lake, 1,900 m) there was a recovery in the ratio of forest taxa to woody non-forest (Golson 1977: 622, using Flenley 1967: fig. 7.5; cf. Walker and Flenley 1979: 320, fig. 12).

Another correlation concerns the end of Kuk phase 4, well dated to around 1200 B.P. This is the point at which pollen diagrams from Enga and Simbu Provinces, as well as from the upper Wahgi itself, register the beginning of that marked rise in the pollen of a small number of quickly growing, light-demanding trees, *Casuarina* in particular, which, as we have already seen, is interpreted as the appearance of the widespread Highlands practice of tree-fallowing on ground going for a long period out of agricultural production. The abandonment of swamp cultivation at Kuk at this time could be connected with the success of this second element in the technical repertory of Highlands farmers for dealing with the problem of productive cultivation in grassland.

The final set of correlations, involving the end of phase 5 and the beginning of phase 6 at Kuk, concerns the sweet potato. Since they are the crux of the argument to be developed, they will be discussed in detail later.

The correlations established between major changes in the natural environment of the Highlands arising from the practice of agriculture, responses evoked by them in the realm of agricultural technology, and aspects of the periodicity of drainage at Kuk have encouraged the search for explanations of the Kuk data so far in ecological terms (e.g. especially Golson 1977). Indeed, there is no doubt from the degree of fit between the environmental and the archaeological sequences reconstructed for the Highlands that the reasons for the periodic use and non-use of the Kuk swamp for agriculture are firmly rooted in complex interrelationships of man and land.

PRODUCTION AND PRODUCTIVITY

In a comprehensive critique of the Kuk interpretations, Modjeska (1977: chs. 2–5) takes basic issue with how this man–land nexus has in fact been treated. He is concerned that the Kuk story has been told essentially in terms of a series of responses (swamp drainage, high-altitude cultivation) and innovations (soil tillage, tree-fallowing, raised-bed planting) in High-lands agricultural practice, adopted in the face of an irreversible and cumulative environmental transformation from forest to grassland brought about by agricultural exploitation of the land. In this process man is accorded an essentially negative role, acting only in reaction to environ-mental changes which, though he was the prime mover, proceeded on an essentially autonomous path.

The environmental changes with which we are concerned result from the fact that orderly forest regeneration after cultivation is susceptible to upset in two main ways: the invasion of cleared areas by fire, a tool com-monly used in hunting as in forest clearance itself; and the renewed clear-ance of the same area at too-short intervals, under land pressures of various sorts. The effects are greater in conditions of infertile soils and climatic disabilities. A number of factors have been invoked in interpretations of Kuk to explain the scale and completeness of the environmental change wrought by agriculture in the Highlands (Golson 1977: 605–8; 1981b). An important one is the slower regeneration of montane forest after clear-ance. Aggravating this is the intolerance of plants like taro and yam of naturally poor and agriculturally depleted soils, which, together with their slower maturation and decreased yield at altitude, may have encouraged, as long as it was possible, expansive use of forest land and frequent pioneering of new forest. Under these circumstances a third factor would have quickly come to bear: the restriction of productive agriculture to a transversely and altitudinally compacted zone between limits set by increasing altitude above and a variety of circumstances below, such as steep slopes, thin soils, cloud cover and unfavourable amounts and distri-bution of rain (see Brookfield 1964: especially 22–3). The implication is that, having reached these limits, agricultural expansion would have been turned back on itself, setting in train the sequence of environmental and agricultural changes which we have described. The underlying assumption is the relentless extension of the agricultural process, the implicit reason for which is steady growth of population. Modjeska has two objections to this formulation: that it takes for granted on the one hand that populations expand rather than stabilise, on the other that production is solely for subsistence.

We thus come to his substantive contribution to the debate. In interpretations of Kuk the drained systems are not looked upon as important in their own right, only as supplements to the dry-land cultivations. Because of the high labour inputs judged to have been involved in their inauguration and maintenance, they were only to be undertaken when the dry-land sector failed to deliver the needed production and were immediately to be abandoned when the problems of the dry-land sector were solved. In contrast, Modjeska proposes that the drained swamps were localised centres of high productivity based on intensive cultivation of taro and surrounded by systems of much lower productivity and complexity. It would have been amongst the compact, populous communities which wetland agriculture supported that there developed the characteristic elements of the contemporary cultures of the region, particularly the mobilisation of resources far beyond the level of subsistence for large-scale political and ritual enterprises involving pigs and other valuables.

There is very little information about the cultivation, wet or dry, of taro in the Highlands, its management, productivity and labour requirements.[5] Yield figures for wet taro are provided by Pospisil (1963a: 444, table 24) for the Kapauku of the Paniai (formerly Wissel) Lakes of Irian Jaya (formerly Dutch New Guinea): they give an average of 12.8 tonnes per hectare. By contrast, for dry-land trials in the Mount Hagen district Clarke (1977: 160, 163, table 1) reports taro yields, with and without compensation for losses due to insect damage, of 5.0–5.3 and 4.4 tonnes respectively per hectare after 12 months' growth on 'good' soil, under long-grass fallow for 8 years, and of less than 1 tonne on 'poor' soil, under cultivation for 10–15 years previously, after 13 months' growth. Sweet potato grown at the Paniai Lakes under exactly the same regime as taro – Pospisil's intensive shifting cultivation on the valley floor (1963a: 103) – yielded 13.8 tonnes per hectare, as against 12.8 tonnes for taro (ibid.: 444, table 24), though labour input was appreciably higher for taro than for sweet potato, which produced 5.6 kg per hour of labour compared with 3.6 kg for taro (ibid.: 423, table 8). In Clarke's dry-land trials near Mount Hagen (1977: 163, table 1), the 'poor' soil gave sweet-potato yields, after 8 months' growth, of 9.3 tonnes per hectare, the 'good' soil, after the same period of maturation, of 18.4 tonnes. Clarke asks us to compare this latter figure with average yields of 20 tonnes per hectare achieved over a number of years at the Highlands Agricultural Experiment Station at Aibura, near Kainantu, Eastern Highlands Province. Kimber (1972: 89–90), who reports these results and considers them a 'fair reflection' of what High-lands gardeners achieve, allows an approximate loss of 31 per cent for inedible tubers, which reduces the edible yield to about 14 tonnes per hectare. The poor-quality portion would, of course, be fed to pigs.

These figures have many implications. They are relevant to later dis-cussion about the change to sweet potato as the subsistence staple. In the present context they would strongly support Modjeska's case for the Wahgi swamps as localised centres of appreciably higher productivity than elsewhere, if it could be shown that taro cultivation took place there. This is in fact the best interpretation of the character of the swamp systems of phases 4 and 5 at Kuk, where, as we have seen, large-scale and coordinated drainage is associated with a repetitive garden pattern defined by long straight ditches intersecting at right angles and thought to reflect the intensive cultivation of a single plant. The whole is reminiscent of the situ-ation described by Yen (1971: 9) for the island of Uvea in western Poly-nesia, where shifting cultivation of yam, banana, taro and *Alocasia* on hill-side and plateau areas is combined with permanent swamp cultivation of taro in the valleys in raised rectangular plots in chequer-board patterns.

Further consideration of Modjeska's arguments requires that we turn to the question of the pig, the focus of so much attention in Highlands societies.

## THE ROLE OF THE PIG

The pig is not an animal native to New Guinea and, given the size and multiplicity of the water barriers between there and its continental base in Southeast Asia, it is not likely to have reached New Guinea independently of man. There are claims for its presence in the New Guinea Highlands by 10,000 B.P. (discussed by Golson and Hughes 1976) and it is certainly in evidence by around 6000 B.P. (White 1972: 92, 108, on the basis of excavations at Kafiavana rockshelter near Goroka). Finds of anything like this antiquity are very few (see S. Bulmer 1966) and in a quantitative sense the situation is not much better for subsequent periods (despite Watson 1977: 61). This is the result partly of the small number of excavated sites, partly of the lag of publication behind discovery (White 1972 is the only detailed treatment). As a result, the archaeological pig bones themselves have very little to contribute to the discussion. A more profitable approach, advocated by Morren (1977), is to look at the place of the pig in the ecology of subsistence.

A number of recent ethnographic studies (e.g. Rappaport 1968, Clarke

Jack Golson

1971, Dornstreich 1977, Morren 1977) have shown the important contribution made by wild resources to the subsistence of gardening communities in New Guinea today, by way of varying the basic carbohydrate diet and supplying essentials in which the staples are low or lacking. Thus Dornstreich (1977: 256—7) reports for the Gadio Enga of the upper reaches of southern tributaries of the Sepik that gathering of leaves, fruits, nuts, tubers and the like and collecting of birds, lizards, insects and fish, though accounting for less than 10 per cent of the diet by weight, supply more than 20 per cent of the protein and almost 25 per cent of the fat, while plant gathering alone provides more than 50 per cent of vitamin A. For hunting and trapping the corresponding figures are 3.4 per cent of calories, 12.6 per cent of protein and nearly 40 per cent of fat, compared with 1.5 per cent of calories, 3.4 per cent of protein and 19.4 per cent of fat provided by animal husbandry.

The resources described in these ethnographic accounts are predominantly those of forest and forest edge, as befits a landmass which falls almost wholly within the perennially wet tropics and has rainforest as its predominant vegetation from sealevel up to the treeline on the highest mountains (3,850—4,000 m under present climate) (see maps in Fosberg *et al.* 1961). Floristically New Guinea is an eastern sub-division of the Indo-Malesian Floral Region (van Balgooy 1976: 13), the resources of whose forests make it the richest in the world in plants useful to man; for New Guinea itself Powell (1976: table 3:1) lists more than 200 species used wild for food, supplying nuts and fruits, leaves, shoots and roots. The vertebrate fauna is closely related historically to that of Australia, but New Guinea animals are essentially rainforest forms, while their Australian relatives are in the main adapted to open forest and dry woodland (Schodde and Calaby 1972: 274; Ziegler 1977).

The ecological changes initiated by man's agricultural activities must have had a significant impact on such plant and animal resources. It is likely that they were favoured by the limited opening up of the forest through bush gardening. The presence of a mosaic of different stages of secondary growth concentrates a wide variety of resources, both plant and animal, in the many induced boundary zones between vegetation communities (Clarke 1976a: 108; 1976b: 253). Hope (1977: 25) suggests this as the reason for the majority representation at one stage of the faunal sequence at the archaeological site of Aibura in the Eastern Highlands Province (White 1972: 57—9) of small scrub wallabies (*Thylogale*), forest and forest-edge animals, which seem nowadays to be nowhere common. In principle the same circumstances are likely to have advantaged feral pigs, which Bulmer (1968: 304, 313) describes as favouring forest edge, disturbed forest and mixed ecological zones containing grasslands, gardens and some secondary bush rather than primary forest; that is, environments associated with agricultural man. Morren's (1979: 6–7) description of the situation amongst the Miyanmin living at between 600 m and 900 m altitude on the northern fall of the central ranges in the West Sepik Province challenges this as a generalisation, but not as a statement about a widespread situation. Here feral pigs subsist for the seven drier months of the year on wild foods in or on the fringes of primary and very old secondary forest, and the Miyanmin settlement pattern is responsive to this fact. However, during the five wetter months, wild foods are scarce and the feral pigs concentrate round human settlements and gardens. In such circumstances of settlement and environmental disturbance by agricultural man feral pig has become a major game animal throughout lowland New Guinea.

It is not known whether in the past feral pig played a similar role in the Highlands, with the possibility that some of the early pig bones in rock-shelters like Kafiavana belonged to feral animals (cf. White 1972: 144). Bulmer (1968: 304) notes that today feral pigs are sparse or absent above about 1,525 m. This is not wholly due to the fact that here occurs the zone of greatest population and severest environmental impact, whose effects we shall shortly be considering. Thus, though there is undisturbed rainforest from 1,525 m to 1,825 m in Tsembaga Maring territory on the northern slopes of the Bismarck Range above the Simbai valley (Rappaport 1968: 34–6), Rappaport (1968: 70) says that feral pigs (males in the specific context) are inclined to stay below 1,000 m. This distribution may reflect the floristic transition from tropical lowland to montane forest described by botanists (e.g. van Balgooy 1976: 14) and emphasised by ethnographers interested in resource distribution (Rappaport 1968: 35; Dornstreich 1977: 249; Morren 1977: 291).

The important point about the Highlands in respect of resources and the effect of human activities on them is that, as we have seen, the environment was not merely modified, it was ultimately transformed. The replacement of forest by grassland meant the removal of forest resources without adequate natural replacement. Straatmans (1967: 17) contrasts the presence of twenty utilisable genera of food plants in the primary forest stage with that of six in the grassland stage, consisting of five additions and only one survivor; his data are inadequate by present standards, but his point is valid none the less. The detailed inventory of marsupials and rodents compiled by Bulmer and Menzies (1972, 1973) for the Kalam (see

Jack Golson

Bulmer 1976: 186 n. 1 for spelling) of the upper Kaironk valley of the Schrader Mountains, covering an altitude range from 1,525 m to 2,625 m and a variety of natural and altered environments, provides ecological information by means of which we may appreciate the effects of forest clearance on wildlife (see table 2 in 1972: 481–3). The authors themselves suggest that clearance which has taken place within living memory between 1,825 m and 2,125 m on the northern side of the valley is responsible for a recent decrease in forest animals and an increase in species like *Rattus exulans* which are adapted to life in gardens and grasslands (*ibid.*: 480). *Dorcopsis* and *Dorcopsulus* wallabies have virtually disappeared over the past two generations (*ibid.*: 493) and been almost totally replaced by domestic pigs for cooking and distribution at the annual harvest-season festival (Bulmer 1976: 174).

As the Kalam example illustrates, losses in the way of natural resources needed to be replaced out of the domesticated sector. The results must have been a greater reliance on garden produce and an increasing need for the more intensive management of pigs. Since the factors that reduced the wild fauna limited the ability of domesticated pigs to forage for themselves, their upkeep became in part a further charge on agricultural production. As pigs became more important, they became more expensive and therefore more valuable.

The nexus between environmental change, pigs and agricultural intensification is clearly set out by Morren (1977: especially 311–13) in a comparison of three montane New Guinea societies for activities bearing on pigs. The Miyanmin of the West Sepik Province, living in a forested environment, practise an extensive pattern of pig management; most of the pork consumed is wild and other wild fauna is exploited, while a negligible amount of effort is expended on domestic pigs, no extra land is brought into production to support them and only about 16 per cent of garden production is eaten by them, in the form of sub-standard taro tubers and kitchen scraps. The domestic pig:human ratio is about 0.1:1 (*ibid.*: 294). The Tsembaga Maring of the Bismarck Mountains, where tracts of grassland have become established and hunting returns in the remaining forest are small, practise a more intensive pig-management system; most pork consumed is domesticated, and, though functioning boars are not maintained, extra land is brought into production to feed a growing herd, with up to 27 per cent of garden produce fed to pigs and allegedly 48 per cent of total work effort devoted to their management. The pig:human ratio varies between 0.8:1 and 0.3:1 (*ibid.*: 299). The Raiapu Enga, living in an environment almost totally transformed to grassland, with hunting negligible and wild fodder for pigs said to be absent, practise the most intensive form of pig management: all pork consumed is domesticated and functioning boars are kept, while more than half the garden produce is fed to pigs and 41 per cent of total effort devoted to them. The pig:human ratio is reported at a maximum figure of 2.3:1 (*ibid.*: 305).

Direct evidence of a decline in faunal resources as a result of environmental change is as yet unavailable but may be provided by the rich faunal sequences from a number of Highlands rockshelters now under active study.[6] Hope and Hope (1976: 49–51) have tentatively attributed indications from widely separated mountain areas of New Guinea for depression of the treeline and downward expansion of alpine grassland following forest burning to an increase in human activities at high altitudes over the last few thousand years. Today these grasslands are used for tracks giving free and unencumbered communication between communities at lower levels, while the transition zone between forest and grassland is an important focus for hunting (*ibid.*: 39–41). Like all ecotones, it concentrates resources and is renewed and expanded by burning. If, as the Hopes (*ibid.*: 51) suggest it could, the history of the treeline reflects its increasing use as a hunting zone, from perhaps in places 5000 B.P., because of increasing populations at lower altitudes, the circumstances fit well the indications of other evidence.

In the upper Wahgi valley the stage of faunal impoverishment had arrived by 2500 B.P. if we correctly interpret the break in the Kuk stratigraphy at that date as reflecting the establishment of stabilised grassland. The conditions had matured therefore for intensive pig husbandry supported on an agricultural base. In terms of the argument that has been developed, we should expect some reflection in the agricultural history of the region. Around 2500 B.P. the third phase of swamp cultivation at Kuk comes to an end because, it is said, the innovation of soil tillage allows productive use of the degraded environments of the dry land. It is not long, however, before the new drainage is undertaken which inaugurates phase 4, at around 2000 B.P. Phase 4, it will be recalled, marks a change in the nature of drainage organisation and garden pattern thought, to register the replacement of smaller-scale units of multicropping by larger-scale systems of monocropping, those of phases 4 and 5 involving taro. Pigs may have accounted for a substantial proportion of the production of these systems.

We have previously argued, following Modjeska, that the swamp systems were centres of high productivity and population surrounded by systems of much lower productivity and complexity, a reconstruction which the few available yield figures for wet and dry taro cultivation in the Highlands support. The people who had access to swampland were greatly advantaged for husbandry of the increasingly valuable pig, because of both the greater productivity of their swamp gardens and the availability of swampland pasturage when the ground was not under cultivation. As a result they are likely to have formed powerful centres of attraction in the region for scarce and exotic items. Both Hughes (1977: 204 etc.) and Strathern (1971: 111) emphasise the variety of goods involved in trade and ceremonial exchange in the Highlands in recent times: salt and other items of localised natural occurrence; animal and plant products of the bush no longer available in the denuded agricultural zone; and true exotics from the lowlands and the coast. Pigs may have played the crucial role in securing such items and with them have opened the way to power and influence, as in later times (e.g. Watson 1977: 63). At the same time, since swamplands, and other ground of high agricultural potential, were localised, it is possible that circumstances of unequal access to them could have engendered those inequalities within and between clans of which Vicedom speaks at the time of European contact. In the interval, however, the sweet potato made its appearance in the Highlands and it is to the circumstances and results of this event that we now turn.

## THE ARRIVAL OF THE SWEET POTATO

Around 250 years B.P. a large volcanic eruption on Long Island off the north coast of New Guinea near Madang produced large quantities of ash, the finer particles of which, transported down wind, darkened the skies over the central highlands for a few days before falling to the ground, giving rise to widespread stories of a time of darkness, with regionally varying accompaniments and effects (Blong 1982; cf. Blong 1975). The ash fall is today locally preserved in depositional sequences in lakes and swamps throughout the Highlands and forms a time horizon of some importance in archaeological, geomorphological and palaeobotanical studies. The ash in question has been called Tibito Tephra, after a creek at Kuk Agricultural Research Station where it was first recognised. Because of the number of radiocarbon dates available for it, from samples collected both on Long Island and at Kuk, it is possible to attempt a conversion of the radiocarbon age of the ash fall to a calendar age by reference to an appropriate table or graph, a number of which are available, all ultimately based on tree rings (refer to note 1). Polach (1982) concludes that the most likely time of the Long Island eruption is mid to late seventeenth century, between A.D. 1640 and A.D. 1680.

Tibito ash is the marker for a series of changes in the sphere of Highlands land use, which fulfil the predictions that have been made for the adoption of the sweet potato (Yen 1971: 7; 1973: 80; Brookfield with Hart 1971: 124n; Clarke 1977) on the basis of its qualities as a cultivated plant. As we have seen, it is more productive and quicker to mature at altitude than the older crops, most of which cease to be productive at all above about 2,100–2,200 m. It is also productive over a longer period than taro and especially than yam (Yen 1974: 72–3): its shallow rooting allows partial harvesting of individual plants; the roots left behind continue to grow; prolific secondary rooting takes place, with the development of new tubers and the possibility of harvesting for up to two years. In addition it is much more tolerant of naturally poor and agriculturally degraded soils. As a result of all these properties, the sweet potato had the capacity to effect what Clarke (1977: 161) calls a spatial and temporal expansion in food production: spatial because agriculture could effectively move into higher altitudes and on to poorer soils; temporal because its tolerance of poorer soils and its longer productivity allowed it to perform the role of a follow-up crop in a rotational system (cf. Kimber 1972: 90–2). This simultaneous more intensive use of ground and more extensive use of country is precisely what is indicated by the changes dated by the coincidental presence of Tibito ash.

Investigations (Oldfield 1977: 59–60;[7] Oldfield *et al.* 1980: 473–5) of lake-bottom sediments in the Southern Highlands at 1,800 m (Lake Egari) and in Enga at 2,500 m (Lake Ipea) show in the former case rapid, in the latter dramatic, acceleration in their rates of accumulation from about the time that Tibito Tephra fell. Chemical analyses of the sediments suggest that this was due to increased erosion of predominantly inorganic soil and substrate in the catchments of the lakes, linked with forest clearance inside the crater at Egari and more intensive land use at both sites.

Pollen analysis results from Enga (Walker and Flenley 1979: 339–40) provide additional information. At the previously mentioned Kayamanda site, Sirunki, a swampy extension of Lake Ipea, renewed forest clearance beginning around an inferred date of 2,000 years ago persisted for 500 years to the top of the Sirunki pollen diagram. There are also indications of clearance about the same time from Lake Inim, 6 km to the west and at a similar altitude. This continued to an inferred date of 500 years ago, when it was intensified, *Casuarina, Trema* and open ground indicators becoming very abundant in relation to canopy trees. If we recognise the imprecision of its dating, it seems very likely that this intensification of forest clearance revealed by the Inim diagram was associated with the arrival of the hardier and more adaptable sweet potato in this high-altitude region.

At Kuk, phase 6 of the drainage sequence, which begins shortly after the fall of Tibito ash, exhibits characteristics which are best explained by the incorporation of the sweet potato in the swamp gardens. As in the two preceding phases, which are thought to have seen intensive cultivation of wet taro, the gardening system is a repetitive pattern of long straight ditches intersecting at right angles, but the network now becomes tighter and more grid-like, taking on the appearance of the chequer-board of gardens and intervening trenches characteristic of dry-land sweet-potato cultivation in the upper Wahgi today. This tightening of the grid would be explained by the need to lower the water table, given the sensitivity of the sweet-potato tuber to moisture. The greater volume of spoil resulting from this operation is disposed of on the surface of the adjacent garden plots, raising their surface, providing tilth for the tubers and distancing them even further from the water table. The main drainage works are intensified at the same time, with the duplication of tributary drains. There is also a dramatic reduction, by two-thirds, in the area of the swamp under drainage, with cultivation now concentrated in the higher part of the swamp adjacent to dry land. This abandonment of swampland would be explained by the ability of the sweet potato to produce better than the older crops at this altitude and across a wider range of soils. Finally, for the first time in the history of cultivation in the Kuk basin, houses appear in the swamp itself. They are of two types, identical in size, shape, interior arrangements and scattered location to the round men's houses and the rectangular women's houses with rounded ends and internal pig stalls, which make up the traditional hamlet and homestead pattern of residence in the upper Wahgi. Charred fragments of sweet-potato tubers have been found during excavations at two of these old house sites in the Kuk swamp.

Watson (1977: 60–1, 64) has argued that the rapid and widespread adoption of the sweet potato, which the evidence from Enga, the Southern Highlands and the upper Wahgi attests, cannot simply be explained by the advantages it confers in the subsistence sphere but becomes comprehensible if the principal attraction of the new crop was as pig fodder. The superiority of sweet potato over all other cultigens as food for pigs would have had irresistible appeal in circumstances where, as today, pigs are highly valued as the means of access into exchange systems of every kind.

We have suggested that the pig is likely to have achieved this role before the advent of the sweet potato, as a result of its growing importance as a domesticated animal in circumstances where the environments for wild animals, possibly including feral pigs, were being destroyed and where for the same reasons pig keeping had increasingly to become a charge on agricultural production. We have also suggested that this charge is likely to have been easily absorbed only by communities in possession of land of greater and longer-term productivity, like those who maintained the swamp cultivations at Kuk. Since such land was unevenly distributed, the possibilities for economic and social inequalities were present at a number of levels, making it possible for advantaged groups to dominate in pig keeping and thereby control the exchanges in other goods which possession of pigs could attract.

The revolutionary element which the sweet potato introduced into this situation was not simply that it was superior pig food, but that it was superior pig food that could be grown more productively over a wide range of soils and altitudes. The yields discussed in a previous section (pp. 124– 5) show not only the decisive superiority of sweet potato to taro in dryland situations, particularly where the soils are poor, but also its advantages over wet taro when grown on good soils. With the sweet potato the agricultural production necessary for pig keeping would no longer have been localised as it was with previous crops. This would create the conditions for challenging the advantages conferred on some groups by previous inequalities of production.

As at a later date when, with the coming of the Europeans, once-scarce shell valuables became abundant in the Highlands and, passing into the hands of men with no access to them before, gave them the opportunity to enter exchange systems from which they had previously been excluded, so the sweet potato, which made it theoretically possible for all men, or at least all married men, to keep pigs, may have tended to democratise institutions depending on control of pig keeping. It is nevertheless clear, from the evidence of Vicedom, that inequality still characterised upper Wahgi society at the time of contact. This is surely because already powerful families were in a much better position to capitalise on the sweet potato when it arrived. Morren's figures (see pp. 128–9 above) show the considerable labour input involved in pig husbandry on any scale and this could be most readily met by men already equipped with polygynous households and control over lesser men's labour and marriages. At a later date, as we have seen (p. 113 above), little men who had become wealthy in pigs and shells through traffic with Europeans were unable to challenge the authority of traditional big-men in Vicedom's day. We may suppose that the big-men of the Ipomoean period were equally tenacious of their position, when their control of pig breeding ceased to be as secure as

Jack Golson

before the arrival of the sweet potato. It may have been in these circumstances that shell came to have the overriding importance in exchange
which it possessed at the time of European contact. In discussing entry
into the socially exclusive *moka* community of the Hageners, Vicedom
(Vicedom and Tischner 1943–8 II: 455) says of the poor that even if
they had pigs they would not have been able to use them to acquire the
necessary pearl shell, which was monopolised by the leading families. As
Strathern (1966: 362) puts it, pigs could be reared by all, but only the
pearl shells carried prestige. They were indeed ideal instruments of social
control, since they were genuinely scarce and their supply was uncertain
(Hughes 1977: 198–202; cf. Strathern 1971: 108–9) until the arrival of
the Europeans. Even the radical erosion of the bases of big-man authority
which the activities of Europeans initiated (see pp. 112–13 above) has not
totally removed the ability of leading families to remain prominent. In a
survey of 97 big-men in 14 clans of three tribes, Strathern (1971: 209–10)
concludes that major big-men have a 3:1 chance of being the sons of big-
men and that there are certain clusterings of big-men within particular
lineages of a clan.

It is less easy to assess developments and identify continuities at higher
structural levels. This is no doubt bound up with the mobility and insta-
bility of named groups in conditions of endemic warfare, to which regular
reference is made in the literature on Highlands societies of the ethnographic period (see Watson 1970). For the Hagen region Strathern (1971:
15–18) notes the great range, from nearly 7,000 to less than 100, in the
population size of 'big-name' tribes, which, he feels, must result from
complex historical events leading to the expansion of some tribes and the
contraction of others through success and failure in warfare. It is possible
to think – much in the manner of Watson (1965a: 307; 1965b: 446–8)
but from different premises – that flux of this type reflects in part the
processes of spatial readjustment by communities taking advantage of the
productive capacities of a new plant in a wider range of environments than
the previous agricultural regime could profitably exploit.

For the Hagen region, however, there are other developments to be
taken into consideration. In an early article on Kuk (Golson 1976, actually
written in 1973) I argued (pp. 216–19) that the exceptionally wide range
of Hagen tribal populations noted by Strathern might be connected with
the abandonment of swamp cultivation in the upper Wahgi before the
arrival of the Europeans. I suggested that the sweet potato was indirectly
responsible for this abandonment, in that the special provision that had to
be made for its wet-land cultivation by way of more intensive drainage

134

created requirements for a type and scale of maintenance that the local political organisation could not effectively guarantee. In these circumstances hitherto productive land fell out of use, to the misfortune of communities on the valley floor, while possession of the sweet potato gave advantage to communities on the valley sides, where indeed, specifically on the slopes of Mount Hagen and the Hagen volcanic plateau (Strathern's Ogelbeng Plain), the largest tribal groupings are to be found (Strathern 1971: 15).

It is more likely, however, that, as is now argued for Kuk (p. 132), most upper Wahgi swampland was abandoned soon after the arrival of the sweet potato and as a direct result of its productivity on surrounding dry land (see discussion in Golson 1977: 627–8; the alternative interpretation discussed there is now preferred: cf. Golson 1981c). Subsequently swampland cultivation ceased altogether. However, according to Gorecki's (1979: 101–5) interpretation of oral traditions both mentioned in patrol reports and collected by himself, it was not only swampland cultivation that was abandoned but valley-bottom settlement as a whole, as a result, he proposes, of the arrival of malaria. This would neatly account for the situation attested for the Hagen area at the point of European contact by all available lines of evidence, of a sparsely inhabited valley floor and a concentration of population on the hills above. Given that the sweet potato was now the staple crop, it becomes clear why the biggest populations and the most powerful tribes should be found on the volcanic plateau at the head of the Wahgi valley and the slopes of the Hagen Range beyond, in contrast to the focus of population and power in the valley itself which we have reconstructed for the pre-Ipomoean period.

Archaeological evidence to test the propositions about the history of Mount Hagen society which have been advanced here will not be easy to come by. In the light of the suggestions that have been made, the most profitable line of approach is likely to be to trace the development of exchange systems through the specialised items involved in them, of which shell and axe stone will be the most prominent archaeologically. Hughes (1977: 198–201) has discussed the occurrence of marine shells in archaeological deposits, but axe stone is a more promising prospect, since it occurs in greater quantites and the quarries from which it was obtained are known (*ibid.*: 132–83).[8]

However, the story that has been told for the upper Wahgi is based upon propositions general to the Highlands as a whole, in particular those relating to the environmental transformation and the responses it evoked in the sphere of land use and production. This being so, we should expect

Jack Golson

that, if our case for Hagen has any validity, the propositions used in its reconstruction would also prove useful in understanding the socio-political situations in other parts of the Highlands.

ACKNOWLEDGEMENTS

The archaeological work described here has been made possible by research permits granted by the Papua New Guinea Government and by the approval of the Department of Primary Industry to work on its Research Station at Kuk. The staff of the Station and the local community at Kuk have given unstinting assistance throughout. Financial support has been regularly provided by The Australian National University, while specific grants have been received from the Wenner-Gren Foundation for Anthropological Research (no. 3016), the Papua New Guinea National Cultural Council, Shell (PNG) Pty Ltd through its Mount Hagen office and the Mount Hagen Local Government Council.

The work has been done in collaboration with Dr P.J. Hughes, Department of Prehistory, Research School of Pacific Studies, Australian National University (geomorphology), Dr R.J. Blong, School of Earth Sciences, Macquarie University (ash-shower stratigraphy), and Dr J.M. Powell, National Herbarium of New South Wales (vegetation history); they have all contributed in important ways to the synthesis presented. Dr Hughes and Dr D.E. Yen, Department of Anthropology, Bernice P. Bishop Museum, now with the Department of Prehistory at ANU, have commented usefully on the present paper. The version here is based on a seminar paper given in the Department of Social Anthropology, University of Cambridge, in 1978 and has benefited from discussions there. Association with Dr T.P. Bayliss-Smith, then and subsequently, has been particularly influential.

# 5 Tribesmen or peasants?*

*Andrew Strathern*

~~~~~~~~~~~~~~~~~~~~~~~~~~~~~~~~~~~~~~~~~~~~~~~~~~~~~~~~~~~~~~~~~~~~

It is commonplace to observe that patterns of economic development
introduced by capitalist agencies possess an extraordinary force to invade
and dominate previously established forms of economic activity. Such
domination tends not simply to reproduce capitalist relations of production in the society affected but to encapsulate earlier relations — hence
'dependency' and 'underdevelopment' theories and the controversies that
have agglomerated around these. Theories which take capitalism as not
only dominant but the only determining force in these situations are likely
to depict indigenous responses to change as at best severely constrained
and indigenous society as in some way 'produced' by the external forces.
This viewpoint, however, is as limited and one-sided as the old 'functioning
community' approach which it attempts to dispose of by straightforward
inversion. While capitalism is very powerful, we need not imagine that it
always works in exactly the same way. Most important, indigenous social
systems do have their own resilience and integrity, which need to be
studied from within.[1] If capitalist relations come to dominate, we must be
able to establish in an exact manner how they do so rather than assuming
that this is in some way inevitable and hence dispensing with the need for
specific analysis. Government legislation and its effects, intended or
unintended, are crucial mediating variables here between outside interests
and the people's own values and aims, and it is important to attempt to
understand how government policy reflects and interacts with emerging
class interests (Barnett 1979).

All observers of societies in the western part of the central Highlands
region of Papua New Guinea have noted a marked emphasis on ceremonial
exchange as a means of achieving status, although there has been less
agreement on the interplay between the achievement of individual and
group status (e.g. Sillitoe 1979). This emphasis has clearly been

*A version of this chapter was first given as a Munro Lecture in Edinburgh on 19 May
1979

137

strengthened as a result of pacification and the cessation of warfare (up to the 1970s), but, again, it is in no sense simply an artefact of colonial administration.

It is of the utmost importance to establish at the outset what kinds of social inequality are encapsulated in these exchange systems and to indicate sharply in what ways they converge with or diverge from the capitalist model. Highlands societies all exhibit forms of competition for status, and the competition is often expressed through a struggle for control over valued scarce goods and their disbursement in reciprocal exchanges. In considering this process, we have to look at cooperation and conflict between (1) men and other men, (2) men and women and (3) groups. The emphases fall differently. Sillitoe, for example, denies that there is much significant intergroup competition in the Wola case (1979). Throughout however, one principle appears to hold: the notion of a true monopoly over the basic means of production by one category, however defined, as against another, is never an overt feature. The basic means of production is, of course, land, and access to land is guaranteed by rights of kinship and residence, denied to no-one. Hence the obvious point that the systems are correctly designated 'pre-capitalist' rather than 'primitive forms of capitalism'.

To say that access to land is guaranteed essentially by the kinship system is not to deny that there can be marked inequality of practical access to the means which are necessary to achieve status.[2] This inequality shows in two categories of relationships: first between men and women, and second between men recognised as big-men and those classified as 'rubbish'. In both instances the relationships are also contained within the structure of kinship relations, but it is significant that they are expressed by the people themselves in general terms, i.e. men versus women, big-men versus rubbish-men. In other words, as established dichotomies, these relationship categories symbolise the idea of inequality, although at the level of practice this idea is constrained by the kinship mould within which it is set. Men as a whole claim superior access to public status by contrast with women; the idea of big-manship is brought further into focus by the opposed notion of the 'rubbish-man'. The concept of achievement is involved here: ideologically, big-men achieve their status and rubbish-men are therefore 'failures'. Since there is a partial approximation between women and rubbish-men, by implication men are seen as more 'able to achieve' than women. As Marilyn Strathern has demonstrated (1978), the two dichotomies are interdependent, at least in Hagen thought.

In order to see the extent to which this ideology corresponds to practice, we have to return to the kinship context. Men do not exercise sway over women or rubbish-men as their 'employers'. Each man instead acts in a role *vis-à-vis* his female kin and particularly his wife; and each big-man attempts to act as a patron, drawing in the labour of less fortunate or less successful men towards his own concerns. The limits on individual exploitation are very clear, and in some ways operate with increased force nowadays. A polygynist can manage only so many wives, and the risks of mismanagement increase sharply as soon as a second wife is taken. He does not have automatic command over the labour of co-residential kin. Even rubbish-men may transfer their allegiance to another big-man or may simply refuse to do much work.[3] Disgruntled wives can neglect pigs or children or leave and go home to their own kin. A seriously disaffected wife or rubbish-man may even, it is thought, turn to poisoning the big-man, perhaps persuaded by outside enemies who are jealous of him. In the past, before pacification and government courts were introduced from the 1930s onwards, a man might beat his wife with greater impunity, and rubbish-men who were refugees from elsewhere had fewer alternative places of residence. Now, a wife may take her husband to court, and a rubbish-man may go off to town or easily move to a new clan-area. Big-men never in any case held exclusive rights to large tracts of customary land, so their capacity to increase production would be limited to their inherited claims, and by their ability to raise a labour force effectively to use these. A big-man with many wives and sons automatically reduces the amount of land available to any one of his successors. But, as is again well known, none of these constraints prevents the phenomenon of big-manship from being reproduced in Highlands societies, so the phenomenon itself must depend on further mechanisms, which enable contenders to build outwards from the marginal advantages available within the system of production into the achievement of inequality through exchange.

While in principle it appears that this must be so in many of the Highlands cases, it seems most evident in Hagen and Enga. In these societies, the rules of exchange are complex and the linkages between individual partners and groups are more ramifying than in the others. There is, moreover, a notion of 'increment' built into exchanges, so that it is possible, by manipulating the timing of activities, to play games of competitive finance through which the ranking of big-men is actually created and maintained. It is noteworthy that in Hagen the big-man is he who can 'find' or 'lay his hands on' wealth, while the rubbish-man is he who seeks — but does not find — (*wuɸkorpa*). Where the status of big-men is most differentiated, a particular category of prestige goods is found to have symbolic importance: the valuable shell, which cannot be directly produced, but must be imported from outside, and was indeed in the past drawn in from a tremendous distance through tortuous trade-routes (Hughes 1977). It is this category which has now largely been replaced by money, although shells are still used in parts of the Southern Highlands, where their numbers were not inflated by European imports after pacification as they were in Hagen and Goroka.

In this kind of society, it is precisely the collective appropriation by all men of transformed or exchanged objects of labour which enables certain individual men to succeed by comparison with others. It is only in this respect that we can argue that men as a whole act as a 'class' in relation to women, and the act of appropriation is also one which is utterly remote from the appropriation of surplus value by a capitalist employer from his workers. The appropriation is realised, as a symbolic act, through public ceremonies, and this is an important part of the meaning of these ceremonies, and a reason why they take place at all, rather than private acts of single re-distribution being predominant. How this works can be illustrated by events at any public killing of pigs, one of the categories of action in the Hagen exchange system. Men are named as those who kill the pigs, produced by the joint labour inputs of their wives and themselves. The wives make initial claims on certain parts of the meat: intestines, sometimes the backbones and heads. But men also claim the whole of the butchered pig as theirs publicly to re-apportion and divide to everyone present and invited. They tell the women and children to sit down and be quiet because dividing out pork is men's work. This, then, is men's 'appropriation', to take hold of the meat and divide it out.

I have deliberately mixed my references to historical time in the account so far, but this is not done with the aim of creating a false 'ethnographic present'. I have not in fact drawn a picture of any one society in full at any given time. Rather, I have been constructing a core of themes around which to build a historical account. The intention is thus, so far, neither synchronic nor diachronic, but outside historical time. In real time, elements of what I have said still hold, or hold in some contexts but not in others where they have been transformed. It is to this process of historical transformation and re-contextualising of relationships that I now directly turn.

The first matter to stress is initial pacification and its subsequent reversal in the 'law and order' problems of the 1970s. In all parts of the Highlands warfare was endemic prior to colonial control.[4] Big-men in Hagen and Enga might owe their position to skill in exchanges rather than to warriorhood as such (although many were also intrepid fighters), but they could never work outside the context of intergroup enmities and alliances. In fact Sillitoe has argued (1978) that they fostered war in order to forestall possible competitors in exchange. In addition, they certainly prosecuted private strategies of revenge on enemies and rivals by means of sorcery, hiring agents to kill on their behalf. If this became known, it would lead to reprisals and hence war also. They risked their own lives reciprocally and, while they could take in refugees if successful, they might find themselves routed at any stage and forced to give up their gardens and pig-herds. They could raise pigs and arrange transfers of shell valuables only if there was peace. Hence it was in the interests of big-men to see that there was an alternation of war and peace. Pacification, as has frequently been noted, froze this situation, but big-men were ready for the change. They now laid stress on their peace-making and exchanging activities, and built the latter into more and more elaborate networks. In areas not suffering from general land shortage the concomitant freezing of land claims could also be accommodated, at least until population pressures increased. Rules of group membership and access to land were flexible, and as long as this flexibility persisted, small-scale readjustments and transfers of claims could occur. The Chimbu land-use system, studied in the late 1950s by Brookfield and Brown (1963), illustrates this point clearly.

In some cases spontaneous migration, or return to areas previously occupied, could happen. This occurred, in two separate phases, within the Dei Council area of Mount Hagen. First, groups re-occupied areas they had earlier lost in warfare, wherever these were not actually colonised by the victors (late 1950s–1960s). Second, at a later stage when cash-cropping was under way, people migrated from hillside territories to flatter places where coffee can be more readily grown (late 1960s–1970s). Often, they were invited by kinsfolk of other groups who had land to spare and wished their friends to occupy claims close to their own rather than having ex-enemies encroach on them. In other words, pacification, while making more difficult the violent eviction of rivals from their land, also brought with it new opportunities of diversifying garden claims in pursuit of increased production. Its effects might thus appear to be wholly benign. Meggitt, however, has argued (1971, 1977) that in the case of the Central Enga population build-up has meant the inevitable return of warfare, as alternative means of coping with the problem of land shortage have been exhausted. Certainly, in the 1970s Enga, Western Highlands Province, and Chimbu experienced the sharpest problems of renewed tribal fighting, and

Andrew Strathern

these are also the provinces with the highest overall population densities. Granted that there are innumerable particular reasons advanced by the people themselves for fighting, and that most of these are governed by the principle of revenge, it still remains a possibility that the intensity of revenge-taking is overall enhanced where land-shortage is experienced; and hence that methods of alleviating such shortage should be regarded as prime factors in reaching a solution to the problem.[5]

Here, of course, the semantics of the term 'land-shortage' must also be scrutinised. Meggitt's argument can be taken on two levels: that the Central Enga see themselves as in need of land and use force deliberately to obtain it, whenever other methods, such as litigation, fail them; or that, whatever conscious reasons they advance for fighting, the rate of inter-group conflict is correlated with the general increase in population pressure. If we take the latter form of the hypothesis, we can operate with statistical patterns alone, filling in the argument with a gesture towards suppositions about psychological tension. If, on the other hand, we wish to concentrate on the people's own view, then two further factors become significant: first, for at least some parts of the Enga area, the persistence of the *tee* exchange system, with its pressure on rearing pigs; second, the universal change in the perception of land as a resource which may be exchanged against money and/or may be used to produce goods convertible into money. Such a perception is itself likely to increase 'land-shortage', if we mean by this people's wish to defend their current claims or to obtain more at others' expense. There can be little doubt that this is a powerful factor everywhere nowadays, even though a general market in land has not developed. Burning or chopping down coffee trees has become a part of warfare, and its clear aim is to cripple the enemy in a way which is much harder to remedy than when swift-growing subsistence crops are involved. The slaughtering of pigs and the burning down of trade-stores have to be seen in the same light. These motives and actions are found in contemporary warfare throughout the Highlands, not simply in the Enga case. Probably the combination of initially heavy population density, a politico-legal structure which emphasised clan solidarity and land re-distribution within the clan but not across clan boundaries (Kelly 1968), and a further injection of pressure from improved health and access to cash-cropping, have all conspired to set the problem in its harshest terms in the Enga area; but the elements are there in other cases also. At one time, commentators were prone to argue that Highlands fighting was a symptom of political uncertainties caused by the withdrawal of the colonial administration and the advent of independence in 1975; but it is

142

no longer possible to stress this point since, five years later, outbreaks of fighting continue, and involve different language and ethnic groups in levels of segmentary conflict which greatly complicate interprovince relations (see Levine and Levine 1979).

It is this turbulent factor of warfare which leads one, as an observer, to think of Highlanders as 'tribesmen'. They have a fierce and continuing concern with intergroup issues, and they are willing to risk life and limb in pursuit of these matters. Conventional court procedures and jail sentences have proved inadequate as deterrents. From the beginning of 1978, therefore, the government introduced an Act, to curb tribal fighting, in which the onus of proof was reversed: persons found within an area designated as a 'fight area' would be presumed guilty of illegal violence unless they could prove otherwise. The legislation has proved controversial (although it was proposed as far back as 1973),[6] and its 'onus of proof' clause has been regarded as unconstitutional, such that it has been hard to apply it effectively, for fear of reversal on appeal. Currently, efforts are being made also to regulate and strengthen procedures for paying compensation for deaths, the only viable alternative to revenge in Highlands terms. Compensation rests on the dual principles of reciprocity and collective liability, just as revenge-killing itself does. If the new legislation is enacted, it will therefore depend on the maintenance of group identity and solidarity; and as much, too, on the continuance of vigorous leadership, for without this the cultural principles I have noted cannot be realised in practice. In brief, both warfare and the measures to date adopted to deal with it rest upon the continuing significance of tribal structures: a fact which is consonant with Meggitt's latest general argument, whatever the exact weighting of the factor of 'land-shortage'.[7]

Yet, if we simply rested at that point, the problems of change would remain opaque. If Highlanders were tribesmen and are tribesmen, and fight for that reason alone, there would be no need to build aspects of change further into our account. It was Meggitt himself, however, who in an earlier article argued that the Enga (and hence other Highland populations undergoing similar processes) were well on the way to becoming peasants, as a result of their dependence on cash and their need to earn it by selling their products, mainly coffee, on the world market. And this characterisation also carries a strong element of truth; though, as with the notion of 'tribesmen', it gives only a partial insight.

What elements of meaning are held to inhere in the term 'peasant'? Meggitt means by it (1) that local people produce crops partly for themselves and partly for monetised exchange with the outside world; (2) that the people are required to pay taxes and have come to depend on services which emanate from the outside, these also requiring expenditure of cash; and (3) that the terms of their exchange with the outside are unfavourable to themselves; in other words, a surplus is now being extracted from them. The crucial variables, therefore, are the exchange of crops for money and the fact that the rates of exchange are set by outside agencies, not by the producers. The same is true of the direct exchange of labour for money which occurs when people migrate elsewhere to work on plantations.

It is interesting to note, for the Hagen area, that Hageners rather rapidly came to perceive the true nature of working on foreign-owned plantations, i.e. that this was no way to become rich, since only the plantation-owners could become wealthy through the process. It is a lesson they have taken to heart and applied in a new way more recently. Their first move was to stop doing contract work on such plantations, confining themselves to piece-work as suited them at times when a coffee flush was on. They early on came to prefer 'independent' migration to towns rather than migration as a part of the Highlands Labour Scheme; even though such independent migration carries with it the risk of not finding a job at all (M. Strathern 1975). There is also a very strong value placed on staying at home and carrying out one's own 'business' of coffee-growing, pig-rearing, running a tradestore and/or a vehicle: in short, anything which is of the 'self-employed' type and largely enables one to stay on one's own ground (cf. Weeks 1977). These are activities which are supposed to 'pull in' money, whereas working for someone else merely enables that person to 'pull' the money to himself.[8] In addition, they are highly critical of the prices paid for their coffee by itinerant buyers. If one stands with a number of sellers at a roadside checkpoint and simply listens to the conversation and comments made, this rapidly becomes clear. 'That's not enough, last week you gave me more, how could the price go down so quickly? Of course, it's good quality and the bag's full: you are giving to us badly and stealing some for yourself.' There is a constant stream of grumbling, which rarely moves the buyer beyond remarking: 'It's not my fault, I only do what my boss tells me.' Either the buyer or his boss is then accused again of 'stealing': usually the buyer, since he is the only agent who is actually seen, and the wider processes involved are genuinely obscure to the bulk of the people. Occasionally, an irate seller will stalk off and threaten to let his coffee rot rather than sell it for a low price. The coffee buyers hit back by pointing out that the standard of coffee beans presented for sale in the Highlands is in fact declining, and by complaining that drivers, who must carry several thousand kina of money with them, are often nowadays assaulted in the Highlands and robbed, to the detriment of the people at large who thus cannot be paid for their coffee.

The point here is to add a dimension to Meggitt's analysis: that of the people's own awareness of their changing situation. If one thinks of peasants as people grimly or sadly accepting their lot, or as treating their lords and masters with careful respect, then this is very far from the mark as far as Hagen is concerned. Hageners do not accept the idea of 'lords', only of 'big-men', and 'big-men' are not fundamentally different from others, hence anything they do may be challenged. Furthermore, there is not yet a clear situation in which their dependence on the outside world is absolute. The fact that they have a low rate of out-migration suggests this. In most clan areas, land for subsistence gardening is still adequate. It is when we expand our perspective somewhat and look at overall patterns of development that a very different picture emerges, for it is Hagen businessmen themselves who are becoming capitalists and employing High-landers from less-developed areas around as their labourers, particularly from parts of the Southern Highlands.

Two separate processes are at work: in one, persons from outlying parts of the Western Highlands itself are migrating into the more fertile and developed areas around the urban centres and attaching themselves via links of affinity or friendship with resident land owners. They are often invited in, as already noted, by people keen to have equable neighbours who will help them with garden work and share the produce of gardens with them in return for the benefits of residence. These incomers are by no means dependent serfs or even clients of their hosts: yet a certain question mark hangs over their security of occupation, a point which can be illustrated by an incident during a phase of conflict between the Kawelka people and Tari settlers on an area of land near to a tea plantation in July—August 1978. After a scuffle over the theft of some pigs, the Tari people invaded the Kawelka area by night and cut down several hundred coffee trees as well as doing extensive damage to bananas and vegetable gardens (total value over K.1,000). We were walking through the gardens assessing and photographing the damage when we met an old Tari man, who is himself resident on Kawelka land. His house had been rifled and all of his money stolen: and he could not be sure whether this had been done by his Tari 'brothers' or by his Kawelka 'hosts'. His ambiguous identity left him doubly weak in the circumstances, and there was little likelihood that he would be indemnified for his loss by either side in the dispute. Others of the immigrants are more secure. They may be married into the Kawelka group or have a strong sponsor. Many of them have planted, and now are able to harvest, their own coffee. Most come from the Tomba/ Tambul region, whose high altitude and cold climate make coffee-growing out of the question. Depending on the way their social relations with the sponsors or kin are managed, they will probably be able to stay permanently and graft themselves gradually into the Kawelka group. Their original language is close to Melpa, and they rapidly learn to be bilingual, if they were not before. It is settlers from different language areas, such as Enga people from Wabag, or Tari people, who are more likely to meet difficulties in future.

All such immigrant settlers are to be distinguished from transient migrant workers, who supply most of the labour for the Western Highlands plantations and also for the smaller work-forces maintained by individual Hagen businessmen. In Dei Council, for example, one prominent local businessman, Goimba-Kot, whose operations have built up from his early involvement in running the business side of the Kotna Lutheran Mission, employs twenty or more young male labourers from Pangia, mostly, as it happens, from the village where my own anthropological work with Wiru-speakers has been done.[9] They pick coffee from the small plantation originally planted for the Lutheran mission congregation which Goimba manages, and they pulp and dry coffee also which he buys with a small fleet of vehicles. Indeed, Goimba also sends his vehicles to Pangia, both to buy coffee there because the Pangia people have fewer marketing outlets, and to obtain new labourers or deliver others back to their homes. The fact that he is able to do this suggests that he makes an overall profit by visiting what is in effect a peripheral area in terms of economic development and purchasing labour and coffee there at favourable rates. He is thus following a pattern established earlier by expatriate plantation-owners and businessmen. It is clear that the more this pattern of labour-extraction between the Western and Southern Highlands is perpetuated, the greater will be the problems of overall imbalance in development. In the meantime the situation of these workers is softened somewhat by the fact that their new employers are socially rather more close to them than Europeans in general have been: for example, workers from Pangia and Kagua, another outlying Southern Highlands area, were included in a distribution of pork when the tribe whose members live around Kotna mission station held a mass pig-killing festival on 21 April 1979. Indeed, Goimba's workers were said to be receiving shares of pork at a family level as well as in the huge public distribution. Capitalist relations of production are thus partly camouflaged by, partly modified by, practices emanating from ideas about kinship and shared ethnicity.

The overall patterns of the movement of labour which I have been sketching can be summarised as follows: in the first phase, lasting from the 1930s to the 1950s, Western Highlanders migrated either to the coast to work on plantations, or to Goroka in the Eastern Highlands, where European enterprise began earlier than in Hagen. In the second phase, from the 1950s to the 1960s, a mixed set of arrangements emerged: some worked on European-owned coffee plantations in the Highlands area itself; some migrated out as independent wage-seekers or on plantation labour schemes as before; some began to build up business enterprises and cash-cropping on a smallholder basis. In the 1970s cash-cropping has grown tremendously, and the money generated by it, along with considerable assistance from government loans, has enabled new corporate groups to be formed for business purposes. These, and their directors, are now essentially taking the place of the expatriate capitalists, and the more this happens the more the whole population becomes more firmly enmeshed in a development process which tends towards the creation and maintenance of wide social and economic inequalities on a scale unparalleled in the pre-contact social systems. The clearest case of this is written large in the situation between the Western and Southern Highlands Provinces. Up to the 1950s Hagen men migrated out in search of, first, shell wealth brought by Europeans from the coast, and, second, money. As soon as cash-cropping and the use of money became established, attitudes to migration switched. Now the emphasis was on locally based development. But the types of enterprise which have been introduced are labour-intensive, just as subsistence techniques also continue to depend largely on hand-labour, and have received little technological input since the initial switch from stone to steel tools occasioned by the arrival of Europeans in the 1930s. Hence, labour power in the form of workers has still to be recruited, whether the plantation-owners are indigenous or foreign. Technically, it would be possible for the corporate groups which are taking over plantation ownership to supply the needed labour from their own membership on a cooperative basis. In practice, they have continued to secure the labour of other groups from outlying areas, thereby reducing the capacity of these areas to produce their own infrastructure for development.

In the initial phases of out-migration of labour and in-migration of European businessmen, economic relations were mediated by the use of shell valuables, as I have noted. These were not only prestige objects, but in the pre-contact societies control over them was largely in the hands of a small elite of men. This was certainly true of Mount Hagen society, as the early ethnographer of the 1930s, Georg Vicedom, clearly reported. Elsewhere, this process has been analysed in detail (A.J. Strathern 1971, 1979b; I. Hughes 1978), but some salient points must be noted here: first, it is important to see that in Hagen the most prestigious forms of shell valuables served to define both the idea of inequality between men and the overall superiority of men *vis-à-vis* women. The first scale of inequality was threatened by the new influx of shells brought by Europeans, for they offered these on a market basis to those who gave them supplies of produce and labour. Undoubtedly the basis for leadership was widened by this process, but the basic structural principles of the society were not, I would argue, altered. The big-men recovered their position in two ways: first by gaining early access to Europeans, approaching them as partners rather than as workers; and second by turning the new supplies of wealth back into the processes of ceremonial exchange, over which they exercised their true dominance. In the case of shells, this was predictable, for shells could not be redeployed in any other way, and the level of manipulation of shells in exchanges simply moved upwards. Those who succeeded in obtaining and giving most shells were still those who had an existing grip on the social networks at large or who developed a flair for exerting such a grip. Big-men thus re-asserted their pre-eminence, but only at a further cost, that of affirming a fundamental new dependence on Europeans as the suppliers of wealth. The point should not be over-stressed, since pigs were in a sense more basic than shells and remained home-produced, their breed improved by mixing with imported strains. Nevertheless, in the people's perceptions, Europeans were identified as the 'wealth people' (*mel-wamb*).

Since it was only men, whether big-men or otherwise, who gained any significant control of valuables, the second scale of inequality, between men and women, was not threatened during the shell boom. Money, however, has produced further changes. To begin with, the pattern of male control was repeated. Vegetables and labour sold by women were paid for with shells, which were then funnelled into exchanges, and this happened in the initial stages of the conversion to money also. But with the proliferation of coffee-smallholdings, both the amounts of money and the amounts of labour required to produce money returns have increased quite sharply, and women are very actively involved in the process of coffee growing and marketing (A.J. Strathern 1979b). They take it to the roadsides and sell it, receiving the money, as a due return for their work of weeding, picking, sun-drying and carrying. Men's response to this has been twofold. First, they remind women that by the rules of land tenure the trees belong to them, since men plant them on their own garden land and it is their wives who do the picking. Second, they say they require the bulk of the money for male-dominated projects: either the purchase of expensive vehicles or the creation of new exchange networks by the use of money in ceremonial prestations. Big-men seek prominence in both spheres, as they must if they are to retain control over money as the successor to shell valuables. Finally, they now spend large amounts of money also on imported foods, mostly canned fish, rice, and frozen beef, and on the commercial purchase of pigs, to be consumed in ceremonies adjunct to the *moka* exchanges.[10] Up until 1978 they also enthusiastically incorporated cartons of beer as items into their public displays; but the new provincial government in 1979 clamped down on off-licence sales of beer, owing to the sharp increase in vehicle accidents and interpersonal violence which inevitably accompanied the diffusion of beer as a consumer good in this way. Drinking was thus mostly confined again to hotels and clubs; and it is also still mainly a male prerogative.

Within what I am depicting as a male strategy of appropriation *vis-à-vis* women, two further features stand out. To begin with, it is worth re-emphasising that the appropriation involved is metaphorical and political. Men do not actually consume any items (except for beer) in an exclusive manner. In fact, there is in Hagen an elaborate etiquette of serving women and children first and grown men last at any occasion when food, including pork, is publicly shared out. But what men do assert is control, decision-making powers. Second, among men themselves it is again big-men who are most concerned to assert this control. They appropriate, not to consume but to distribute and to engage in further exchanges. Exchange is seen as a kind of consumption by those receiving a gift. Men used to indicate their mouths in telling me that they would soon be receiving a *moka* gift of shells, for example, and would say 'Soon we shall eat them.' But from the giver's viewpoint the shells or pigs are, of course, an investment, designed to draw in a potentially bigger return later. Similarly, spending money is described as 'eating' it, but giving it away in *moka* is 'planting' it, so that it will grow and bear fruit which can then be harvested. Here is where big-men may deplore women's forms of consumption involving regular private expenditure on foodstuffs and clothing for themselves and their children. Women, on the other hand, criticise younger men's consumption patterns, by which money is wasted on beer, card-playing and chasing after loose girls. It is this, among other processes, that big-men in Hagen are forestalling by retaining control of the major forms of investment and by not laying themselves open to accusations of private consumption. Thus they attempt to maintain their ideological supremacy. At times the process may also bring them into conflict with mission adherents.

The big-man with whom I have been sharing a settlement since 1974, Ndamba, for example, sees his continuing practice of *moka* not just as a means of keeping individual control over events but as the expression of his commitment to a whole way of life, and he tries to include money in *moka* as a new kind of valuable. Within his own lineage there is a split between himself and his elder brother Wømb. Wømb would probably be regarded simply as a 'rubbish-man' were it not that he has a cash income from coffee and has been baptised into the Lutheran mission along with his whole family. One of his sons leads the prayers in the local church on Sundays and has tried to start some adult evening classes also. He solicits money contributions for the building of a permanent-materials church to replace the present building of thatch and cane. Ndamba's family quietly oppose all these moves, although no overt issue is ever made of the matter, and one by one more people in the clan, including some other big-men, are either becoming baptised or talking of it. Ndamba says that Wømb 'never does anything, but wanders around in the undergrowth', that is, he spends most of his time on garden work and does not make *moka* or public speeches. Ndamba also disapproves of his own daughters going to the introduced evening classes (as well as to 'social nights' run by the local primary-school teachers), arguing that what they learn at these is how to fornicate and flout his authority. Nikint, one of Ndamba's sons, adds that the mission people are good at consuming food and receiving gifts but poor at organising their own shows and at paying back their debts. On 18 April 1979 Ndamba put on a special killing of pigs in order to consecrate a new ceremonial ground he had laid out and to bring his ancestral ghosts in as witnesses to his act in setting up a new *pokla mbo* there. (The *pokla mbo* is a specially constructed tub, planted with cordylines and packed with ritually prepared secret ingredients which act as magic to maintain a big-man's personal success in 'pulling in' wealth to the men's house before which the tub stands.) At the killing, just after Ndamba had made a ringing invocation to the ghosts, Wømb appeared as a visitor and was struck with a severe headache half-way up the ground. The whole occasion was an affront to Wømb's conversion to Christianity and a reminder that in terms of the old values he was 'rubbish' while his brother was 'big'. Little wonder he had a headache, for Ndamba had deliberately revived an ancient custom to make his point. Ndamba kindly met Wømb and asked after his health, and later put aside a very large leg of cooked pork for him. Others commented directly 'Wømb feels badly against Ndamba, and Ndamba did this to make him feel better.' After all, Wømb too will be a ghost later and has to be kept in good humour. Ndamba also set up, in 1973, a cult site of the Female Spirit just next to the site chosen for the 'new village' of persons converted to the Lutheran mission. Thus in every way he has politely maintained his own traditions in the face of religious encroachment from outside, and he sees the use of money in *moka* as a part of this overall strategy.

There is another line of potential division. Younger men, outside the mission network and within Ndamba's own support-group, see the build-up of investment of money in ceremonial exchange which he advocates as rather irksome. They would prefer, they say, simply to do 'business', that is, make money and spend it as they themselves see fit rather than having to save it and contribute it to enterprises in which he is the leader. In part, these views emanate from a section of the group which has no separate big-man of its own and in which the two brothers who form its nucleus would like to have more independence from Ndamba than they are able to achieve. But in part, also, it undoubtedly represents one possible choice for the future, in which public political life would lose its character and private enterprise, investment and consumption would loom much larger.[11]

It is interesting to reflect that this is precisely the attitude which early agricultural extension officers in Hagen saw themselves as attempting to inculcate. One such officer, for example, told me in 1969 at a conference that social life had been based too much on clanship and his department was now trying to develop a more individualistic set of values among the people, since this was the only way development could take place. 'Favour the entrepreneur' was thus his policy, and at this stage the Australian administration also advocated the introduction of individual freehold tenure as a means of stimulating indigenous business activity. Here, then, lies another important theme in the study of development: government legislation and the attitudes of government officers.

The colonial administration attempted to introduce, just before self-government in 1973, legislation designed to make such freehold tenure possible and to stimulate a market in land transactions. The bill failed owing to opposition from members of the House of Assembly who had been alerted to its possible dangers partly by a campaign conducted by a New Zealand academic, Dr Alan Ward. He cited the case of the Maori experience, and warned that the result of such an Act could be the creation of a landless proletariat with which no government could effectively deal. Briefly, he warned it would lead to revolution. Both liberal and conservative politicians clearly saw the dangers of this, and voted the bill out.

Alan Ward was soon appointed as an adviser to a national Commission

151

of Enquiry into land matters, and the Commission produced an influential report during 1973 which became the basis for a very different land policy of the new national government. The chief aim of the report was to recommend the protection of indigenous land rights and the substitution of a communal rather than an entirely individualistic model of development. The recommendations suited the mood of the country's new rulers, and generated, during a very fruitful period of legal drafting from 1974 to 1975, a series of Acts designed to give more authority to local leaders in settling land disputes and to enable traditional groups such as clans to set themselves up as legal entities for the purpose of doing business, including land development. The intention was to do away with cumbersome and inappropriate laws enacted to run companies, partnerships, or cooperatives, and to give a simpler basis in law for already existing groups to run businesses: to harness, that is, the indigenous potential for cooperation and organisation. During the same period, also, the Village Courts Act gave to local groups considerable powers to elect their own magistrates and settle most disputes (other than questions of land ownership, serious crime and traffic offences) according to customary rules. All these Acts can be seen as attempting 'to give back power to the people' and as built on the assumption that indigenous rules and principles of organisation could be sufficient to handle even the new situations brought about by prior economic and political change. From time to time, also, the new government instituted a policy of making funds available in large amounts to indigenous bodies, enabling them to take over expatriate plantations, thus beginning a process which is well under way in the Western Highlands.

What have been the effects of these laudable policies and liberally conceived new Acts? It is not easy to assess the picture overall. For one thing, the new business groups have not entirely replaced individual initiatives by private businessmen, whether citizens or expatriates. For another, they themselves are set up with rather varying constitutions. Some, for example, are much more oriented towards big business and profit than are others. In the same way, Village Courts have worked with variable success. But one general point does stand out, from the perspective of events within Dei Council during the last three years: that the liberal aims of the mostly expatriate advisers and lawyers who drafted the new Acts have not been, in any simple way, realised. Rather, there are indications, not as yet conclusive, that overall economic forces have proved stronger than the intentions of the law-makers.

For example, a major aim of the Village Courts legislation was to enable people to settle disputes more in accordance with procedures of mediation and by payments of compensation rather than by fining or by jail sentences. Magistrates were encouraged to hear cases in informal settings and to allow persons litigating to approach settlement through lengthy debate and discussion. But in practice the courts in Dei have not done this. Magistrates have acted in a very formal way, have demanded respect from litigants, have tended to use fines rather than mutual exchanges of goods as a means of settlement, and have consistently sought to put offenders in jail where they see fit. Altogether, they have been concerned to assert their authority, not in the image of the big-man or the community counsellor, but rather as local equivalents of alien, town-based magistrates (Fitzpatrick 1980). Again, prominent local business leaders have been active in setting up groups for development and these have indeed been based on collections of clans, as envisaged in the Acts. They have, however, been established on quite a large scale, and the aim of their leaders has been to take over large-scale enterprises previously developed to a point of profitable efficiency by expatriate companies or individual businessmen.

The first of these groups to be formed in Hagen was that known as Pipilika, based on an ancient dispersed category of peoples now divided into different local tribes. Founded through the inspiration and hard work of a magistrate and a law graduate, this development group has had an astonishing success.[12] It began by obtaining a large grant to take over a coffee plantation. It now owns the prestigious Hagen Park Motel also, and has obtained, with massive bank support, the very largest and most profitable plantation in the northern part of Hagen district (Gumanch). Soon after Pipilika came into operation in this way, two further groups were founded in implicit rivalry with it from inside Dei Council. One is centred on the Dei United Party M.P., Mr Parua-Kuri, and represents an alliance between himself and the businessman Goimba whom I have mentioned earlier. It is known as Raembka, and potentially unites all nine clans of the Tipuka tribe with supporters from their ancient pair-group, the Nelka, and the Tipuka's current allies, the Kawelka. The other large group is called Welyi-Kuta, and centres on a businessman, Mr John Maes, and several clans from among three tribes all traditionally opposed to the Tipuka—Kawelka pair in warfare: that is, the Welyi, Kombukla, and Minembi groups. Maes stood as a Pangu candidate against Parua in the 1977 national elections and was runner-up, so there is a certain influence from national politics which is also involved in the constellation of these groups.[13] Large numbers of persons rather informally contribute money as 'shares', and the totals collected are given as evidence of serious intentions and capacities so as to persuade the government to advance loans for the purchase of plantations.

Andrew Strathern

Welyi-Kuta have in this way taken over several hundred acres of coffee land situated on land traditionally owned by the Welyi (Penga and Bitam). Since government policy officially is to favour those who have such traditional land claims in moves to re-purchase the land, this means that the Welyi are in a very powerful bargaining position, and have demanded that the vast majority of shares in the new enterprise should belong to their own development association rather than agreeing to an arrangement including Raembka. No doubt their aim is to redress an imbalance caused by the dominance of Raembka directors within yet a third corporate enterprise, this time run by a formally constituted company which is the business arm of the local government council. This is the Dei Development Company, which administers the finances of Tigi Plantation, bought in 1975. Tigi was originally founded, some twenty years ago, by an energetic Australian, John Collins, and the Council obtained it a few years after his unexpected early death. Despite the need to pay off a government loan in excess of K.300,000, the plantation quickly showed a profit, and in 1977 its directors were able to distribute K.125,000 for use on general road improvements throughout the council area.[14] As I noted, Raembka men are rather predominant in running Tigi, and situations of this kind undoubtedly sharpen suspicions and rivalry within the Council, even though profits have not been assigned only to projects which will improve the lot of Raembka people at large. Indeed, it was notable that they were not assigned to help with road assistance among the Kawelka, a principal set of allies of the Raembka.[15]

My general observation can now be made quite simply. The intention of legislators in providing for business groups was to encourage communal action and prevent a polarisation between 'evolved' big-men as entrepreneurs and 'peasantised' masses. However, another potential context of inequality was not envisaged, although it should have been, given knowledge of the competitive principles of local social structure: that is, the likelihood that business groups would become new and powerful competitive units. The new groups are based on only a selection of the total set of clans in an area, and within these effective membership depends on taking out numbers of shares. Further, only those development groups with firm traditional land claims to areas occupied by coffee plantations stand a chance of acquiring these immensely valuable assets. It becomes clear, then, that the groups and individuals who do not belong to these new associations or have little standing in them will gradually become poorer by comparison with those who are members or, especially, hold positions of control within them. The associations do not exclude indi-

154

vidual businessmen, of course, but they can, through their corporate structure, build up a level of financial influence which no individual could hope
to match.

Further, as it happens, there are likely to be geographical correlates of
this situation. Plantations were made on flatlands rather than on hillsides,
hence the traditional flatland-dwelling groups are the ones which will
effectively inherit these rich resources rather than the hill dwellers.
Ndamba and his Kawelka clansmen, with whom I live, are hill dwellers,
and as it happens their only chance of participating in this new phase of
development is blocked, since the Kawelka land at Kuk which was earlier
alienated was purchased not by an expatriate businessman but by the
government's Ministry of Agriculture as a Research Station, and the
Department of Primary Industry has refused to release even as yet
undeveloped portions of the Station (remaining unused several years after
purchase), on the grounds that they are needed for future research purposes. Annoyances and concern have predictably built up over this issue,
and over related unsuccessful attempts to acquire remaining lots of
government-owned land nearby.

The mention of land problems brings me back to the other side of the
picture of corporate organisation. While, in the first phase of development,
officials were interested in promoting individualisation, it is obvious that
this policy never proceeded to the point of breaking down all aspects of
corporate identity; indeed, the flexible re-shaping of corporate identities,
around emergent big-men who combine aspects of modern and traditional
status, has been strikingly clear. Such identity is shown both in collective
displays of decoration and ceremony at *moka* or pig-killings and, under
stress, also in the collective violence of fighting and full-scale warfare.
Despite the overt aim of individualisation, the overall policies and changes
brought by the administration themselves led inevitably to this resurgence,
as an answer in some places to pressure of land shortage (Meggitt 1977),
or simply in response to the inadequacy of mechanisms for settling other
disputes over previous killings, compensations, abductions or insults,
matters which are the stuff of intergroup politics whether land is short or
not. It was within this context that the new development associations
came into being after independence as bodies prepared now to wage rivalry
on an economic scale not known before. And it is inside these that new
and more hidden processes of individual economic differentiation have
also begun. The biggest 'big-men' will be those who combine formal offices
within these associations and other useful government connections; and
the processes whereby they become rich will be less evident to the bulk of

the people than is the case for big-men in the traditionalist mould, such as Ndamba, who work in their own gardens, build their own houses and rear their own pigs. Moreover, the new business associations provide plenty of scope for the educated elite to participate as accountants, managers, and overseers, so employment will be available for the educated children of the successful land owners. If this happens, a clear economic class structure will emerge. One big obstacle to its emergence, the lack of a market in land, has now begun to crumble, through the availability of government land leased for development purposes.

It is also clear, however, that there are other possibilities. For instance, the development associations could mitigate their new aggressively capitalistic stance by deliberately fostering projects with wide significance for community welfare. Ceremonial exchanges with money also provide a very valuable way both of re-distributing cash at random to its original locus of production and of keeping money *out* of investment in inequality-producing business activities. Perhaps provincial governments could play a role in seeing that traditional groups all share some kind of access to new sources of monetary income. If this is not done, there will be further problems. Those groups which eventually see themselves as disadvantaged will fight for their share, and may continue to do so unless they are heavily contained by police forces. Tension and hostility already exist and spark into killings between immigrant settlers and land owners around them in the Wahgi valley; and this pattern could be written much larger if conflict over control of lucrative plantation land were to grow.

Further, the whole pattern of prosperity in the Western Highlands has come to depend somewhat artificially on inputs of labour from poorer or more overcrowded areas to the west, east and south of the province. This is because, I have argued, the big plantations are labour-intensive, and because Western Highlanders have preferred to inherit the colonial pattern of employing labour to which they were themselves originally subjected, rather than undertaking the work themselves. If relations between immigrant workers and local people were to decline severely, or the immigrants were to withdraw their labour on the grounds that they needed to build up their own provinces, the current pattern in the Western Highlands could be threatened. It is possible to argue that this is in fact what should happen, at least gradually, for the Western Highlands cannot indefinitely contain labour immigration, and its effect is also to make the Western Highlands richer and the surrounding areas poorer, a situation with its own further dangers at many levels, from the familial context up to the level of inter-province politics. At all events, I suggest that economic planning will have to consider seriously the social impact of continued labour migration and the potential dominance of development associations. As an attempt, therefore, to redress the interprovince imbalance, the 'corporate plantations' project now being run in the Southern Highlands as a means of holding labour there is basically sound, although in the longer run it could possibly also lead to an internal repetition of the type of new circumstances I have sketched for the Western Highlands.

I have discussed in this paper some emerging patterns of inequality in Highlands societies. The twin themes of class and capitalist structure have been much to the forefront. In speaking of these as 'dangers' for the Highlands, I have not intended my remarks to be taken as either paternalistic or romantically nostalgic, but would merely stress that the potentially permanent, large-scale, and hidden forms of inequality which can be brought about by capitalist enterprise also bring with them the potential of severe and society-wide conflicts which are of quite a different order from those engaged in by big-men in the Hagen *moka*. Yet it would be foolish for planners or anthropologists to deny to Highlanders their vigorous sense of competition in economic and political affairs, a sense which certainly does show in the *moka*, and which cheerfully accepts in principle the notion that some will succeed and others must fail. When Ndamba set up his magical powerhouse at his new ceremonial ground in 1979, he drew me aside and whispered to me: 'You understand, Andrew, that this is all done to prevent our rivals from catching up with us. We shall make money-*moka*, buy vehicles, build stores, do all these things, and stay ahead, so that people will be envious and angry with us. Be careful, then, as I have often told you, for they may kill us.'[16] The urgent spirit of competitive risk-taking and achievement breathes through these words and no doubt spurs on, equally, the leaders of the new development corporations, although the objective effects of Ndamba's practices are entirely different from those of plantation acquisition and profit-making. Thus, his whole aim is to maintain exchange partnerships, to keep wealth flowing and to make generous distributions of pork to his kin and neighbours. If others are envious of him, it is not envy of a more comfortable life-style or a larger bank balance, or of ownership of more land, it is envy simply of his personal capacities to speak and act, and thus to justify his name as a true big-man in the Hagen style.

# NOTES

~~~~~~~~~~~~~~~~~~~~~~~~~~~~~~~~~~~~~~~~~~~~~~~~~~~~~~~~~~~~~~

## 2 Two waves of African models in the New Guinea Highlands

1 The issues raised by Barnes have been very extensively debated in relation to the typological question of whether Highlands groups are to be described as lineages and whether 'descent' is to be seen as unilineal. Investigators have also seen, however, the need to move from typological to processual questions (see La Fontaine 1973; de Lepervanche 1967–8; Mandeville 1979; Watson 1970; A.J. Strathern 1972). It is here that, as Langness argued, close attention to the significance of warfare, and therefore also of pacification, is needed (Cooper and Rodman 1979). Of Barnes' propositions, those dealing with group-segmentation and with the lack of storage practices in relation to crops have received surprisingly little close examination. The first is crucial to the study of how leaders establish followings (A.J. Strathern 1971). The second is even more crucial, since it is pertinent to the ways in which a 'surplus' can be built up and disbursed in prestige-seeking activities. Basically, there is a familiar conversion of subsistence products into prestige objects achieved through the constant direction of women's labour, since women do the major work in managing and harvesting the staple sweet-potato crop and in feeding it to herds of pigs reared for use in exchange festivals. When pigs are further exchanged for shells, which men treat as objects entirely at their disposal, the conversion from women's labour to men's prestige is completed.

2 Meggitt's particular proposition has, of course, been heavily criticised. The most sophisticated discussion of the whole issue is still Kelly 1968. Recently, Brown and Podolefsky have elucidated a new approach by tackling a more rigorous set of comparative materials than Meggitt was able to do in 1965 and establishing possible relationships between population density, agricultural intensity, the sizes of social groups, and the degree of individuation of land-holding. Their overall finding is that 'individual land tenure is a product of short fallow and frequent land use' (Brown and Podolefsky 1976; Brown 1978: 111). This certainly fits with the Chimbu data, although a complex notion of what constitutes 'land tenure' is required here, for the obvious reason that communal land rights operate at a different level from rights governing the everyday use of land.

3  It is a mistake to make a model of this kind and expect it to hold equally and in all respects for the African cases themselves. The actual constraints on the effective affiliation of persons to defined *local* groups and on the segmentation of such groups over time would appear to be quite different in the separate cases of the Nuer, Tallensi and Tiv. *A fortiori*, then, it is wrong to expect that the model will apply *in toto* to any given Highlands case. The most that can be said for it is that it provides a kind of typological check-list. The more difficult problem arises out of Langness' early call for an alternative 'whole-system' model of Highlands societies. 'Descent' and 'unilineality', taken in the strict sense as propounded by, for example, Fortes for the Tallensi, have proved inadequate concepts by which to explain the total operation of Highlands groups; although the study of how descent constructs are actually used turns out to provide important clues in the search for such an explanation. Finally, Maurice Godelier (this volume) neatly points out how the 'big-man' model of Melanesian societies has itself obscured features of societies such as the Anga where big-manship is not highly developed.

4  By April 1979, however, Namba appeared to have 'settled down'. His new wife proved hard-working and home-keeping, and she bore him a son, who was called 'Senis' (which means 'in the place of'): that is, when the boy grows up, his name will be 'Ongka', after his grandfather. Namba is due to inherit most of his father's land claims at the settlement Mbukl, whereas Ongka himself has planted coffee and provided land for most of his younger children at his own father's original settlement, Poklɸk, near to Kuk (see A.J. Strathern 1972: 37, 82). Here, Ongka relies greatly on female labour; whereas at Mbukl Namba and other young men cultivate gardens which require a greater input of tree-felling, trenching and fencing.

5  This proliferation of comments closely parallels an earlier profusion of discussions on the agnates versus non-agnates issue, resulting from the 'first wave' of African models in the Highlands. In both cases the controversies may be slightly misplaced, since in their initial form they drew attention away from analysis of other features of the societies in question. The 'agnates' issue implied a definition of descent as a recruitment rule, which has proved inapplicable to the Highlands. And the 'exploitation' issue similarly depends on conflicting definitions of what the terms 'exploitation' and 'class' actually mean. Douglas (1978) attempts to subsume both African and Melanesian cases into her general grid/group paradigm, but this also falls foul of typological reification, which reduces its explanatory power.

6  An empirical matter, which would be worthy of close comparative examination, is the extent to which greater or lesser numbers of these *kintmant* are/were found in particular Hagen groups; and, more broadly, the extent to which there are comparable categories of 'workers' in other societies in the Highlands. In the Wiru language (Pangia, Southern Highlands Province) there is a term *tiobango* which

glosses as 'little man, stunted man', and this is usually applied to mature bachelors of small build who help established householders with their garden work. But, as a term, it does not automatically carry the connotation of 'worker for a big-man' in the way that the Melpa term *kintmant* does. Correspondingly, the big-man complex is less developed among the Wiru than in Hagen (cf. Bowers 1965).

Analysis of exploitation in the African cases, also, would be improved by attention to the question of control over marriage and whether certain men remain unmarried and have no recourse but to 'work for' others. This would enable us to evaluate the proposition, that all juniors become seniors, more closely.

7　The situation continued into 1979, and indeed warfare in the Western Highlands appeared to have intensified following the establishment of an interim government at province as well as national level. In the 1979 fighting very considerable damage − of up to K.50,000 or more (K. is the PNG kina currency: £1 sterling equals about K.1.4) − to crops, livestock, and houses was reported from both the Western Highlands and Enga Provinces, and interprovince hostility was also on the increase. It is obvious that, whatever the underlying reasons for these periodic resurgences of warfare, one result of war is to destroy some of the assets built up by individual entrepreneurs, and hence to delay the emergence of such entrepreneurs as a dominant class. One can expect the businessmen also, as a proto-class, vigorously to call on the state to protect their assets, something which so far has not been effectively done despite the enactment of tough legislation early in 1978 to punish intergroup fighting and the declaration of a national emergency in the Highlands in 1979. By 1981 the situation had become more calm; but the competition for land, to be used for development, intensified.

8　Rubel and Rosman (1978) have made the analysis of exchange structures centring on marriage patterns the core of a significant set of comparisons of societies within Papua New Guinea, particularly from the Sepik and Highlands areas. They also propose a 'generative model' of how an 'original' structure may have become transformed over time into contemporary societies. There are many problems with their presentation, but it does have the prime merit of taking exchange as its main concept, and in this sense it is a genuine attempt to answer Langness' call for concentration on Melanesian structures themselves without an 'African mirage' in front of them. However, the principal drawback of their structuralist approach is that it tends to remain typological and configurational, with the result that the *processes* which lead to the transformations they suggest are not fully hypothesised. Hence also, the directions for post-colonial change cannot be derived from their models. It would be unfair, however, to argue that they are unaware of the need for models of process. They see exchange systems as *sui generis* structures, which make 'demands on the system of production in a society' (p. 343). They thus invert the simple marxist approach to produce a simple structuralist one. The correlation they note between 'the most intensive form of sweet-potato production' and the Enga *tee* exchange system can be read in terms of continuous interaction between variables rather than one-way determination, of course, and the most plausible historical guess is, as they formulate it, following Meggitt, that the *tee* 'probably evolved out of ceremonial payments of homicide compensation' (p. 345).

9  A masterly synchronic synthesis of approaches via both descent and exchange models is provided by Kelly in his account of the Etoro, which was not available when Rosman and Rubel wrote their book (Kelly 1977). It is likely that a distinctive set of models is required to portray the features of low-population-density societies such as the Etoro, Daribi, Kaluli, Samo, Biami and Onobasulu, who all live in the southern interchange region between the Papuan coast and the central Highlands (see Brown 1978: 35–6).

## 3  Production and inequality: perspectives from central New Guinea

1  My thanks to the Australian National University, Macquarie University, and the Australian Research Grants Committee for supporting fieldwork at various times between 1969 and 1979. Irari Hipuya of Horailenda parish has been my host and close colleague in ethnographic endeavour from the beginning. Andrew Strathern, Bill Clarke, Jack Golson, Maurice Godelier, Brian Fegan, Annette Hamilton and Eugene Ogan have all offered helpful criticism of my thesis. Strathern and Roger Keesing have read an earlier version of this chapter and I include here some of their more valuable comments.

2  Kelly's (1977) excellent analytic description of Etoro gardening, for example, reveals that sweet-potato gardens are often neglected in favour of hunting, sago production and the cultivation of mixed gardens. Sweet-potato gardening, far from dominating the annual cycle of productive activity, seems but poorly integrated into the subsistence pattern and would appear to be a relatively recent addition.

3  Compensation is, however, a recognised practice in low-production societies as well (e.g. Schieffelin 1976 and 1980). In suggesting that the problem should be theorised in terms of a sequence beginning with reciprocity based on identity and not yet including the possibilities of compensation (a non-identical and therefore less desirable form of reciprocity), I am here bending ethnographic facts to the progressions of a logical-historical method ('. . . the historical method, only stripped of the historical form and diverting chance occurrences' – Engels, quoted in Meek 1977: 135).

Notions of compensation have of course been generalised throughout post-colonial Papua New Guinea and are today the basis for monetary claims arising from motor accidents and other mishaps involving people from diverse linguistic and regional backgrounds in conflict (cf. Strathern 1974). As a result of a hunting accident in Duna country in 1978, the local parliamentary member for the Kopiago-

Koroba region was reported to have demanded payment of 54,000 kina compensation from the Premier of Simbu (Chimbu) Province. I was told that if the demand were not met a 'pay-back' killing would even the score between 'the lineage (*lain*) of the Southern Highlands' and the 'lineage of all Chimbu'. Here the mechanisms of pay-back and compensation have been combined to regulate relations between post-colonial regional groupings (conceptualised in the segmentary idiom) and to initiate massive financial 'exchanges' between them.

4   'societies of the type under examination': that is, societies capable of producing a sufficient surplus of economic values, separable from the immediate needs of subsistence, and circulatable in exchange against values derived from the claims of kinship. In societies below this level the 'kinship system' consists of a more or less direct exchange of rights in persons against rights in other persons (e.g. bride-service rather than bridewealth). See Siskind 1978 and Turner 1979. Turner's formulation of Gê and Bororo societies (which lack domesticated livestock) as 'political economies based on social rather than material production' (p. 168) could no doubt be profitably applied to low-production societies in New Guinea as well.

5   Fortes (1978: 17) authoritatively states that, far from lineages providing the basis for production units in the Ivory Coast, 'actual production is undoubtedly a function of the domestic family'. He further generalises that 'the operating units in all pre-capitalist economies are individuals and domestic families'. Although Fortes may be correct, I have nevertheless taken the lineage–communal basis of work groups as reported for the Guro and Mbum as if empirically correct for the purposes of establishing a contrast.

Fortes' empirical objection leads him to quibble that: 'It is therefore only in the sense of its being the legally empowered corporate holder and allocator of productive resources that the neo-marxist concept of "the lineage mode of production" may be descriptively appropriate.' I agree, but the emphasis should be inverted: although there is a question concerning lineage versus communal ownership of land (see below), lineages in both Africa and New Guinea are legal constructions to which the control and ownership of human beings are attributed. (See for example Schneider 1970.) 'Lineage mode of production' seems a necessary and sufficient designation for such systems.

6   Several informants recalled clearing gardens on their own with stone tools, although the introduction of steel tools has no doubt further encouraged the practice. A contrast is provided by the Trobriand example of gardening teams coordinated under the authority of a garden magician. Roger Keesing (RK) notes that 'the larger production units might be consequence, not cause, of the larger-scale political units'. This speculation is applicable in the African cases as well.

7   This is not to suggest that surplus can be objectively defined in relation to some absolute, 'pre-social' level of essential consumption.

Although I follow orthodox marxist thought in regarding surplus as a relative and historically determined concept, taking all levels of pig production as surplus to a hunting and horticulture base-line offers an attractive, albeit theoretically flawed, simplification for developmental modelling requiring comparisons between societies.

8 'Cf. the double-tuskers in the New Hebrides that are left to die, or the consecrated Kwaio pigs that may die of old age' (RK). Such practices are unheard of among the Duna and, I think, elsewhere in montane New Guinea.

9 This judgement is based on Duna accounts of their *Palena Nane* cult, which fell into desuetude in the late pre-colonial period. Michael Wood (personal communication) finds no false appropriation of the labours of unmarried young men in hunting among the Kamula of the Papuan Plateau. On hunting as a submerged mode of production, see next note.

10 However, the initiation-based, low-production formations are precisely those where young men are expected to devote much of their energy to hunting rather than horticulture. Further analysis in terms of a subsidiary mode of production might be fruitful (Balibar 1970; O'Laughlin 1975). The transition from a system in which hunting dominates over horticulture to a system with horticulture and pig husbandry in dominance would seem to require the sort of dual-mode (or dominant and subsidiary mode) analysis first proposed by Meillassoux for the hunting and farming activities of the Guro. Meillassoux has been criticised for falling into a 'merely technicist' conception of the mode of production, but the question is whether distinctively different modes of economic relationship accompany hunting and horticulture as subsistence methods (cf. Lee 1980).

11 'The difference here, I think, is iron tools (in Africa). Wherever tribal peoples used stone tools they apparently defined secondary growth as corporate property of the descendants of those who first cleared it. With iron tools, secondary growth becomes a free good in many places (e.g. southeast Asia)' (RK).

Among the Duna (and generally in the Highlands), women are recognised as holding some rights in land by descent. But owing to virilocal residence these rights rarely have *de facto* significance. Presumably the *de jure* principle is a factor in the insistence among men that it is not good to reside on your wife's ground (see next note), although Duna say it is because the men of the affinal host-lineage 'pull' all of a man's wealth so that he neglects his own 'brothers'.

12 Throughout this essay I use the term 'lineage' in a generalised sense, compatible as much with the cognatically conceived and constructed descent groups of the Duna and Huli as with the more strictly patrilineal units of the Mae Enga. The Duna term *damene*, 'related kind' or 'species', is used in speaking of both ego-centred groups and networks as well as groups conceptualised in terms of descent from ancestors. A man will refer to his homestead group as his *damene*, including his wife, although he will point out that she is also of a

different *damene*, the *damene* of her ancestors. Similarly, a man may refer to any of his consanguines, wherever they live, as his *damene* (*no damene*, my related-kind) − although his *damene* is also the *damene* of his ancestors, who necessarily cannot be the ancestors of all of his consanguines. Thus not only is the contrast between agnatic and non-agnatic cognatic descent not important, but also the distinction between descent and egocentric kinship has little relevance in most contexts.

Jackson (1970) has challenged Glasse's (1968) characterisation of the Huli descent system as cognatic, and I understand that Lawrence Goldman in his forthcoming book dealing with the Huli of the Koroba area (bordering on Duna country) again seriously questions the idea that Huli social structure is cognatic. Although Duna do not practise simultaneous multi-local residence as do the Huli, I have otherwise found Glasse's description of the principles and operation of Huli descent structure and local grouping largely congruent with Duna notions and practices. A formulation that would emphasise the functional similarity of Huli and Duna groupings with the more strictly lineal systems of neighbouring peoples would be desirable, but I do not think denying the importance of cognatic descent will clarify matters. Duna stress descent through any combination of genealogical links as the individual's means of finding security and social rights in a plurality of communities, and thus as his means of geographic mobility and assurance against excessive demands for financial contributions to local group/lineage affairs. Similarly, from the point of view of the collectivity, cognatic connection provides an avenue for the recruitment of new residents and external supporters. When I explained Meggitt's (1965) thesis to Irari Hipuya, he replied that Wabag people didn't have enough land, but in Duna country the problem was shortage of people.

Duna place little emphasis upon the jural distinction between *anoaga'ro* (those descended through men only) and *imaga'ro* (descended through one or more women). Since they usually practise virilocal residence they recognise that *anoaga'ro* will have a better knowledge of past land use and political events concerning the interests of the locally based, territorial community. But the cardinal jural distinction for them is between descendants of whatever connection and affines. Men emphasise that it is good to live with kin wherever one has rights by descent; it is not good to live with one's wife's people.

13 'Also, I think, the intensity of warfare is a factor both in polarising the sexes (with the weapons in male hands) and in rendering in-marrying women "spies" from the enemy camp − partly Meggitt's and Langness' arguments' (RK).

However, the evidence of Kelly (1976) and Barth (1975) suggests that while sexual segregation is as much a feature of low- as of high-production central New Guinea societies, the prevailing ideology of low-production societies stresses the antithesis of male and female sexuality rather than feminine inferiority. The intensity of warfare may be an important factor in the apparent differences between Africa and New Guinea, but I doubt if this argument can be extended successfully to account for sex-status differences between New Guinea societies. The women as 'spies' argument evidently has some salience in the Enga case, but has less applicability for the Duna (and the Huli — Glasse 1974). With a greater degree of segregation in everyday life, women are less likely to overhear men's plans, while at the same time men are much more aware of conflicting loyalties among themselves on the basis of their cognatic descent ties.

14  Terray (1979: 39) has recently stressed the importance of interlineage conflict in Africa as well: 'It is possible to suggest that the lineage mode of production is but a particularly effective theatre of illusion in which contradictions inherent in exploitation are relegated to the ranks of secondary contradictions, the principal contradiction being that which opposes productive units [lineages] to each other . . . this illusion is the best guarantee of the elders' power and the perenniality of exploitation.' One might reflect that the same is true of our own world, the principal contradiction being that which opposes nation-states and economic systems to one another.

15  Subjects and instruments of labour: see Marx, *Capital*, vol. I, ch. VII, section 1, 'The labour-process or the production of use-values'.

16  Men's work and travelling time in maintaining pandanus, hunting and so forth is clearly productive. Time spent in arranging financial transactions is productive only in the sense that exchange and sacrifice 'produce' sociality and so reproduce the conditions necessary for production. Of course the data here can no more than suggest the likely shape of pre-colonial patterns when warfare, ritual and stone technology were all factors.

17  My characterisation of the Botukebo system as low-production is based on the low pig:person ratio and the dependence upon land-extensive shifting cultivation for the bulk of sweet-potato cultivation. Waddell (1972) suggests a rather different characterisation by emphasising the presence of labour-intensive cultivation techniques, although these account for only about 10 per cent of total production.

18  Or is it that Kapauku individualism, like Guro communalism, should be taken as a reflection of the ethnographer's ideology rather than an objective characterisation?

19  'Does this imply an Ipomoean counter-revolution?' (RK)

20  The analysis here supersedes that of appendix 2 in my thesis where I unwittingly predetermined much of the result by setting the initial values for male and female labour units differently in different age brackets. Age weightings here are the same for both sexes: ages 11–17 = 0.5 unit, 18–54 = 1.0 unit, 55–65 = 0.5 unit, 66 and over = 0.25 unit. I am grateful to Ross Homel (Macquarie University) for extensive consultation on statistical problems.

21  By including data on men's reputations for wealth and speech-making a multiple regression equation accounting for 51.8 per cent of the

observed variance in homestead pig production can be derived. However, reputations for wealth would be expected to correlate with pig production. Leaving aside data on reputed wealth, reputations for 'helping' others by contributing pigs for payments and distributions prove a poor predictor of reported pig production. Reputations for speaking ability taken together with the product of male multiplied by female labour account for 45.5 per cent of the variance. See next section.

22 'Belief in one's spiritual efficacy and magical power becomes a self-fulfilling prophecy, just as failure breeds failure – the Oceanic concept of *mana* is a nice *post hoc* rationalisation of differential success' (RK).

23 'patriarchy': any system in which men dominate through their social roles as actual or metaphorical 'fathers'. The kinship basis of patriarchy is important, since it is closely linked with men's claim to 'own' women and children, and thus with patriarchy's distinctive articulation of economic and kinship practices.

24 'Male chauvinist pig appropriation . . . ' (RK).

25 Note the contrast with Enga (and Hagen) practice, where a newly married couple begin pig production with breeding stock from the wife's family.

26 'This is the ultimate Melanesian problematic: the construction of a universe in which women's false-consciousness is rendered a social imperative and a cosmic certainty' (RK).

27 My formulation here has derived inspiration from Nicolaus (1972).

28 The positive attributes of pre-eminent men are largely denied to women. Women are not wealthy on their own behalf, nor can they exchange or speak publicly except on behalf of fatherless sons. Women do, however, acquire local reputations commensurate with their feminine roles: some women are said to be good at gardening ('pigs and sweet potato grow on their skins'), others are good at raising children; some women are known to be obedient, others are condemned for their self-willed behaviour.

29 'I suspect that the stereotypic highlands "big-man" is partly a product of the colonial period, and that success in entrepreneurship and deeds in war were more differentiated than the literature suggests. The "big-man" is an ideal type that has somehow been elevated into a real human: a walking abstraction, it seems to me' (RK). Certainly colonial developments have had their effect, but perhaps Keesing is reading Highlands ethnography through Kwaio glasses, since Kwaio (like Duna) lack the elaboration of exchange practices characteristic of high-production societies. Enga and Hagen big-men are a product not only of ethnography but also of the social environment in which they are found, a social environment profoundly structured by the totalising activity of massive ceremonial exchange. Strathern's contrasts between big-men in high and middle-range production systems (1969, 1979b) are corroborative.

30 Ritual performances were generally held in abeyance after 1954 when

government patrols began regularly to enter the area, and all pre-colonial cults were explicitly abandoned as 'the work of Satan' after the missions arrived in 1961.

31 '. . . a crucial element of the domination of elders in Melanesia as in Africa' (RK). Yet secret/sacred knowledge among the Duna seems to have been more an assurance against neglect in old age than a key to dominance. In any case it is notable that Terray and Meillassoux have tended to neglect the role of magic and ritual knowledge in supporting the domination of the elders. Again one is faced with the question whether this reflects a greater rationality in social life or an inclination on the part of the ethnographers to idealise tribal communities and to emphasise the economic at the expense of the ideological.

32 'Look-alike children: the Wiru say the same (another medium-intensity production people like the Duna)' (AS) (Andrew Strathern). On parental ambivalence towards children as successors see also Fortes 1974 and Keesing 1976: 194. What needs to be explored in this respect is the political economy of reproduction and demography, particularly in its ideological aspects (e.g. Heinsohn and Steiger 1980). In the pre-colonial period Duna pollution beliefs supported a late age of marriage by encouraging young men to 'think of their skins' and avoid women. This can be seen as a means of limiting access to pig production and hence political power, but it also has demographic implications. Since the Enga and Huli with earlier average ages of first marriage share similar beliefs, the thread of reasoning becomes tangled here, yet it remains an attractive hypothesis that older men exercised some influence over population growth through their promulgation of ideas about sexuality.

33 There is a common attitude among Duna men associating feminine sexuality with loss of masculine resources, although the voracious vagina symbolism in this behaviour was, I think, preconscious. Duna men are mostly circumspect in their speech: 'In the past you would have to pay a pig to any *palena* bachelor who heard such talk' remarked another man present at the time.

34 Sillitoe (1978) arrived at similar conclusions in a comparative study.

35 Money's devilish qualities in pre-capitalist social relations are explored in a fascinating essay by Taussig (1977).

36 Strathern's argument is that shells aid in the mystification of exchange-values by abstracting them from women's labour. I would suggest that shells be seen as part of a series: human life-values (or concrete labour power and reproductive capacity) → pigs → shells → abstract exchange-value. The Ekari (Kapauku) provide an interesting case in this respect, since Pospisil's ethnography reveals them as poor in pigs yet deeply engaged in financial transactions calculated in terms of (cowrie) shell values. It is as if the expansion of real production has been blocked and a reified culture of finance developed instead. In my thesis I have examined the Kapauku case as a form of fetishisation.

LeRoy's (1979) account of Kewa practices in exchanging shells against pigs suggests further implications of shell manipulation. The generation of exchange-values in an economy requires the 'crossing-over' in transaction of at least two commodities. In a hypothetical system producing only pigs, exchanges must, by default, be made against human life-values, articulating pig production with the production of 'kinship' (as proposed here for the Duna). By exchanging shells directly against pigs (as ceremonial exchange and not simply trade), the Kewa in effect create an expanded sphere of financial activity apart from direct involvement in relations of kinship. *Moka* and *tee* also achieve this, but they require the further institutionalisation of a deferment in the opposition scenario, viz. delayed exchange. Deferred returns must depend on the trust that people are able to place in their exchange relationships, and here there is a tendency to re-introduce kinship through affinal partnerships. Kewa exchanges also put men's trust to the test, but it is only a short-term affair. None the less, the exercise is central to the development of a reliable social order: 'If the spectator sees bungling and disputes, he is liable to think that the entire group of pig killers is of unsound constitution . . . : "If someone from a different village were to see us now in our confusion, he would think that some of us might get sick or die" ' (*ibid.*: 206).

37  Suggestively, a few informants recalled that at some time in the past there had been an attempt to restore fertility to the whole of Duna country by performing rituals which required that a pig be passed from parish to parish the entire length of the Tumbudu valley from Huli country to the Strickland river. The attempt failed, as was often the case, owing to insufficient cooperation between parish groups. One may see in these recollections a ritualistic (or imaginary) prefigurement of enchained exchanges of the sort actually achieved by the Enga in the *tee*. On ritual enchainment see Meggitt (1973).

38  Assembling a compensation or marriage payment among the Duna does in a sense depend upon 'finance', since men do not rely on their own homestead production alone. But there is little reliance upon the manipulation of debts in assembling these payments. Contributions are made on the basis of generalised kinship or friendship rather than particularised exchange-partnership.

39  The statistic of association is Cramer's *phi* (Hays 1973: 745). Homel performed a log linear analysis of a three-way contingency table of wealth ratings by speech ratings by 'helping' ratings using the program GLIM (Nelder and Wedderburn 1972). The results indicated that the correlation between any pair of attributes is independent of the level of the third. The correlation between wealth and speech ratings is of questionable significance, such that it might be due to their separate correlations with 'helping'. By this analysis, 'helping' would be an independent variable determining men's reputations for both wealth and speaking. This seems unlikely. Alternatively, the correlation between wealth and speaking may be accepted as significant, in which case all attribute pairs are correlated and the rather low correlation between wealth and speaking is independent of the level of 'helping'.

40  'The criterion of "speech-making"/"talk" as the crowning character-

istic of big-men is one which Hagen big-men, such as Ongka, also claim
for themselves, as in the phrase *ik-e na mint tep mor*: "only I hold the
talk" ' (AS).

41 'There is something interesting here, as though the ancestors were on
the side of women. They too want to eat and don't like men giving
away all those live pigs or pork for others to eat!' (AS).

42 'In Wiru, pig-kills also coincide with *taim hangri* [periods of food
shortage] sometimes, for the reasons that you have advanced for
Duna' (AS). In the post-colonial period Duna have rejected the notion
that the ancestors require sacrifices, and pig-kills are now planned
events anticipated a month or more in advance. Usually the date is
agreed upon with local missionaries to commemorate church events.
(On one occasion, following a period of bad weather, a missionary was
urged to move forward the date because sweet-potato supplies were
running low.) During the lead-up to the event no local pigs are killed
and people work hard in anticipation of eating pork. People recall
how in former times when a compensation payment was being readied
women were constantly urged to work harder. Tempers frayed and
witchcraft accusations sometimes resulted. With the payment made
people could relax and dance, but there was little pork to eat. What is
not clear is the extent to which the 'bad times' which forced decisions
for sacrifice may have been brought on by passive resistance or even
sabotage of production by women, rather than the external factors of
disease and bad weather, brought on by the ancestors, as claimed by
the men.

43 Rubel and Rosman's analysis of sacrifice depends particularly on
material from Rappaport on the Maring which differs on several significant points from Duna practice. I regret that there is not space
here to comment on their valuable work and develop a comparative
theory of sacrifice.

44 The following story of an incident in the wartime period reveals the
importance and depth of the desire:

> Five airplanes came. All men had very great fear. 'All men will
> die; we aren't sure,' they thought . . . Many men also thought
> the same; now is the time for utterly dying. 'Having eaten only
> one pig we will die,' they thought. So the men, having killed all
> the pigs, only seared them over the fire [didn't cook them
> properly] and ate them. Many other men did the same. Hanging
> oneself was known. Many men did this. Many many pigs and
> much sweet potato were eaten. 'Having filled our stomachs we
> will die,' they said.                     (Cochrane and Cochrane 1966)

45 The large-scale communities of the Sepik pose different problems.
Sago production supports large populations but pig-production is low.
Tuzin (1976) argues that the projection of a terrifying village super-
ego (the *Ngwal* of the *Tambaran*) combined with the complexities of
symmetrical (moiety-based) segmentation, realised through the
initiation systems of these communities, function to maintain social

order in circumstances otherwise beyond the capabilities of the Melanesian polity. My suggestion is that production-based exchange and accompanying rationalisation of social relationships occur in complementary variation with ritual elaboration as basic modes of social integration. Sepik communities fit this generalisation, although their inclusion in the general model proposed here would require a revision of the use-value nexus of pig-production and population growth.

## 4 The Ipomoean revolution revisited: society and the sweet potato in the upper Wahgi valley

1 B.P.: Before Present, which is the radiocarbon reference year of 1950. Dates given in this form, however, are in radiocarbon years, not calendar years, and there is a variable relationship between the two because of variations in the amount of radioactive carbon in the atmosphere over time. Conversion of radiocarbon years into calendar years is currently a matter of much specialist discussion which, for our purposes, can be disregarded since, with one exception, we do not need the degree of precision in dating which is at issue. The exceptional case, discussed later in the paper, is the subject of a publication by Mr H.A. Polach, head of The Australian National University's Radiocarbon Dating Laboratory (Polach 1982). I wish to thank Mr Polach for his personal help on this particular issue of interpretation and both him and his staff for the long-term contribution they have made to the Kuk project in matters of dating.

2 The Manton site, on Warrewou Tea Plantation, is named after Mr Ivor Manton, who kindly gave permission and assistance for excavations to be carried out in 1966, while he was establishing the plantation. For allowing the partial re-opening of the 1966 trenches in 1977, when tea bushes were well established on the site, I wish to thank Mr David Little, acting on behalf of the new owners, Warren Plantation (Mount Hagen) Pty Ltd.

3 The Kaugel site was brought to our attention in 1976 by Mr Martin Gunther, then in charge of the High Altitude Research Station of the Department of Primary Industry at Tambul, as a result of the discovery of a wooden spade during drainage on the Station. A report is in preparation.

4 Mr Ben Probert, Patrol Officer at Tari, wrote to me in late 1977 about the discovery of wooden implements during drainage at Mogorofugwa. I was able to visit the site in early 1980, at the time of renewed drainage under the supervision of Mr Robert Campbell, Department of Primary Industry, Tari, thanks to Dr Bryant Allen, Office of Environment and Conservation, Port Moresby, and Mr Andrew Wood, Department of Geography, University of Papua New Guinea, who were doing fieldwork in the Tari basin at the time.

5 Dr T.P. Bayliss-Smith, Department of Geography, University of Cambridge, began research into these questions in the Western High-

lands Province, as a visitor to the Australian National University while on sabbatical leave during 1980.

6 The most important are Dr S.E. Bulmer's sites of Kiowa (Simbu Province) and Yuku (Western Highlands Province) and Ms M.-J. Mountain's Nombe site (Simbu Province), first investigated by White (1972: 127–41) under the name of Niobe. The collections are respectively in the Department of Anthropology, University of Auckland, and the Department of Prehistory, Research School of Pacific Studies, Australian National University.

7 The 'uppermost ash' reported in this preliminary statement as 60–110 years old by lead isotope dating (Oldfield 1977: 59) has subsequently been shown (by Dr R.J. Blong) to be Tibito Tephra. Recalculation of the lead isotope results has brought them close to the age estimate based on radiocarbon determinations (Oldfield *et al.* 1980: 466–7).

8 Mr J.E. Burton, Department of Prehistory, Research School of Pacific Studies, Australian National University, is currently engaged on research into this topic.

## 5 Tribesmen or peasants?

1 For an apparently opposed viewpoint see Kahn 1978. The theoretical issues involved require much more thorough discussion than my brief statement here suggests. In particular, we have to distinguish between what is autonomous and contingent in a people's response to outside forces and what is genuinely inevitable given a constellation of external factors.

2 Also, as Modjeska has stressed for the Duna, women do not possess all the tools and techniques needed to clear land for gardens (Modjeska 1977).

3 Onombe, who works for the big-man, Ndamba, in Kawelka Kundmbo clan, told me that he sees himself as 'helping' Ndamba voluntarily with all of his projects. Earlier, he left the household of another Kundmbo big-man, Roltinga, because Roltinga refused to repay a debt in pigs. Young men of Kundmbo explain how Onombe sometimes gets cross and refuses to do things for Ndamba and how he may help himself to large amounts of pork at a distribution if he feels annoyed over some issue. All these signs of 'grumpiness', taken in good humour by Ndamba, are clearly a result of his occasional displeasure at the numbers of tasks he is asked to do. Since he is a co-clansman of Ndamba and has few, if any, remaining connections outside the clan, it is unlikely that he would leave Ndamba's household. Ndamba himself still works hard in his gardens, and Onombe is deputed especially to assist one of Ndamba's wives.

4 Godelier, in an article critical of the use anthropologists have made of the concept of 'tribe', argues that we must be suspicious of the idea of 'tribalism', since it may be used as a tool by the 'powers who dominate and oppress the young nations of the Third World'. He argues that tribal conflicts are 'explainable primarily by reference to colonial

domination' and should not be seen as having an origin 'in the functioning of pre-colonial structures' (Godelier 1977: 96). However, for the New Guinea Highlands at least, this viewpoint is hard to accept in totality. It is patent that contemporary conflicts in the Highlands are due partly to new economic pressures and partly to previously established cultural values.

5  A grave difficulty here for policy-makers is that it is precisely in areas where re-settlement blocks have been set up in order to facilitate in-migration from areas experiencing land-shortage that new problems of social control have arisen. Many Enga farmers, for example, have migrated into the Kindeng re-settlement area in Hagen, only to find, as a result of deaths in road accidents, that they are at loggerheads with the surrounding Kuli people. In mid-1979, as a result of an escalation of violence, many Enga began leaving the Western Highlands and returning to their own Province, itself by no means free from repeated bouts of severely damaging warfare.

6  See P. Paney *et al.* 1973.

7  I am referring here to the discussions in Meggitt's 1977 book, which in part reverses the implications of his 'From tribesmen to peasants' article of 1971.

8  Indigenous magical practices, designed to 'pull' wealth at the expense of other rivals, have probably enabled Hageners to formulate this view.

9  Tunda village, comprising Tunda proper, Andua, Tarini, Andayapu, Makuliyondo, Mandaiyawane and Kerepali.

10  By April 1979 people had begun to grow tired of imported beef and were returning to their own pork, which they had decided was sweeter in taste after all.

11  By April 1979 one of these younger men, Parle, had built a special house for rearing chickens for sale, which he proposed to share with Nikint. I myself had helped considerably in building a new tradestore near to Ndamba's ceremonial ground. Ndamba was not disturbed by these trends. On the contrary, he thought that plans for extra money-making were very welcome, and he consecrated the entrance-way to the new store by placing the jawbones of pigs from his sacrifices at the ceremonial ground on a special pair of cordyline plants, bound together in a symbolic arch to prevent any ill-luck from passing into the area. For him there is no perceived conflict between business and *moka* since money from the former can be used to augment the latter. Younger men see the issues differently. (By 1981 the chicken-rearing enterprise had collapsed, and tradestore profits had not proved very significant.)

12  Mr Andrew Kei and Mr Michael Mel. Both also held offices in local government or in parliamentary politics. This combination of political and economic activity is typical of the new Highlands elite. (By 1981 the two leaders were in conflict, and Mr Kei had joined the Welyi–Kuta corporation in opposition to Pipilika.)

13  Parua has always stood as a United Party candidate, and this is the party which has been in chief opposition to the ruling Pangu coalition

with the People's Progress Party up to 1978. Late in that year, however, the PPP leader took his section out of the government and the United Party leader, Mr Raphael Ndoa, stepped into the breach, gaining a position for himself as Minister of Health. In 1977, however, the United Party and Pangu had still been prime opponents, and the competition between Parua and J. Maes reflected this, the pre-contact Tipuka–Kombukla enmity and the 1970s expression of this in rivalry between Raembka and Welyi-Kuta. (By 1981 the PPP party had displaced Pangu, and Parua in turn had joined the new government.)

14  Plantations taken over in this way are usually run by expatriate managers, who work either directly for the owners or on contract from a management company run by a large-scale plantation-owner, Mr Miles Barnes. The same company advises Dei Development also. It is apparent that, aside from the shift in ownership, these plantations are run in exactly the same ways as before.

15  This has also caused some criticism of the M.P., whose job is seen as including a watching brief on matters such as roads. In fact, the Council had money allocated for this road since mid-1978 but in April 1979 had not yet organised its proper repair and reconstruction. The M.P. then lobbied to get this done, and the job was completed by mid-1980.

16  It is notable that Nikint, whom Ndamba regards as his potential successor (cf. Chapter 2), had never watched the *pokla mbo* ritual before, as it was last performed when he was a child some twenty-five years prior to 1979.

# BIBLIOGRAPHY

Allen, M.R. 1967. *Male cults and secret initiations in Melanesia.* Melbourne.

Amarshi, A., Good, K. and Mortimer, R. 1979. *Development and dependency.* Melbourne.

Balgooy, M.M.J. van. 1976. Phytogeography. In *New Guinea vegetation,* ed. K. Paijmans, pp. 1–22. Canberra.

Balibar, E. 1970. On the basic concepts of historical materialism. In *Reading Capital,* ed. L. Althusser and E. Balibar. New York.

Barnes, J.A. 1962. African models in the New Guinea Highlands. *Man* o.s. 62: 5–9.

Barnett, T. 1979. Politics and planning rhetoric in Papua New Guinea. Unpub. seminar paper.

Barrau, J. 1957. L'énigme de la patate douce. *Etudes d'Outre-Mer* 40: 83–7.

Barth, F. 1975. *Ritual and knowledge among the Baktaman of New Guinea.* Oslo.

Bateson, G. 1936. *Naven.* Cambridge.

Blong, R.J. 1975. The Krakatoa myth and the New Guinea Highlands. *Journal of the Polynesian Society* 84: 213–17.

1982. *The time of darkness: local legend and volcanic reality in Papua New Guinea.* Canberra.

Bohannan, P. 1957. *Justice and judgement among the Tiv.* London.

Bonte, P. 1977. Classes et parenté dans les sociétés segmentaires. *Dialectiques* 21: 103–15.

1979. Marxist analyses and social anthropology: a review article. *Critique of Anthropology* 4(13–14): 145–63.

Bourdieu, P. 1977. *Outline of a theory of practice* (trans. R. Nice). Cambridge.

Bowers, N. 1965. Permanent bachelorhood in the upper Kaugel valley of Highland New Guinea. *Oceania* 36(1): 27–37.

1971. Demographic problems in montane New Guinea. In *Culture and population,* ed. S. Polgar, pp. 11–31. Cambridge, Mass. and London.

Brookfield, H.C. 1961. The Highlands peoples of New Guinea: a study of distribution and localization. *Geographical Journal* 127: 436–48.

1962. Local study and comparative method: an example from central

New Guinea. *Annals of the Association of American Geographers* 52: 242—54.

1964. The ecology of Highland settlement: some suggestions. In *New Guinea: the central Highlands*, ed. J.B. Watson. *American Anthropologist* 66: 20—38, special publication.

Brookfield, H.C. and Brown, P. 1963. *Struggle for land*. Oxford.

Brookfield, H.C. with Hart, D. 1971. *Melanesia: a geographical interpretation of an island world*. London.

Brookfield, H.C. and White, J.P. 1968. Revolution or evolution in the prehistory of the New Guinea Highlands: a seminar report. *Ethnology* 7: 43—52.

Brown, P. 1963. From anarchy to satrapy. *American Anthropologist* 65: 1—15.

1978. *Highland peoples of New Guinea*. Cambridge.

Brown, P. and Podolefsky, A. 1976. Population density, agricultural intensity, land tenure and group size in the New Guinea Highlands. *Ethnology* 15: 211—38.

Brunton, R. 1975. Why do the Trobrianders have chiefs? *Man* 10(4): 544—58.

Bulmer, R.N.H. 1968. The strategies of hunting in New Guinea. *Oceania* 38(4): 302—18.

1976. Selectivity in hunting and in disposal of animal bone by the Kalam of the New Guinea Highlands. In *Problems in economic and social archaeology*, ed. G.de G. Sieveking, I.H. Longworth and K.E. Wilson, pp. 169—86. London.

Bulmer, R.N.H. and Menzies, J.I. 1972, 1973. Karam classification of marsupials and rodents. *Journal of the Polynesian Society* 81: 472—99, 82: 86—107.

Bulmer, S.E. 1966. Pig bone from two archaeological sites in the New Guinea Highlands. *Journal of the Polynesian Society* 75: 504—5.

Chowning, A. 1977. *An introduction to the peoples and cultures of Melanesia*. California.

Clarke, W.C. 1966. From extensive to intensive shifting cultivation: a succession from New Guinea. *Ethnology* 5: 347—59.

1971. *Place and people: an ecology of a New Guinea community*. Berkeley, Los Angeles and Canberra.

1976a. The maintenance of agriculture and human habitats within the tropical forest ecosystem. In *Report of symposium on ecological effects of increasing human activities on tropical and sub-tropical forest ecosystems (University of Papua New Guinea, 28 April—1 May 1975)*, pp. 103—14. Canberra.

1976b. Maintenance of agriculture and human habitats within the tropical forest system. *Human Ecology* 4: 247—59.

1977. A change of subsistence staple in prehistoric New Guinea. In *Proceedings of the Third Symposium of the International Society for Tropical Root Crops*, ed. C.L.A. Leakey, pp. 159—63. Ibadan.

Clarke, W.C. and Street, J.M. 1967. Soil fertility and cultivation practices in New Guinea. *Journal of Tropical Geography* 24: 7—11.

Clastres, P. 1977. *Society against the state* (trans. R. Hurley). Oxford.

Cochrane, D. and Cochrane, N. 1966. *Yunaya haga giniu* 3 [Duna literacy primer]. Summer Institute of Linguistics. Ukarumpa.

Conklin, H.C. 1963. The Oceanian–African hypotheses and the sweet potato. In *Plants and the migrations of Pacific peoples: a symposium*, ed. J. Barrau, pp. 129–36. Honolulu.

Cooper, M. and Rodman, M., eds. 1979. *The pacification of Melanesia.* Studies in Pacific Anthropology. Michigan.

Craig, R. 1969. Marriage among the Telefolmin. In *Pigs, pearlshells and women*, ed. R.M. Glasse and M.J. Meggitt. Englewood Cliffs.

de Lepervanche, M. 1967–8. Descent, residence, and leadership in the New Guinea Highlands. *Oceania* 38: 34–58 and 163–89.

Denevan, W.M. and Turner, B.L. 1974. Forms, functions and associations of raised fields in the Old World tropics. *Journal of Tropical Geography* 39: 24–33.

Dornstreich, M.D. 1977. The ecological description and analysis of tropical subsistence patterns: an example from New Guinea. In *Subsistence and survival: rural ecology in the Pacific*, ed. T.P. Bayliss-Smith and R.G. Feachem, pp. 245–71. London, New York, San Francisco.

Douglas, M. 1978. Cultural bias. R.A.I. Occasional Paper 35. London.

Dunn, S.P. 1979. The position of the primitive–communal social order in the soviet–marxist theory of history. In *Toward a marxist anthropology*, ed. S. Diamond. The Hague.

Engels, F. 1884. *The origin of the family, private property and the state.*

Evans-Pritchard, E.E. 1940. *The Nuer: a description of the modes of livelihood and political institutions of a Nilotic people.* Oxford.

Feacham, R. 1973. The Raiapu Enga pig herd. *Mankind* 9: 25–31.

Feil, D.K. 1978a. Enga women in the *Tee* exchange. In *Trade and exchange in Oceania and Australia*, ed. J. Specht and J.P. White. Special issue, *Mankind* 11(3): 220–30.

    1978b. Holders of the way: exchange partnerships in an Enga *Tee* community. Ph.D. thesis. Australian National University.

Finney, B.R. 1973. *Big-men and business: entrepreneurship and economic growth in the New Guinea Highlands.* Hawaii.

Fitzpatrick, P. 1979. The political economy of dispute settlement in Papua New Guinea. Unpub. paper, Cambridge Criminology Conference Workshop on crime and justice in the Third World.

    1980. *Law and state in Papua New Guinea.* London.

Fitzpatrick, P. and Southwood, J. 1976. The community corporation in Papua New Guinea. I.A.S.E.R. Discussion Paper 5, Port Moresby.

Flenley, J.R. 1967. The present and former vegetation of the Wabag region of New Guinea. Ph.D. thesis, Australian National University.

Fortes, M. 1945. *The dynamics of clanship among the Tallensi.* London.

    1949. *The web of kinship among the Tallensi.* Oxford.

    1953. The structure of unilineal descent groups. *American Anthropologist* 55(1): 17–41.

    1974. The first born. *Journal of Child Psychology and Psychiatry* 15: 81–104.

1978. An anthropologist's apprenticeship. *Annual Review of Anthropology* 7: 1–30.

Fosberg, F.R., Garnier, B.J. and Küchler, A.W. 1961. Delimitation of the humid tropics. *Geographical Review* 51: 333–47.

Foucault, M. 1979. *The history of sexuality* 1(4), ch. 2: Method (trans. R. Hurley). London.

Glasse, R.M. 1968. Huli of Papua: a cognatic descent system. *Cahiers de l'Homme*, n.s. 8. Paris.

1974. Le masque de la volupté: symbolisme et antagonisme sexuels sur hauts plateaux de Nouvelle-Guinée. *L'Homme* 14: 79–86.

Godelier, M. 1969. Land tenure among the Baruya of New Guinea. *Journal of the Papua New Guinea Society* 3: 17–23.

1971. 'Salt currency' and the circulation of commodities among the Baruya of New Guinea. *Studies in Economic Anthropology*, AS7: 52–73.

1973a. Outils de pierre, outils d'acier chez les Baruya de Nouvelle-Guinée. *L'Homme* 13(3): 187–220 (en collab. avec J. Garanger). (English trans.: Stone tools, steel tools among the Baruya of New Guinea. *Social Science Information* 18(4–5): 633–78.)

1973b. The visible and the invisible among the Baruya of New Guinea. In *Perspectives in marxist anthropology*, pp. 196–203. Cambridge.

1976. Le sexe comme fondement ultime de l'ordre social et cosmique chez les Baruya de Nouvelle-Guinée. In *Sexualité et pouvoir*, ed. A. Verdiglione, pp. 268–306. Paris.

1977. The concept of the tribe: a crisis involving merely a concept or the empirical foundations of anthropology itself? In *Perspectives in marxist anthropology* (trans. R. Brain). Cambridge.

Golson, J. 1976. Archaeology and agricultural history in the New Guinea Highlands. In *Problems in economic and social archaeology*, ed. G.de G. Sieveking, I.H. Longworth and K.E. Wilson, pp. 201–20. London.

1977. No room at the top: agricultural intensification in the New Guinea Highlands. In *Sunda and Sahul: prehistoric studies in Southeast Asia, Melanesia and Australia*, ed. J. Allen, J. Golson and R. Jones, pp. 601–38. London, New York, San Francisco.

1981a. Agriculture in New Guinea: the long view. In *A history of agriculture in Papua New Guinea: a time to plant and a time to uproot*, ed. D. Denoon and Catherine Snowden, pp. 33–41. Port Moresby.

1981b. Agricultural technology in New Guinea, pp. 43–54 of Denoon and Snowden as above.

1981c. New Guinea agricultural history: a case study, pp. 55–64 of Denoon and Snowden as above.

Golson, J. and Hughes, P.J. 1976. The appearance of plant and animal domestication in New Guinea. In *La préhistoire océanienne* (symposium XXII of IX Congress of Pre- and Protohistoric Sciences, Nice, September 1976). Centre National de la Recherche Scientifique, Paris (also in *Journal de la Société des Océanistes* 69 (vol. 36) 1980: 294–303).

# Bibliography

Golson, J., Lampert, R.J., Wheeler, J.M. and Ambrose, W.R. 1967. A note on carbon dates for horticulture in the New Guinea Highlands. *Journal of the Polynesian Society* 76: 369–71.

Good, K. and Donaldson, M. 1980. Development of rural capitalism in Papua New Guinea. Institute of Papua New Guinea Studies Occasional Paper 1. Port Moresby.

Gorecki, P.P. 1979. Population growth and abandonment of swamplands: a New Guinea Highlands example. *Journal de la Société des Océanistes* 35: 97–107.

Gray, B.M. 1973. The logic of Yandapu Enga puberty rites and the separation of the sexes: responses to ecological and biological pressures in New Guinea. M.A. thesis. University of Sydney.

Hamilton, A. 1981. The unity of foraging. Paper presented at the Department of Anthropology, University of Sydney, March 1981.

Harris, E.C. and Hughes, P.J. 1978. An early agricultural system at Mugamamp Ridge, Western Highlands Province, Papua New Guinea. *Mankind* 12(4): 437–44.

Hatanaka, S. and Bragge, L.W. 1973. Habitat, isolation and subsistence economy in the Central Range of New Guinea. *Oceania* 44: 38–57.

Hau'ofa, E. 1975. Anthropology and Pacific Islanders. *Oceania* 45(4): 283–9.

Hays, W.L. 1973. *Statistics for the social sciences*, 2nd edn. New York.

Heinsohn, G. and Steiger, O. 1980. Birth control, witch trials and the demographic transition. *Diskussionsbeitrage zur Politischen Oekonomie* 33. Universitat Bremen.

Herdt, G.H. 1977. The shaman's 'calling' among the Sambia of New Guinea. *Journal de la Société des Océanistes* 33: 153–67.

Hogbin, I. 1978. *The leaders and the led: social control in Wogeo, New Guinea.* Melbourne.

Hope, G.S. 1980. Tropical mountain forest in retrospect and prospect. In *Of time and place: essays in honour of O.H.K. Spate*, ed. J.N. Jennings and G.J.R. Linge, pp. 153–69. Canberra.

Hope, J.H. 1977. The effect of prehistoric man on the fauna of New Guinea. In *The Melanesian environment*, ed. J. Winslow, pp. 21–7. Canberra.

Hope, J.H. and Hope, G.S. 1976. Palaeoenvironments for man in New Guinea. In *The origin of the Australians*, ed. R.L. Kirk and A.G. Thorne. Human Biology Series 6. Canberra.

Howlett, D. 1980. When is a peasant not a peasant? First thoughts on proletarianisation in Papua New Guinea. In *Of time and place*, ed. J.N. Jennings and G.J.R. Linge, pp. 193–210. Canberra.

Hughes, I.M. 1977. *New Guinea stone age trade.* Research School of Pacific Studies, Department of Prehistory, Australian National University. *Terra Australis* 3.

1978. Good money and bad: inflation and devaluation in the colonial process. In *Trade and exchange in Oceania and Australia*, ed. J. Specht and J.P. White. *Mankind* 11(3): 308–18, special issue.

Jackson, G. 1970. Review article: Glasse, the Huli and descent. *Journal of the Polynesian Society* 79: 119–32.

James, W. 1978. Matrifocus on African women. In *Defining females: the nature of women in society*, ed. S. Ardener. London.

Kahn, J.S. 1978. Marxist anthropology and peasant economics: a study of the social structures of underdevelopment. In *The new economic anthropology*, ed. J. Clammer, pp. 110–37. London.

Keesing, R.M. 1971. Descent, residence, and cultural codes. In *Anthropology in Oceania*, ed. L.R. Hiatt and C. Jayawardena, pp. 121–38. Sydney.

1976. *Cultural anthropology: a contemporary perspective.* New York.

Kelly, R.C. 1968. Demographic pressure and descent-group structure in the New Guinea Highlands. *Oceania* 30: 36–63.

1976. Witchcraft and sexual relations. In *Male and female in the Highlands of New Guinea*, ed. P. Brown and G. Buchbinder. *American Anthropologist*, special publication.

1977. *Etoro social structure.* Ann Arbor.

Kimber, A.J. 1972. The sweet potato in subsistence agriculture. *Papua New Guinea Agricultural Journal* 23: 80–102.

La Fontaine, J. 1973. Descent in New Guinea: an Africanist view. In *The character of kinship*, ed. J.R. Goody, pp. 35–52. Cambridge.

Lampert, R.J. 1967. Horticulture in the New Guinea Highlands: C14 dating. *Antiquity* 41: 307–9.

Langness, L.L. 1964. Some problems in the conceptualisation of Highlands social structures in New Guinea. In *New Guinea: the central Highlands*, ed. J.B. Watson. *American Anthropologist* 66(4): 162–82, special publication.

Lawrence, P. 1967. Land tenure among the Garia. In *Studies in New Guinea land tenure*, ed. I. Hogbin and P. Lawrence. Sydney.

1975. The ethnographic revolution. *Oceania* 45(4): 253–71.

Leach, E.R. 1962. On certain unconsidered aspects of double descent systems. *Man* o.s. 62: 130–4.

Lee, R.B. 1980. Is there a foraging mode of production? ms. (A French version appears in *Anthropologie et Sociétés* 4 (1980) Special issue on hunting/gathering societies. Dept. of Anthropology, Université Laval.)

LeRoy, J.D. 1979. The ceremonial pig kill of the south Kewa. *Oceania* 49: 179–209.

Levine, H.B. and Levine, M.W. 1979. *Urbanization in Papua New Guinea.* Cambridge.

Lévi-Strauss, C. 1969. *The elementary structures of kinship*, ch. 29: The principles of kinship. London.

Lloyd, R.G. 1973. The Anga language family. In *The linguistic situation in the Gulf District and adjacent areas, Papua New Guinea*, ed. K. Franklin. Linguistic Circle of Canberra (Pacific Linguistics, Series C, 26): 31–111. Canberra.

1974. Baruya kin and kith. In *Kinship studies in Papua New Guinea*, ed. R.D. Shaw, pp. 97–114. Papua New Guinea.

Mandeville, E. 1979. Agnation, affinity and migration among the Kamano of the New Guinea Highlands. *Man* 14(1): 105—23.

Marecek, T.M. 1977. Shifting cultivation among the Duna of Papua New Guinea. *Tools and Tillage* 3: 78—90.

Marx, K. 1857. Grundrisse: general introduction. In *Grundrisse*, trans. and ed. D. McLellan. London.
   *Capital* I and II. Moscow. 1965 and 1966.

Mead, M. 1940. The Mountain Arapesh II: supernaturalism. Anthropological Papers of the American Museum of Natural History 37(3): 317—451.

Meek, R.L. 1977. *Smith, Marx and after*. London.

Meggitt, M.J. 1964. Male—female relationships in the Highlands of Australian New Guinea. In *New Guinea: the central Highlands*, ed. J.B. Watson. *American Anthropologist* 66: 204—24, special publication.

   1965. *The lineage system of the Mae Enga of New Guinea*. Edinburgh.

   1967. The pattern of leadership among the Mae-Enga of New Guinea. *Anthropological Forum* 2(1): 20—35.

   1969. Introduction. In *Pigs, pearlshells, and women*, ed. R.M. Glasse and M.J. Meggitt. Englewood Cliffs.

   1971. From tribesmen to peasants: the case of the Mae-Enga of New Guinea. In *Anthropology in Oceania*, ed. L.R. Hiatt and C. Jayawardena. pp. 191—210. Sydney.

   1973. The sun and the shakers: a millenarian cult and its transformations in the New Guinea Highlands. *Oceania* 42: 1—37, 109—26.

   1976. A duplicity of demons: sexual and familial roles expressed in western Enga stories. In *Male and female in the Highlands of New Guinea*, ed. P. Brown and G. Buchbinder. *American Anthropologist*, special publication.

   1977. *Blood is their argument: warfare among the Mae-Enga tribesmen of the New Guinea Highlands*. California.

Meillassoux, C. 1964. *L'Anthropologie économique des Gouro de Côte d'Ivoire*. Paris.

   1967. On the mode of production of the hunting band. In *French Perspectives in African studies*, ed. P. Alexandre.

   1975. *Femmes, greniers et capitaux*. Paris. (English translation *Maidens, meal and money*, 1981. Cambridge.)

   1979. Historical modalities of the exploitation and overexploitation of labour. *Critique of Anthropology* 4(13—14): 7—16.

Modjeska, C.N. 1977. Production among the Duna: aspects of horticultural intensification in central New Guinea. Ph.D. thesis. Australian National University.

   1980. Review of: *Etoro social structure* by R.C. Kelly. *Oceania* 50: 239—40.

Molyneux, M. 1977. Androcentrism in marxist anthropology. *Critique of Anthropology* 9 and 10(3): 55—82.

Morren, G.E.B. 1977. From hunting to herding: pigs and the control of energy in montane New Guinea. In *Subsistence and survival: rural*

*ecology in the Pacific*, ed. T.P. Bayliss-Smith and R.G. Feachem.
London, New York, San Francisco.

1979. Seasonality among the Miyanmin: wild pigs, movement and dual
kinship organization. *Mankind* 12(1): 1–12.

Nelder, J.A. and Wedderburn, R.W.M. 1972. Generalized linear models.
*Journal of the Royal Statistical Society*, ser. A 135: 370–84.

Nicolaus, M. 1972. The unknown Marx. In *Ideology in social science*, ed.
R. Blackburn. Glasgow.

O'Laughlin, B. 1974. Mediation of contradiction: why Mbum women do
not eat chicken. In *Women, culture and society*, ed. M.Z. Rosaldo
and L. Lamphere. Stanford.

1975. Marxist approaches in Anthropology. *Annual Review of Anthropology* 4: 341–70.

Oldfield, F. 1977. Lake sediments and human activities in prehistoric
Papua New Guinea. In *The Melanesian environment*, ed. J.H.
Winslow, pp. 57–60. Canberra.

Oldfield, F., Appleby, P.G., Brown, A. and Thompson, R. 1980. Palaeo-
ecological studies of lakes in the Highlands of Papua New Guinea. 1:
the chronology of sedimentation. *Journal of Ecology* 68: 457–77.

Paney, P. *et al.* 1973. *Report of the Commission to Investigate Tribal
Fighting*. Port Moresby.

Ploeg, A. 1973. Feasting for gain and help. *Mankind* 9(1): 15–24.

1975. Spontaneous rural resettlement in and near the Chimbu District
in 1972–3. New Guinea Research Unit Discussion Paper 5. Port
Moresby.

Polach, H.A. 1982. Radiocarbon dating of Long Island and Tibito tephras.
In *Cooke–Ravian volume of volcanological papers*, ed. R.W.
Johnson, pp. 108–13. Geological Survey of Papua New Guinea,
Memoir 10. Port Moresby.

Pospisil, L. 1963a. *Kapauku Papuan economy*. Yale University Publi-
cations in Anthropology 67. New Haven.

1963b. *The Kapauku Papuans of west New Guinea*. New York.

Powell, J.M. 1976. Ethnobotany. In *New Guinea vegetation*, ed. K.
Paijmans, pp. 106–83. Canberra.

Powell, J.M. and Hope, G.S. 1976. Vegetation history. In *New Guinea
vegetation*, ed. K. Paijmans, pp. 101–4. Canberra.

Powell, J.M., Kulunga, A., Moge, R., Pono, C., Zimike, F. and Golson, J.
1975. Agricultural traditions of the Mount Hagen area. Department
of Geography Occasional Paper 12, University of Papua New Guinea.

Radcliffe-Brown, A.R. 1930–1. The social organization of Australian
tribes. *Oceania* 1(1): 34–65; 1(4): 444–56.

Rappaport, R.A. 1968. *Pigs for the ancestors: ritual in the ecology of a
New Guinea people*. New Haven and London.

Read, K.E. 1959. Leadership and consensus in a New Guinea society.
*American Anthropologist* 61: 425–36.

Reay, M.O. 1959. *The Kuma: freedom and conformity in the New Guinea
Highlands*. Melbourne.

1964. Present-day politics in the New Guinea Highlands. In *New*

    *Guinea: the central Highlands*, ed. J.B. Watson. *American Anthropologist* 66: 240–56, special publication.

Roheim, G. 1945. *The eternal ones of the dream*. New York.

Rossi-Landi, F. 1979. On the dialectic of exogamic exchange. In *Toward a marxist anthropology*, ed. S. Diamond. The Hague.

Rubel, P.G. and Rosman, A. 1978. *Your own pigs you may not eat: a comparative study of New Guinea societies*. Canberra.

Sahlins, M. 1961. The segmentary lineage: an organization of predatory expansion. *American Anthropologist* 63: 322–45.

    1962–3. Poor man, rich man, big-man, chief: political types in Melanesia and Polynesia. *Comparative Studies in Society and History* 5: 285–303.

    1972. *Stone age economics*. Chicago.

Salisbury, R.F. 1962. *From stone to steel: economic consequences of a technological change in New Guinea*. Melbourne.

    1964. Despotism and Australian administration in the New Guinea Highlands. In *New Guinea: the central Highlands* ed. J.B. Watson. *American Anthropologist* 66: 225–39, special publication.

Scheffler, H.W. 1966. Ancestor worship in anthropology: or, observations on descent and descent groups. *Current Anthropology* 7: 545–51.

Schieffelin, E.L. 1976. *The sorrow of the lonely and the burning of the dancers*. New York.

    1980. Reciprocity and the construction of reality. *Man* 15: 502–17.

Schneider, H.K. 1970. *The Wahi Wanyaturu: economics in an African society*, ch. 7: People as wealth. Chicago.

Schodde, R. and Calaby, J.H. 1972. A biogeography of the Australo-Papuan bird and mammal faunas in relation to Torres Strait. In *Bridge and barrier: the natural and cultural history of Torres Strait*, ed. D. Walker, pp. 257–300. Research School of Pacific Studies, Department of Biogeography and Geomorphology Publication BG/3, Australian National University.

Schwartz, T. 1973. Cult and context: the paranoid ethos in Melanesia. *Ethos* 1: 153–74.

Sexton, L. 1980. From pigs and pearlshells to coffee and cash. Ph.D. thesis. Temple University.

Sillitoe, P. 1978. Big-men and war in New Guinea. *Man* 13(2): 252–71.

    1979. *Give and take: exchange in Wola society*. Canberra.

Sinclair, J. 1966. *Behind the ranges*. Melbourne.

Siskind, J. 1978. Kinship and mode of production. *American Anthropologist* 80: 860–72.

Standish, W. 1973. The Highlands: *'Ol i no save harim mipela'*. *New Guinea* 8(3): 4–30.

    1978. The big-man model reconsidered: power and stratification in Chimbu. I.A.S.E.R. Discussion Paper 22. Port Moresby.

Steadman, L.B. 1971. Neighbours and killers: residence and dominance among the Hewa of New Guinea. Ph.D. thesis, Australian National University.

Steensberg, A. 1980. *New Guinea gardens: a study of husbandry with parallels in prehistoric Europe.* London.

Straatmans, W. 1967. Ethnobotany of New Guinea in its ecological perspective. *Journal d'Agriculture Tropicale et de Botanique Appliquée* 14: 1—20.

Strathern, A.J. 1966. Despots and directors in the New Guinea Highlands. *Man* 1: 356—67.

  1969. Finance and production: two strategies in New Guinea Highland exchange systems. *Oceania* 40(1): 42—67.

  1970a. The female and male spirit cults in Mount Hagen. *Man* 5: 571—85.

  1970b. Male initiation in New Guinea Highlands societies. *Ethnology* 9: 373—9.

  1971. *The rope of moka: big-men and ceremonial exchange in Mount Hagen, New Guinea.* Cambridge Studies in Social Anthropology 4. Cambridge.

  1972. *One father, one blood: descent and group structure among the Melpa people.* Canberra.

  1974. When dispute procedures fail. In *Contention and dispute: aspects of law and social control in Melanesia,* ed. A.L. Epstein. Canberra.

  1977. Contemporary warfare in the New Guinea Highlands: revival or breakdown? *Yagl-Ambu, P.N.G. Journal of Social Sciences and Humanities* 4(3): 135—46.

  1978. 'Finance and production' revisited: in pursuit of a comparison. *Research in Economic Anthropology* 1: 73—104.

  1979a. 'It's his affair': a note on the individual and the group in New Guinea Highlands societies. *Canberra Anthropology* 2(1): 94—113.

  1979b. Gender, ideology, and money in Mount Hagen. *Man* n.s. 14: 530—48.

  1979c. 'We are all of one father here': models of descent in New Guinea. In *Segmentary lineage systems reconsidered,* ed. L. Holy. Queen's University Belfast Papers in Social Anthropology, 4: 145—56.

  forthcoming. 'A brother is a creative thing': conflict and change in a Melpa family. In *The family: material interests and emotions,* ed. H. Medick and D. Sabean.

Strathern, M. 1972. *Women in between: female roles in a male world: Mount Hagen, New Guinea.* London.

  1975. *No money on our skins: Hagen migrants in Port Moresby.* New Guinea Research Bulletin 61. Port Moresby.

  1978. The achievement of sex: paradoxes in Hagen gender-thinking. In *Yearbook of Symbolic Anthropology,* ed. E. Schwimmer. 1: 171—202. London.

Tanner, N. 1974. Matrifocality in Indonesia and Africa and among Black Americans. In *Woman, culture and society,* ed. M.Z. Rosaldo and L. Lamphere. Stanford.

Taussig, M. 1977. The genesis of capitalism amongst a South American peasantry: devil's labor and the baptism of money. *Comparative Studies in Society and History* 19: 130–55.

Terray, E. 1972a. *Marxism and 'primitive' societies. Two studies.* New York.

1972b. Historical materialism and segmentary lineage-based societies. In Terray 1972a.

1975. Classes and class consciousness in the Abron kingdom of Gyaman. In *Marxist analyses and social anthropology*, ed. M. Bloch. ASA Monographs. London.

1979. On exploitation: elements of an autocritique. *Critique of Anthropology* 4(13–14): 29–39.

Townsend, P. 1971. New Guinea sago gatherers: a study of demography in relation to subsistence. *Ecology of food and nutrition* 1: 19–24.

Turner, T. 1979. The Gê and Bororo societies as dialectical systems: a general model. In *Dialectical societies: the Gê and Bororo of Central Brazil*, ed. D. Maybury-Lewis. Cambridge.

Tuzin, D.F. 1976. *The Ilahita Arapesh: dimensions of unity.* Berkeley.

UNESCO. 1962. Symposium on the impact of man on humid tropics vegetation, Goroka, Territory of Papua New Guinea, September 1960. Canberra.

Vicedom, G.F. and Tischner, H. 1943–8. *Die Mbowamb: die Kultur der Hagenberg-Stämme im Östlichen Zentral-Neuguinea*, 3 vols. Monographien zur Volkenkunde 1. Hamburg.

Waddell, E.W. 1972. *The mound builders: agricultural practices, environment and society in the central Highlands of New Guinea.* American Ethnological Society Monograph 53. Seattle.

1975. How the Enga cope with frost: responses to climatic perturbations in the central Highlands of New Guinea. *Human Ecology* 3: 249–73.

Walker, D. and Flenley, J.R. 1979. Late Quaternary vegetational history of Enga Province of upland Papua New Guinea. *Philosophical Transactions of the Royal Society of London, B. Biological Sciences* 286: 265–344.

Ward, A. 1972. Agrarian revolution: handle with care. *New Guinea* 6(1): 25–34.

Watson, J.B. 1965a. From hunting to horticulture in the New Guinea Highlands. *Ethnology* 4: 295–309.

1965b. The significance of a recent ecological change in the central Highlands of New Guinea. *Journal of the Polynesian Society* 74: 438–50.

1967. Horticultural traditions in the Eastern New Guinea Highlands. *Oceania* 38(2): 81–98.

1970. Society as organized flow: the Tairora case. *Southwestern Journal of Anthropology* 26: 107–24.

1977. Pigs, fodder, and the Jones Effect in post-Ipomoean New Guinea. *Ethnology* 16: 57–70.

Weeks, S. 1977. Why leave? My village is a good place: factors contributing to minimal migration in eight villages in the Highlands. In *The rural survey 1975*, ed. J. Conroy and G. Skeldon. Supplement to *Yagl-Ambu* 4: 67–86, special issue.

White, J.P. 1972. *Ol tumbuna: archaeological excavations in the eastern central Highlands, Papua Guinea.* Research School of Pacific Studies, Department of Prehistory, Australian National University. *Terra Australis* 2.

Worsley, P. 1956. The kinship system of the Tallensi: a revaluation. *Journal of the Royal Anthropological Institute* 86: 37–75.

Wurm. S.A. 1975. *New Guinea area languages and language study*, vol. 1. Pacific Linguistics C–38. Canberra.

Yen, D.E. 1971. The development of agriculture in Oceania. In *Studies in Oceanic culture history* 2, ed. R.C. Green and M. Kelly. Department of Anthropology, Bishop Museum, Honolulu. Pacific Anthropological Records, 12.

1973. The origins of Oceanic agriculture. *Archaeology and Physical Anthropology in Oceania* 8: 68–85.

1974. *The sweet potato and Oceania: an essay in ethnobotany.* Bishop Museum Bulletin 236. Honolulu.

Ziegler, A.C. 1977. Evolution of New Guinea's marsupial fauna in response to a forested environment. In *The biology of marsupials*, ed. B. Stonehouse and D. Gilmore, pp. 117–38. London and Basingstoke.

# INDEX OF PERSONS

# INDEX OF PLACES

## INDEX OF PEOPLES AND GROUPS

## INDEX OF TOPICS

For EU product safety concerns, contact us at Calle de José Abascal, 56–1°,
28003 Madrid, Spain or eugpsr@cambridge.org.